AND GLADLY TEACH

Reminiscences of Teachers from Frontier Dugout to Modern Module

AND GLADLY TEACH

Reminiscences of Teachers from Frontier Dugout to Modern Module

Edited by James Smallwood

UNIVERSITY OF OKLAHOMA PRESS
NORMAN

Library of Congress Cataloging in Publication Data
Main entry under title:

And gladly teach.

1. Education—Oklahoma—History. 2. Teachers —Oklahoma—Correspondence, reminiscences, etc.
I. Smallwood, James.
LA349.A63 370'.9766 75-40961
ISBN 0-8061-1340-5

 Composed and printed at Norman, Oklahoma, U.S.A., by the University of Oklahoma Press. First edition.

PREFACE

This volume is an effort to record for posterity some of the experiences of pioneer teachers in Indian Territory and the State of Oklahoma.

Many former teachers have long felt it was important that the activities and experiences of pioneer teachers be recorded and preserved for the information and enjoyment of the present and future generations.

As teachers in a young and pioneer state these people have witnessed and have contributed to the greatest period of technological and social development the world has ever known.

While serving as president of the Oklahoma Retired Teachers Association, we were challenged by Mary Mullen, then president of the National Retired Teachers Association, to collect reminiscences from retired teachers and bind them in a scrapbook for display at the Association's Biennial Convention in Houston Texas. The Oklahoma Retired Teachers Association accepted the challenge and, through a state committee, set out to collect stories from retired teachers throughout the state.

The state committee, with enthusiastic support of local committees in every county of the state, received responses from more than five hundred retired teachers. With this accumulated wealth of material and the enthusiasm of the leadership of the state association, it was decided to explore the possibility of a published book gleaned from these reminiscences.

We approached Odie B. Faulk, head of the History Department of Oklahoma State University, and Leroy H. Fischer, Oppenheim Regents Professor of History there, for their counsel and guidance, and to our delight we found them very much interested in our project. With their assistance and encouragement, Dr. James Smallwood, Assistant Professor of History at Oklahoma State University, most graciously did the editing and provided guidance in the publication of the volume. We are also indebted to Merrilyn Irby for contributing the art work.

This volume is a tribute to the efforts and contributions of Oklahoma retired teachers, some nearing the century mark, and to the co-operation and support of the state's two major universities in the editing and publication of the book.

If the readers of this volume find it interesting and worthwhile, then the Oklahoma Retired Teachers Association will feel well rewarded for their time, efforts, and money involved in collecting the materials and sponsoring the publication.

J. CONNER FITZGERALD, *State Director*
National Retired Teachers Association

Stillwater, Oklahoma
February 15, 1976

ACKNOWLEDGMENTS

The editor wishes to thank the many people whose support helped bring this project to completion. The officers and members of the Oklahoma Retired Teachers Association conceived the idea of collecting teacher reminiscences as a Bicentennial project. Special appreciation goes to the ORTA "Pride in America" Committee which co-ordinated the collection of memoirs—Letha Campbell, chairwoman; Mary McCain, co-chairwoman; J. C. Fitzgerald, co-chairman; and other members of the committee: Lucile Claiborne, Kathryn Rogers, Doris Brown, and Jessye Moore. ORTA President Byron L. Shepherd should also be recognized. Additionally, Dr. Fitzgerald (a past-president of the ORTA and presently the Oklahoma State director of the National Retired Teachers Association) helped the editor in various other ways, by attending to some of the details which arose as the project progressed.

The editor would also like to thank the staff of the University of Oklahoma Press for their efforts; Kelley Vogt of the Oklahoma State University History Department staff for typing rough copy and final manuscript; and good friends, Professors Odie B. Faulk, Carl N. Tyson, and LeRoy Fischer, whose encouragement and support facilitated the development of this project from beginning to completion. My wife, Mary Anne, who helped me in ways too numerous to mention, has my deepest appreciation.

JAMES SMALLWOOD

Stillwater, Oklahoma
January 9, 1976

CONTENTS

	Preface	*page* *v*
	Acknowledgments	*vii*
I.	Education in Oklahoma: An Overview	3
II.	On the Other Side of the Desk	15
III.	The Territorial Years	38
IV.	Early Statehood	72
V.	The Depression	138
VI.	The Modern Era	180
VII.	A Funny Thing Happened on the Way to School	231
	List of Project Contributors	239
	Index	253

AND GLADLY TEACH

Reminiscences of Teachers from Frontier Dugout to Modern Module

I

EDUCATION IN OKLAHOMA AN OVERVIEW

Today's generation of students and some of their younger teachers do not remember the days of frontier education in Oklahoma. Forgotten are the one-room sod, dugout, or log schoolhouses where the teacher's first duty of the day was to sweep mountains of dust not only from the floor but also from the tops of crude, handmade benches used for desks and chairs. Forgotten are the two- and three-mile treks to class. Forgotten are the daily trips for water to a well or to a stream that might be one or more miles from the schoolhouse. Forgotten are the days when "wild" Indians or suspicious whites might bring children to class on the first school day and remain for hours, standing at the back of the room, inspecting and evaluating the schoolmarm or the headmaster. Forgotten are the days when a teacher's only supplies consisted of slates and chalk and the only equipment the blackboard. Forgotten are the old outhouses—one marked clearly for "girls only" and the other for boys. But Oklahoma teachers and students who grew to maturity in the state's formative years remember; they witnessed the transition from one-room dugouts to consolidated school districts to the modern facilities of larger cities and towns.

Oklahoma education has its roots in the Indian era. Between

1820 and 1837 the Five Civilized Tribes were forced to accept reservations in Indian Territory, present-day Oklahoma. When they reorganized their society after the trek across the Mississippi River, they quickly re-established their schools. Missionaries, who had worked among the tribes even before removal, followed them westward, instructing them in the Christian religion and providing them with the rudiments of an Anglo-American education. In addition to subsidizing the many mission schools, the tribes very early organized a system of public education. The Cherokees established rural schools, most of which were administered by Indian teachers. Further, the Cherokees established two seminaries—one for males, one for females—for advanced training. The Choctaws also founded public schools immediately after reaching Indian Territory. By 1848 the Choctaws supported nine boarding schools and by 1860 reported that a total of nine hundred children attended their boarding and neighborhood institutions. The Creeks, Chickasaws, and Seminoles also organized schools, although the Seminoles probably had fewer than the other tribes. Like the Cherokees, the other tribes established advanced academies. The schools of the Nations also included institutions for orphans, the blind, the deaf, and the mentally ill.

The curriculum of the Indian schools included traditional subjects such as spelling, reading, history, Latin, English, and arithmetic. Girls attended special classes in child care, sewing, and cooking. Vocational subjects taught in some schools included agriculture, animal husbandry, carpentry, and mechanical arts. Mission schools also stressed biblical instruction. With funds always a problem, the expenses for operating the Indian schools came from annuities paid by the United States for cession of Indian lands in the East and from interest on monies deposited in the United States Treasury. Monies received from fees, fines, and philanthropic societies represented some of the other sources of income.

After the Civil War an ever increasing number of whites began venturing into Indian Territory. Since the Nations did not provide for the education of whites, most Anglo children had little opportunity to attend school. White children were taught at home by their parents; in some cases, well-to-do families hired tutors. Increasingly, subscription schools became popular. To begin these schools, parents first found a building which could be used as a classroom, made or purchased furniture, and then employed a teacher, who received pay in the form of monthly tuition for each child enrolled.

The creation of Oklahoma Territory in 1890 ushered in a period of progress in education. The territorial legislature created a public school system which provided for a territorial superintendent and local superintendents for all organized counties. Each county was divided into small school districts, usually less than five miles square, which were controlled by an elected board. By the fall of 1891, four hundred districts had been organized to cater to the needs of the 22,590 school-age population. Approximately 10,000 students attended Oklahoma schools this first year.

In Oklahoma's expanding educational system, teachers remained in short supply. Of the 438 men and women who taught in the territory's first public school system, most were recruited from among the settlers themselves. Many had little more than an eighth-grade education, but they managed nevertheless to give their charges instruction in basic education. To insure a continuing high quality of instruction, the territory provided for certification of teachers. The First Territorial Legislature required the teaching of spelling, penmanship, reading, arithmetic, geography, English grammar, United States history, the Constitution, and physiology and hygiene. Later legislatures expanded the list of courses required at various graded levels.

The earliest certification program provided for three types of graded certificates in addition to a temporary license. After a two-week summer normal held in each territorial county, participants could take examinations to qualify for one of the certificates. A first-grade certificate required that a candidate be at least twenty years of age, have twelve months' teaching experience, and make an average score of at least ninety over an examination of required subjects. First-grade certification was valid in all counties and remained in force for three years, renewable once on completion of another summer normal institute. Second-grade certification followed the same guidelines, but the age limit was reduced to eighteen, experience necessary to three months, and the average required to eighty. Moreover, a few subjects were dropped from the examination schedules. Second-grade certificates were effective for only two years and were valid only in the county where issued and in adjoining counties. Still lower requirements were set for the third-grade and temporary certificates. For the former, the age limit was sixteen, and an average of seventy was required on an examination over fewer courses than for first- or second-grade certificates. A third-grade certificate remained effective for one year, only in the county of issue. Temporary certification, granted in cases of emergencies, remained valid in a designated district, but only until examinations were next given by county boards.

The school system of Oklahoma Territory expanded rapidly. By 1895, 79,665 youngsters were attending classes. By 1898, all cities and towns provided graded instruction through high school. Progress was also seen in old Indian Territory. The Curtis Act of 1898 contained a provision transferring control of tribal institutions to the federal government. More facilities were founded to serve the needs of both Indian and white children. By 1905 a total of 445 day schools operated in Indian Territory. Over one hundred other day schools served Indians but barred whites, as did an additional thirty-three boarding schools. Yet another seventy-eight schools served the black community exclusively.

Leaders in Oklahoma Territory did not ignore higher education. The first legislature passed enabling acts founding the University of Oklahoma at Norman, Oklahoma Agricultural and Mechanical College at Stillwater, and Central State Normal at Edmond. All three were in operation in 1892. To provide for black students and to train the Negro community's teachers, the legislature in 1897 established the Colored Agricultural and Normal University at Langston. Other colleges established by the territory included Northwestern State Normal at Alva (1897), University Preparatory School at Tonkawa (1901), and Southwestern State Normal at Weatherford (1901).

The end of the territorial days found 3,220 public schools in operation in Oklahoma's 3,093 school districts. Over 151,400 pupils attended classes in the 1906–1907 term. Teachers, still in short supply, found that their salaries had soared to an average of $40.22 per month for men and $36.61 per month for women.

In launching a state system of public education, leaders built on the already functioning territorial system. The state constitution classified Indians with white citizens and integrated the schools into one system. Separate "minority" facilities were provided for Negroes, under the stipulation that "like" accommodations, "impartially" maintained should be available for them. The first fifteen years of statehood wrought changes for Oklahoma's educational system. By 1908, the state had over 5,600 rural schools, not counting city and graded systems. That year the legislature authorized the consolidation of school districts. By majority vote, the citizens of any two or more adjacent districts could unite to form a consolidated district, which oftentimes allowed for a more efficient use of monies for facilities, supplies, and salaries of instructional personnel. Yet, significant progress in consolidation did not materialize until the depression years when tax collections shifted to state from local sources. Then the consolidation movement reduced the total number of the state's districts, as small one-room schools joined with those of adjacent areas to create larger districts.

The first years of statehood also brought changes in higher education. The early state-supported schools had all been located in old Oklahoma Territory. Indian Territory originally had no colleges, but the extension of the public school system into the eastern part of the state necessitated the founding of colleges in old Indian Territory to train the teachers who were now needed more than ever. In 1909 the legislature created Southeastern State Normal at Durant, Northeastern State Normal at Tahlequah, and East Central State Normal at Ada. Established at the junior college level, the three normals were raised to senior, four-year rank in 1919.

Progress came rapidly to the new state's system of public education. In 1911 the legislature created the state board of education to replace an earlier ex officio board. Among its other duties the board was empowered to make rules regarding licensing of teachers. Investigations disclosed that county agencies were sometimes lax in screening, evaluating, and examining individuals for teacher certification. Consequently, a new school code of 1913, passed by the legislature, provided that teachers must be at least eighteen years of age, allowed for the abolition of county normals and the substitution of teacher training programs, and provided that after 1916 all scholars must have high school or normal school training to teach. By 1914 the "model school" program was also begun, with the board hoping to upgrade rural facilities by establishing a "model school" in all counties. To become models, institutions must meet state standards, which emphasized the physical plants of the institutions.

From 1910 to 1920 a teacher shortage and proliferation of one-room or two-room rural schools appeared to be dominant characteristics of the state system. By 1915 the state had 5,845 districts, of which 5,397 were rural. The state had 12,390 teachers, 7,333 of whom administered to the rural schools. Scholastic enrollment totaled 459,722, with 289,209 of that number attending rural facilities. City systems normally operated their institutions for a full term of 180 days, while village schools averaged just over 165 days and rural schools only 100 days. During the World War I period, the junior high school became popular. Thus, under the "six-three-three plan," many children remained in school even if they had originally planned to drop out after the eighth grade. More secondary schools were being organized. As early as 1916 the state had accredited 136 four-year, 23 three-year, and 17 two-year high schools.

The decade of the 1920's saw continuing progress in the school system. For the session of 1919–20 and again in 1920–21, state aid was voted for districts unable to keep schools open for a full term of instruction. The aid allocated was $100,000 per year, but that amount grew in subsequent appropriations and allowed improvement in rural school instruction and administration. New laws also strengthened compulsory attendance rules. By 1922 schools statewide were crowded to capacity. More money, more teachers, and more facilities were needed. The legislature responded with emergency appropriations and a "free textbook bill," to provide books for grades one through eight, inclusive, but not for high schools. In subsequent action, the 1925 legislature repealed the free textbook law. That same year, the state department of education made a detailed, county by county study of public education and found that poverty remained the basic cause of the inadequate school system. The legislature responded with increased aid, appropriations totaling $1,500,000 for the 1926–28 biennium.

The disastrous effects of the great depression were felt throughout Oklahoma, particularly in its school system. Local ad valorem taxes had provided schools with approximately 90 per cent of their funds. In the depression, not only did property valuations decline but taxes often were not paid in full. Many counties found themselves without operating money to run schools for a full term, and teachers found themselves holding pay warrants which might be discounted up to 50 per cent when cashed. Children often went hungry, finding that they received their best meal of the day at school when sympathetic teachers—using state, federal, and local aid—started hot lunch programs. Yet county governments sometimes reduced costs at the expense of schools. During 1931 the state's common schools received over 41 cents from each property-tax dollar. By 1933 schools received an average of only 10 cents from each dollar. The legislature passed new tax-raising measures in 1933, but financial hardships forced still more facilities to close before completing a full term. The federal government intervened in 1934 with $1,200,000 emergency aid and also established a fund to put unemployed teachers back to work. In 1935 the state assumed greater responsibility for education, with the legislature appropriating $8,200,000 for common schools. Moreover, a minimum salary schedule for state-aided schools gave teachers a wage of $50 to $100 per month, depending on the type of certificate held. Later, emergency appropriations followed the original grant. Such aid allowed completion of the 1935–36 term. Finally, continuing New Deal aid provided for such improvements as construction of new school buildings—classroms, teacherages, gymnasiums, and auditoriums.

The 1940's opened with a continuing shortage of funds and teachers. The United States' involvement in World War II heightened the teacher shortage as men resigned their posts to join the service or to answer the draft. Yet the over-all qualifications of teachers improved during the decade. In 1940 over 69 per cent of the state's teachers were college graduates, and by

1948 the figure had risen to over 79 per cent. Legislative appropriations for schools and teachers' salaries also continued to rise, with the 1949 appropriation reaching $26,000,000. Salaries remained generally low compared to those in other states, but in 1942, by constitutional amendment, voters approved a teacher retirement law, which the legislature vitalized in 1943. Three years later, four "better school" amendments became part of the state constitution, after a hard-fought campaign supported by such organizations as the state's Parent-Teacher Association and the Oklahoma Education Association. The amendments permitted local districts to increase the tax levy for schools from ten to fifteen mills with the approval of the voters; granted county commissioners the power to levy one mill for separate school building; provided that legislative appropriations for education must total at least $42 per student enrolled in the state's system; and provided that the state adopt a free textbook program for the common schools. In addition, by 1949 the legislature had prepared Oklahoma's first comprehensive school code, one that would be revised frequently until 1971, when a new code was adopted.

A number of organizations have helped to improve the quality of education in Oklahoma. One of the most important is the Oklahoma Education Association, organized in 1889. In the state's formative years the OEA lobbied for compulsory attendance laws, a teacher retirement system, higher salaries for instructors and administrators, increased legislative appropriations for schools, a unified school code, and many other reforms. The association supported, for example, the "better school" amendments of the 1940's. Today, it continues to strive for innovative, progressive reforms in the state's educational system. Another important organization is the Parent-Teacher Association. Local parent-teacher clubs sprang up in Oklahoma as the first schools began operation, and the state PTA was organized in

1922. Through the years the PTA has supported and actively worked for the same types of improvements favored by the OEA. Moreover, at local levels the PTA has organized free hot lunch programs, has tried to insure that children have frequent physical and dental examinations, has begun special assistance programs for less fortunate children, and generally has promoted progress at the grass-roots level.

Public education in Oklahoma made remarkable strides from the 1950's to the 1970's. Whereas in 1946 only 73.5 per cent of Oklahoma's teachers held bachelor's degrees, by the mid-1950's teacher qualifications had improved tremendously. Of 20,512 public school instructors, only 312 (1.5 per cent) remained on temporary certificates. All others had at least a bachelor's degree. Salaries for classroom teachers and for principals had increased to an average of $3,703. But Oklahoma's pay schedule still averaged $432 below the national average, and the state ranked twenty-eighth in the nation. The trend toward school consolidation continued, with state regulations forcing many one- and two-room rural schools to combine or to close.

The state continued to appropriate record amounts of money to improve the education of Oklahoma's youth. In the fiscal year 1960–61, for example, funds for public schools totaled $115,432,000 from all sources. Consolidation reduced the number of school districts from the unwieldy 4,450 of 1948 to 1,274 in 1960. There remained less than 300 one-room schools in the state by 1961. The average salary of teachers continued to rise—to slightly over $5,200 per yearly contract by 1962. By the mid-1970's appropriations reached new highs. State appropriations in 1974 topped $192,000,000, with $5,000,000 of that total marked for the free textbook program. The federal government added over $40,000,000, including more than $16,000,000 for the school lunch program. The trend toward consolidation of public schools continued, with the state showing 456 independent and 178 dependent school systems for a total of 634 districts. Average salaries for teachers and administrators increased, as did their qualifications. By 1974, a total of 11,596 teachers in the state's public school system held master's degrees.

Like the public schools, the system of higher education continued to expand. By mid-decade, the state's system of higher education included thirty-five colleges and universities, community colleges, and constituent agencies. Enrollment continued to increase, with totals reaching 110,586 in the fall semester of 1974, totals which reflected an 80 per cent increase over the figures of the mid-1960's. By 1974 budgeted monies for the state's schools topped $157,000,000, an increase of 170 per cent over a ten-year period.

The selections which follow capture something of the excitement of education in Oklahoma's formative years, something of the problems involved, and something of the hopes and dreams of those who manned the schools. The first section, organized topically, explores motivation, certification, and the ofttimes restrictive early contracts. Thereafter, organization is chronological, with respective sections examining the territorial years, early statehood, the depression, and the modern era. A final, short section contains a selection of the humor which, as all teachers know, emerges in the classroom. Of course, many of the reminiscences cover a broad panorama of topics, and some span more than one time-period. In these cases, the editor has tried to place an individual narrative in the chapter which most nearly fits the focus of the selection. A brief introduction precedes the narratives in each chapter. Occasionally the original narratives have been altered slightly for consistency in spelling and punctuation and for brevity; but in the main, the reminiscers speak for themselves. While limitations of space made selectivity a necessity, it should be pointed out that all of the reminiscences contributed for this project contained a wealth of material. All were valuable, but only a sampling could be included in this volume. All of these narratives will remain in the archives of the Oklahoma Historical Society for the use of researchers. At the end of this volume may be found the names of those who contributed to the project. In the selections reported in this study, contributors are identified by name, with their present home town (if known) immediately following. In addition, if pertinent, the town or county where particular experiences took place is mentioned. In a few instances parts of an original narrative are separated for use in different chapters. In these cases, only the contributor's name and home town are repeated. In selecting the material to be presented here, attempts have been made to choose representative samples from as many areas of the state as possible. But responses to our questionnaire remained more numerous for some regions than for others. Nevertheless, the selections found herein do reflect the experiences of Oklahoma's teachers. This is their volume. They still hold the future in their hands.

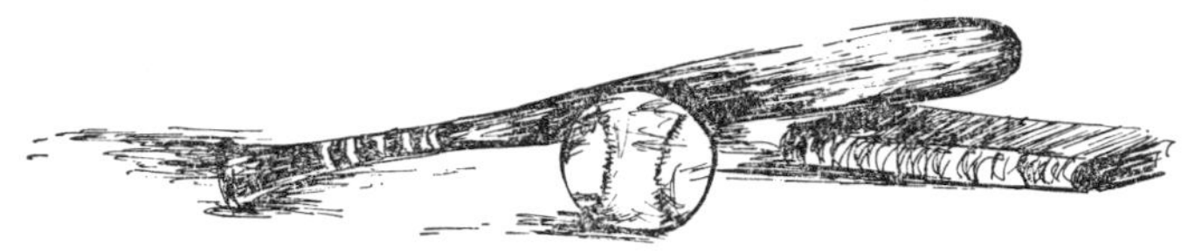

II

ON THE OTHER SIDE OF THE DESK

Individuals chose teaching careers for a variety of reasons. Rather than monetary considerations or status, most of those who wrote their reminiscences for this project stressed service to their communities as a motive for teaching. True, some found themselves faced with unpleasant alternatives. A. D. Hefley of McAlester, for example, decided that teaching was more attractive than picking cotton or plowing all day. Yet Hefley and most others had a sincere desire to help society, particularly underprivileged children who needed the guidance, friendship, and security that good teachers could help parents provide.

After selecting their careers, Oklahoma's teachers found themselves confronted by questions of certification. Local requirements were ever changing, as were territorial and, later, state requirements. Teachers in Oklahoma's formative years found that they must continuously attend summer institutes or add college credits each year to remain qualified in their fields. Finally, standardization came, when the state began requiring college degrees for permanent certification.

Once certified, the would-be instructor began "that" search for "that" first job. And when the search resulted in an offer of employment, teachers usually gazed in horror at the first contract. Not only was the pay low and the hours long, but school boards oftentimes attempted to regulate the private lives of teachers in their contracts. A "positive good" in the eyes of the typical school board, the restrictive contracts remained a "necessary requirement" for many teachers, with restrictions sometimes only tolerated because employment was needed.

The following chapter offers selections which deal with the issues of motivation, certification, and "that" first contract.

A. D. Hefley of McAlester had a special reason for deciding to become a teacher.

The date was July, 1910. I was fourteen years old and had never been to school. My parents were sharecroppers, and father thought it was about time that I enter school so I could learn to read and write and do a little "figgerin'," so I would not get cheated when I sold my cotton. It was three miles to the little pine box, one-room school where John Banks was teaching a two-month summer session. Mr. Banks was standing in the door of the building when I approached from the playground. He motioned to me to come to him. I started toward him, trembling with fear. I couldn't imagine what he wanted. "Come and let's sit on the well curb; I want to talk with you," he said. We sat down. Then, he turned to me and said, "I want you to enroll this morning and study to be a teacher; maybe you'll end up being president of the United States like Old Abe, who never got but three months schooling in his life," he told me. I had never thought of it before, but somehow I detected a ring of sincerity in his voice. What if I could better my condition? I was tired of eating corn pone and blackstrap for breakfast and plowing all day in the hot, blazing sun. At the end of the season, we had to give half of everything we made to the landlord. Maybe Mr. Banks was right; maybe I could go to school, learn to be a teacher, and improve my way of living.

Mr. Banks' words of encouragement had changed the entire course of my life. Never again would I be content to grub sassafras and plow all day in the hot sun.

Lloyd Bateson, Prague, adds an interesting comment on the question of "why teach?"

I began teaching school during the depression years for $55 per month. Since I had been born and reared on a farm, I thought I'd teach school instead of picking cotton.

Arcie Alice McFalls, Idabel, was always interested in children, and her interest in them prompted her to choose teaching as a career field.

When I was a child in grade school, I saw children less fortunate than I pushed in a corner of the building; no attention was paid to them. I started having daydreams: "When I get to be a teacher, I am going to teach all children." And that dream stayed with me until I became a teacher.

Faye M. Duke, Alva, remembers that she decided in early childhood to become a teacher.

I think my urge to teach might have come when I first saw the light of day. At any rate, according to my parents, I had my first teaching experience when I was not yet old enough for present-day kindergarten. In a simulated classroom set up the way I imagined a classroom to be from what my brothers had told me about school, I daily taught fifteen "pupils"—my fourteen dolls of assorted sizes and my constant companion, Tom. Tom was a big cat, white with yellow spots, and was possessed of the most amiable disposition in feline history. The epitome of patience and obedience, he became a stellar actor in whatever role I cast him. From this prophetic beginning, I came to realize my dream some fifteen years later. Armed with a first-grade certificate earned by taking an examination, I taught my first three years in the lower grades, teaching through the school term and working during summer terms toward my degree.

Vivian Smith, Elk City, gave this answer when asked why she became a teacher.

I think that the ability to teach was a talent I was born with. I decided to make teaching my occupation when I was in the second grade. I had a hard time getting my education. We were poor, a high school was fourteen miles away, and we didn't have the money to pay board and room. I worked my way through high school and college. My greatest satisfaction was doing the job right and, later, seeing my school children growing up and spreading out in the way they chose for their life's work. Some made preachers, teachers, doctors, dentists, housewives, farmers, and lawyers. They often came back to me and told me how I had helped them get started in life. My most memorable students were the ones who made good at the occupation they chose for their life's work.

On the question of motivation and certification, Zelma Bickers, McAlester, adds:

My reason for choosing the teaching profession may be considered light, but a high school principal urged me to do so, and my father promised me a wrist watch, which I wanted very much. Father thought the business world was no place for ladies. At that time, we could take a county examination on basic subjects. This I did and obtained a first-grade certificate which was considered the highest level, and I could teach any grade up to the ninth grade.

At first undecided about a college major, Arthur C. Brodell of Cleveland, Oklahoma, was influenced by a book on education which he read early in his college career.

When I left my farm home in 1907 at the age of fifteen to enter the subfreshman class at Oklahoma A. and M., I knew a few things about farming. I had no idea what other occupations had to offer. During my freshman year, I roomed at a place where there was a senior enrolled in education. One day while visiting this senior, I picked up a book dealing with one of his educational subjects. The book was so interesting that I decided to become a teacher.

Eunice Heizer, Blackwell, was influenced by her father and the high ideals of the teaching profession.

I suppose that most of us sometime in our life have wondered just why we chose to do the things that we did, or why we developed a great desire to do certain things. But as to teaching, it was no problem to choose. My father had grown up in a big family where ideals were high, but opportunity for higher education was lacking. So he had very little formal training, but what he did have was a practical nature, and it was enough for him to make a good living for his family and be a well-respected citizen. But, too, it gave him a desire for more, which he attained in possible ways as he went along.

In those days, a person with a profession was looked up to, honored, and respected. And as you know, teaching remained one of the few professions open to women. A teacher was to be revered, was wise, and was beyond reproach. In fact, a teacher could be thrown out of her school if she showed any sign of immorality. So, what more could a father want for his only daughter? And as for me, I dearly loved every teacher I had and wept bitterly every time school was out. It seemed as if I lived for just one thing—to be a teacher.

Some individuals appear to have been "born" to teach. Addie Pettit of Hartshorne comments on her decision to enter the profession.

My earliest recollection of my dreams for the future was that I was to teach. My most vivid memories of childhood are "playing school." Anyone could guess who the teacher was: I ruled the other "kids" and my two sisters with a power that was almost unbelievable. In the summer time, the "schoolhouse" was under the trees in our yard, and in the winter the bedroom was converted to a classroom. During all of the trials of growing up—puberty, adolescence, hoeing corn, picking cotton, milking cows, churning, washing and ironing clothes, and the hundreds of other chores that are a part of life on a farm—I always knew that some day I would be a teacher. This overwhelming desire probably accounts for the fact that the Sunday afternoon in May, 1930, when I signed a contract to teach a school was the most exciting experience thus far in my young life. In the spring of my senior year of high school, I took the county teacher's examination in the county superintendent's office in McAlester, and I passed it. This qualified me for a third-grade teacher's certificate.

May Parry Forneris, Coalgate, adds:

Through the years, I never had a thought other than to be a teacher. My first pupils were a mother cat and her rather unwilling litter of kittens. Later, when I began to read and love school more and more each day, my pupils became the younger children on the block. After college, I was home again and teaching the children of friends with whom I went to grade and high school; soon, it became the second and third generation. I taught for thirty-eight years.

Edna Donley of Oklahoma City, a past-president of the Oklahoma Education Association, relates some of the phases that teacher certification has gone through since 1913.

Teachers are born, not made. I'm sure you have heard this

statement many times in your life. However, those of us who have spent many years in the classroom know that the kind of preparation we receive is so very important. In 1913 my first grade teacher, who was a first-year instructor in a one-room school with all eight grades, had a third-grade county certificate issued to her by the county superintendent after she had taken an examination in the basic subjects. Her license was effective for one year. My sixth grade teacher in a two-room school had a first-grade certificate which she had received by taking the county examination in more subjects than had my first grade teacher, and she had made a grade of at least 90 per cent average on them. Her certificate was in force for three years. Most of my high school teachers had earned from thirty to sixty hours in an "approved program" at one of the state colleges.

I started my teaching career at eighteen years of age, with a life certificate. In 1926 this meant that I was qualified to teach any subject at any grade level. However, two years with those sixth and seventh grade students convinced me that I needed much more preparation to be as effective a teacher as I thought I could become. Perhaps it was because so many of us felt the same way that we united our efforts through our national and state professional organizations to do something about teacher standards and certification.

We had to begin where our certification process had been established. Prior to 1920, the power to certify teachers had rested primarily with county and city superintendents. However, beginning in 1913 the approved program approach was widely adopted. This plan required persons to complete certain approved courses, with certificates issued by the State Board of Education. In 1929 legislation abolished the county and city examining boards and gave the State Board of Education the legal authority of certification. Licensing power still remains with that state agency.

World War II interrupted our certification program. The war took many teachers from the classrooms, women as well as men. Some women joined the WACs, and others went to defense factories. Many remained in the classroom where they felt teaching youth was still top priority, but because of the great shortage of teachers, "war emergency certificates" were issued to new instructors. This emergency plan brought into the classrooms persons with less than a high school education who had taken some short courses in the summer. In 1943–44 there were 905 emergency certificates issued. After the war it became evident that some kind of teacher involvement was seriously needed for raising the standards for certification. In an effort to increase participation, the State Department of Education and the Oklahoma Education Association jointly created the Teacher Education and Professional Standards Commission (TEPS) in February, 1947. This commission's philosophy included the belief that the profession should assume responsibility for the competence of the members and for their performance and that there should be improved communication between institutions that prepare teachers and the schools which employ them. This commission became a powerful force in discontinuing the war emergency certificates and the life certificates and in raising the minimum requirement from sixty semester hours in 1947 to a bachelor's degree in 1957. Because of these far-reaching decisions, Oklahoma ranked first in the nation with the percentage of teachers with a bachelor's degree. In less than five years nearly 40 per cent had a master's degree. These are distinctions of which we can be justly proud! Improved standards were adopted for counselors, for school administrators, and for others in special areas. Efforts were made to get all teacher preparation institutions accredited by the National Council for Accreditation of Teacher Education (NCATE). By 1962 almost 87 per cent of all instructors were graduated from such institutions. In 1971 the state legislature created the Professional Standards Board, composed of twenty-six members with the responsibility for providing leadership for the improvement of standards for the certification of teachers and other educational personnel. The standards board also served in an advisory capacity to the State Board of Education. This gave the profession a legal voice in setting standards.

As I reflect upon the changes that have taken place in certification since I started my own education in 1913, I'm proud of the advancements which have been made; and I'm proud to have had a part in them. Yes, there were heartaches; tempers often flared up; opinions differed; and yet through it all, there was an honest desire to improve standards. Our differences were in how it should be done. I'm pleased to have served on the TEPS Commission as a classroom teacher, and as an OEA staff member, I was privileged as a part of my assignments to serve as consultant. Also, I wrote the original bill that created the Professional Standards Board. It was because of the excellent working relationship that existed between the leadership of the State Department of Education and the Oklahoma Education Association that the profession has had a meaningful opportunity to develop and recommend standards.

Chelsea O. Burkett, born and reared in Cleveland County, tells of a teacher's seemingly constant progression through the different levels of certification.

With a high school education, I decided to apply to teach in one of the seventy rural schools in Cleveland County. At that time, 1925, there was still a rural school every three miles—checkerboard fashion—over all the county. I took an examination in the county superintendent's office for a third-grade county certificate. I passed, went to the rural South Gale School, applied, and got the job; and I was on my way, teaching for a living. My third-grade county certificate soon expired. I then took another test, this time for a second-grade certificate. I passed and then was on my way for another two years. But these certificates were very temporary, so teachers as a group—not just me—started slowly to move forward in their qualifications: We all wanted to secure college credits. My first two college credits were acquired in an extension class from Edmond which was held in the county superintendent's office. The next two semester courses were on school law. That was my start, my first college hours. Then we set sixteen college hours for a goal, which would allow us a two-year extension on our teaching certificate. We met that goal.

The state department set thirty-two hours for a goal, which would give us a five-year certificate. With night classes, Saturday classes, and correspondence courses we reached that goal. Then, we were told that a life certificate would be issued on sixty semester hours. The idea of county certificates was being shunned for college training. When some reached sixty hours of credit, they stopped to catch their breath. But by now, summer school terms at all colleges were popular with teachers. We began a system of going to summer terms and teaching during the fall, winter, and spring—then doing it all over again.

By December 1941, with no school terms missed, I had worked out 109 semester hours. On December 7, Pearl Harbor Day, I had a conference with my wife. I secured a substitute teacher to finish my term. I went to the University of Oklahoma for one semester to finish my hard-earned degree in elementary education. In 1948 I secured my master's degree in secondary education and began a new career—secondary teaching and administration. Continuing to attend classes under the G.I. Bill while I was securing my master's degree, I finished all of my course work on my doctor's degree with some 200 semester hours. I saw that I must stop either teaching or going to school, as the year-round job with no let-up was too much; so I settled down as a junior high and then a senior high school principal at Lexington High, where I worked until my retirement in 1968, having taught forty-two years.

The career of Nettie Mitchell Parker, Mangum, shows the patterns of certification as many teachers worked their way through various grades.

Nettie Parker taught with every kind of certificate that the state issued. After finishing high school in May, 1927, she started teaching the next term with a third-grade county certificate. In 1928 she received her two-year state certificate; then she acquired a five-year license in 1930. She received her life certificate in 1931. She was awarded a B.S. degree in 1936 from Southwestern State College at Weatherford. In 1947 she received her master of education degree from the University of Oklahoma at Norman.

At twenty years of age, Fern Folger McCormick graduated from Morrison High School, Morrison, Oklahoma. She tells how she acquired certification.

The summer of 1924 I went to Phillips University, where I received my first eight hours of college credit. I took a state teaching examination in the county superintendent's office which entitled me to a third-grade teaching certificate. It made me eligible to teach my first rural school at Wing Spring, a little one-room schoolhouse which was located back in the blackjacks southeast of Perry. I taught twenty-some-odd boys and girls—all eight grades for $85 a month. At the end of the second summer, I completed another eight hours, passed another state examination, and received my second-grade teaching certificate. My parents moved to Perry that summer, and I was able to drive to Wing Spring where I taught my second year for $95 a month. In 1926 I transferred to Central State Teachers College. At the end of the summer work, I again took the state teaching examination and received my first-grade certificate, which was good until I received my life certificate by completing ninety hours by attending summer school and doing extension work for the next eleven years.

Jess Hudson, Tulsa, is pleased that requirements have become stricter over the years.

During my forty-four years of service in the schools of Oklahoma, I have seen a number of changes in public school education, most of which have been good. One of the most significant improvements that comes readily to mind is the increased professionalization of education. My own personal experience is a case in point and is the basis for my views. My earliest awareness that there might be some requirements for teaching was when I finished the eighth grade. Our superintendent proudly told the class that we were all qualified to teach school on a third-class certificate.

Prior to my graduation with a degree from a small liberal arts college, I had not intended to make teaching my career and consequently had only one hour of credit in education. That hour consisted of a brief overview of the history of education which was offered in the history department. There was no department of education. As graduation approached, a friend who was superintendent of schools at Headrick, Oklahoma, wrote me offering me a job at $90 per month. I decided to accept the offer but found that there were some certification requirements. Even though I had no professional training, I was issued a temporary one-year certificate with the provision that the following summer I enroll in eight hours of education at the University of Oklahoma if I expected to continue teaching.

Before I had completed my first year at Headrick, I was called into military service during World War I and was sent overseas. In the summer of 1919, near the end of my service, I was offered the superintendency at Headrick, but the fact that I had not completed the requirement of eight hours of professional training confronted me; consequently, hoping to get a postponement of the requirement for one year, I wrote to the state superintendent of schools presenting my case and asking for a deferment of the requirement. Apparently feeling a great surge of patriotism, the superintendent wrote to me saying that in view of my services to my country, all certification requirements would be waived; and I would be granted a life certificate to teach all subjects in all grades. I could hardly believe he meant it. But on my way to Headrick, I stopped at his office, presented my letter, and picked up the certificate.

I used this gratis certificate for eleven years without any professional education. During this time, I thought of teaching as a temporary vocation. I planned to complete a doctorate in chemistry and enter the field of industrial chemistry; consequently, I saw no need for professional education courses. During these eleven years, I taught Cicero, German, French, algebra, plane and solid geometry, general science, physics, and economics. My only qualifications for teaching were a fairly good academic background in all the subjects except economics, in which the superintendent knew I had not an hour of credit. Never did I have the opportunity to teach chemistry, though I had completed a master's degree in the field.

At the end of the eleven years of teaching, I was offered an elementary school principalship in Tulsa provided I enroll in elementary education and begin work toward the master's degree in education. The offers for beginning positions in commercial or industrial chemisty at that time were less lucrative than that of a principalship; consequently, I abandoned for all time the idea of chemistry in favor of a career in education. The requirement of a master's degree in education for the principal's job was only a local school district's move toward greater professionalization, but the idea of a certificate good for all grades for life was becoming unacceptable to the profession as a whole.

From the 1920's to the present there have been many changes in certification requirements which I will not detail. The approach to change has been two-fold: first, restriction of certification to major and minor fields with greater emphasis on academic preparation; and second, increased requirements in professional education. Now one must be certified to teach a specific subject in secondary schools, to teach elementary subjects, or to be a counselor. One must obtain a special certificate to be an elementary school principal, another to be a secondary school principal, and still another to be in general administration. No more significant change in the forty-four years of my school experience occurs to me than the growth in professionalization from my gratis certificate granting me for life the right to teach any subject in any grade to the highly specialized certification of the present.

Mabel Baldwin Couch, Chelsea, also comments on early certification.

I went to classes in country schools until I finished the eighth grade. I rode horseback eight miles to Centralia, Oklahoma, to take my examination for my eighth grade diploma. We lived too far from a high school for me to go without staying away from home; being only fifteen years old, I continued studying the eighth grade. But in 1917, as soon as I was eighteen years old, I went to Nowata, Oklahoma, and took the teacher's examination for a third-grade county certificate. My joy knew no bounds the day I received that license. Later permits—including a second- and first-grade county certificate, a bachelor's degree of science, and a master's degree of teaching—never gave me half the thrill of that "first permit" to teach.

Jessie May Hines of Chickasha, who has been at Cameron University for the past twenty-nine years, remembers the strict provisions of her first public school contract which attempted to regulate aspects of her private life.

When I signed my first contract, I agreed that I would not smoke, dance, play cards, or leave the community for more than one week end a month. One example of the restrictive atmosphere in which I worked occurred when a minister was visiting in the home of one of his members and saw a bridge table sitting in the room of the two teachers who roomed there. He did not ask about its use. The teachers had "kitchen privileges" but would eat from that bridge table in their room. The minister reported to the school board and wanted the teachers fired because they were "playing cards." They were called before the board, but they were not fired—just reprimanded. Contracts now simply state that we have been approved and that we shall receive the stated salary, "if funds are available." There is still protection for administrators and boards concerning salaries but nothing to assure teachers that they will receive all salaries. But we are on the way toward even more improvements in many areas.

Joyce Bradfield, Ponca City, taught her first school in Blackwell, Oklahoma, and once signed a contract which prohibited her from marrying.

I received a two-year temporary certificate and a first grade job at a salary of $76.70 per month for nine months, with the stipulation that I was to attend summer school each summer thereafter until I had acquired a college degree. My contract also read in the fine print that I was not to indulge in dancing, smoking, or marriage and that I must spend my week ends for the most part in the service of the community in which I taught.

Gertrude Gates Patton, Duncan, briefly recounts the requirements in her first contract.

My 1919 contract specified that I must be in the town at least three week ends each month and take part in church activities. Also, I must not marry through the school year. Really, these were not hardships, as was the no smoking requirement a bit later.

Jontie Combs, who taught at Hominy (Osage County) from 1929 to 1934, remembers that her first contract stipulated no card playing, no dancing, and no smoking.

The school board also hired a man to watch the boarding places of teachers. His job was to report to the board if the contract were broken. In addition, he was to report the names of the men who called on the young lady teachers and the time they left. Our salaries were so low between 1924 and 1934 that nine teachers lived in four bedrooms with one bath.

Jane E. Davis, Norman, began teaching in 1923 in Grady County. Her first contract contained a list of at least one dozen "don't's."

I was born, reared, and educated in Oklahoma. I started to class in a one-room school in Grady County, called the Ireton District, which was five miles northeast of Alex. I went to Alex for my high school education and to Central State Teachers College at Edmond long enough to earn a third-grade teacher's certificate. I began teaching in 1923 in Grady County in a two-room school in the Valley View District. I taught there only for two years because that was as long as any teacher could teach in one district at a time. Another teacher taught for three months with me, got married, and forfeited her contract; so I had to teach all eight grades alone to finish out the term for $75 a month. The next year they renewed my contract and raised my salary to $100 a month if I would continue teaching all eight grades. I agreed. I am saying this to let the teachers of today realize what teachers earned back in the "good old days" and how well off they are today.

In the early days, the teacher's contract was really something to talk about. As I recall, here are some of the requirements: 1. This contract is null and void if the teacher marries. 2. Do not keep company with men during the school week. 3. Be home between the hours of 8:00 P.M. and 6:00 A.M., unless in attendance at a school function. 4. If teaching in town, do not loiter downtown in ice cream stores or cafés. 5. Do not leave town at any time without permission of the chairman of the board of trustees. If teaching in the country, do not go to town without permission of the chairman of the board of trustees. 6. Do not smoke cigarettes. 7. Do not drink beer, wine, or whisky. 8. Do not dress in bright colors. 10. Do not dye hair. 11. Wear long dresses, not more than two inches above the ankle. 12. Do not use face powder, mascara, or paint on the lips. I'm just wondering how a contract like this one would go over in our day of teaching in 1975.

The first contract of Nell Terrill Burton Welch, Tulsa, contained the following restrictions: no card playing, no marrying, no dancing.

Once I danced—the "Home Sweet Home Waltz." Some of my high school pupils saw me. If they had told, I would have been fired. Two girls of my eleventh grade class asked me a question. If they had a party in their home on Friday night, with parents in attendance, could they dance. I answered that I felt the parents and not the school should decide. The party was given, they did dance, and they were called into the superintendent's office for interrogation. One question was, "Did any faculty member know about the party?" The girls replied, "We cannot answer your question unless you call Miss Burton to hear our answer." I was not called. Another time, after a basketball game on Friday evening, some players went to a dance. They were suspended from school. My wish was that the little daughter of that superintendent would grow up to be a dancer. I hope she did.

Mabel Couch remembers one of the early contracts she signed in a Rogers County school district.

I recall the stiff contract I signed when I taught in the Talala school. It stated that teachers would not be permitted to date on school nights; and on Friday, Saturday, or Sunday nights, teachers must be at home or in their boarding place by 10:00 P.M. Gentlemen were not to be allowed in a lady's room unless properly chaperoned by the landlady. Once I broke that rule by attending an ice cream social to raise money for the school. A young gentleman and I were met at the door by the clerk of the board, T. Dawson. He promptly asked if I remembered what my contract said about dating. I assured him that I did but that I assumed under the circumstances it would be overlooked. He very sternly advised me not to let it happen again. He said, "Contracts don't make way for assumptions, whatever the circumstances." Thereafter, I missed attending many school functions like ball games, programs, ice cream socials, and other events because I dared not risk losing my contract—and school.

Other provisions of that same contract stated: Teachers were not to use tobacco in any form. Teachers were not to dance or play cards. Teachers were expected to attend church and Sunday school and to take part in civic affairs, as long as it did not interfere with their teaching. Teachers were to teach and accept their responsibility by always setting a good example for their pupils. Teachers must dress neatly and becomingly. Jobs were scarce—so we signed the restrictive contracts and, for the most part, followed them to the letter.

Katharine Clark Moore, Sapulpa, began teaching in 1928, and here comments on her first position (Okfuskee County), certification procedures, and contracts typical of the 1920's and 1930's.

I started my teaching career in a three-teacher rural school in July, 1928. I had finished high school in May, and my only teaching credential was a two-year certificate issued after passing a state teacher's examination in February of that same year. At that time, many rural schools had a two-month summer session and dismissed classes during September and October so students could pick cotton. My summer experience in trying to teach first, second, and third grades proved to me that I needed some "know how." So in September, I enrolled in a nine-week teacher-training course at East Central State Teachers College. During this time, teachers' colleges were on five nine-week terms and a three-week August term. After ten years of summer school, extension classes, and correspondence courses I earned a bachelor of science degree and had progressed to a small-town school where I continued teaching for thirteen years until World War II began. Many teachers began teaching careers just as I did; teaching and working on college hours in order to earn a degree.

During the 1920's and 1930's there were no tenure laws, and teachers were never sure they would be re-employed for the next year. Most teachers, including principals, were single women; and if they married, their contracts were immediately cancelled. Our contracts contained many rigid requirements, such as no dancing, no smoking (for women), and no dating through the school weekdays. We must attend all school activities whether or not they pertained to our teaching assignment. And it was mandatory that we attend church at least three Sundays out of four. Salaries for elementary teachers ranged from $70 to $90 per month for nine months. High school teachers were paid a little more. In the early 1930's the school district where I taught didn't have enough money to finish out the term; teachers were asked to donate their services for the last month of school. Of course, we did, otherwise we would not have been reinstated for the next year.

Some strict demands were made by superintendents and principals. Faculty meetings were held at 7:30 A.M. No teachers were permitted to visit in the halls or on the playground. We were on hall or playground duty every week. If we were on hall duty, we ate our lunch in the hall. The same for playground duty! When on bus duty, we stayed until 6:00 P.M. and sometimes until 7:00 in bad weather. We were required to remain in our classrooms at least one hour after the students were dismissed to work on the next day's preparations. Principals checked to see that we did! We made detailed lesson plans, and the principal checked to see if we carried them out. All of these things we accepted with little question because this was part of our assignment.

In their quest for education and later in their search for that first job, many teachers received aid from their parents. Ruth Rice of Pauls Valley was one young scholar who had such help. Note the unusual way in which her father assisted in finding Ruth her first assignment.

I am the last child of nine children, all of whom were girls except one. My parents believed in getting an education, so five sisters ahead of me were school teachers, and I followed the pattern. In those days, if you were a teacher you walked a straight and narrow line and you were respected in your community.

After finishing high school during the depression years (which was a struggle), I went to the nearest teacher's college and got a job with a nice family, mostly taking care of childrn who were in the elementary grades. My parents helped me with my tuition, which was $5.00 per semester, bought me a few clothes, and gave me $1.00 or $2.00 for books and spending money. My mother cooked for roughnecks working on an oil well near our home to get the money. The summer rolled around, and one of my sisters loaned me $50 to light-housekeep in one room. The end of that summer I received my two-years certificate.

My Dad had a friend or two who were on the school board, one of whom owed him $100. My Dad forgot the $100 in exchange for the teaching position for me with the school.

III

THE TERRITORIAL YEARS

Many of Oklahoma's earliest teachers had a childhood which included a trip by wagon to "the territories," life in a temporary sod house or dugout, and the otherwise austere life of pioneers. Their education oftentimes consisted of training in early subscription schools or perhaps in Indian institutions, where they learned the rudiments of reading, writing, and arithmetic. Their pioneer beginnings made them tough and strong-willed and most capable of meeting the challenges which they would find in Oklahoma's first, crude, underfinanced schools.

After receiving their basic education in early territorial schools, Oklahoma young people who chose the teaching profession joined a hearty brotherhood. Joining ranks with older instructors who perhaps had had a few years' experience before moving to "the territories," the inexperienced teachers usually began their careers in the impoverished surroundings of the one-room sod or log school. Many teachers started their life's work in education as teenagers, some as young as fifteen years of age. Many were not certified. Hence, it often took years of part-time study, including participation in summer normals, for teachers to progress from temporary or third-grade county certification to lifetime certification, a task made more difficult because of the frequent upgrading of requirements by the territorial (later state) board of education.

Many of the selections below recount, from both "sides of the desk," early experiences in the schools of Oklahoma.

Lottie Ross, of McAlester, was given her early schooling by her father because there was no school near her first home in Whitefield, Indian Territory (Haskell County). She received her first teaching appointment in 1899 at a Choctaw Indian school near Byrds Mill (Coal County).

I was born on a farm, February 10, 1880, near the little town of Whitefield, Indian Territory. It was considered a very lawless part of the county. Robbers and marauding bands often invaded the country. Belle Starr, leader of one gang, often came to town, but no officer tried to arrest her because she would shoot to kill if apprehended. But aside from that fact, there was a certain amount of charm to the country. It was there the buffalo grazed on the prairies; the deer scampered about in the woods and became so tame in the winter time they would come right up to a farmer's cow lot to pick up a few corn shucks that had been blown over the fence by the wind. Wild turkeys made the morning air ring with rapture, and the toms strutted around with their long tail feathers spread in a fanlike shape in order to win the love of the hens.

There were no rural schools near where we lived, so my father taught me himself. One hour, after supper, every night was set aside for school work. We used *Swinton's Readers*, *Ray's Arithmetic*, and the *Blue Back Spelling Book*, and Father's own copies of penmanship. After our lessons were over, Father coached me on public speaking, which came in very handy at an early age and, in fact, for all my life.

When I was ten years old, Father decided I had better be in school with other children; he and the family moved to Texas, and I started to a rural school. Several years passed, and I graduated from the Alamo Institute at the age of eighteen. I wanted to become a schoolteacher, and I thought the schools in the Indian Territory were more in need of teachers than any place I could think of, and I persuaded my parents to go with me back to the land of my dreams.

One day in June, we put a few things in a covered wagon drawn by two big bay horses and set out from Texas toward the Indian Territory. After traveling seven days, we entered the territory and settled in a small town called McMillan, named for a prominent Indian who lived there. I inquired as to whom to see in regard to getting a school. I was told that if I wanted to teach in the Choctaw schools, I would have to see a Mr. Martin Chigley, who was superintendent of the schools. I went to see Mr. Chigley and made application for a school. He told me that all of the contracts had been filled except one for a remote one-room school. He then looked straight at me for a few minutes as if he were considering my age and ability to teach and then said, "I wouldn't advise you to take the school." I asked why, and he said, "The men who patronize the school like what they call firewater; and when they drink it, they go to the schoolhouse and run the teacher off. No teacher has ever taught a nine-month school there." But I was so desirous of becoming a teacher that I said, "I'll take it."

I went before the examining board, got a certificate, signed a contract, and prepared to teach my first school. The place was near Byrd's Mill, sixty-five miles from where I lived. There was no rail connection, so my father drove me over in a buggy. It took twelve hours to make the trip. When I got there, I went to the house of the Byrds to ask about getting a place to stay while teaching the school. They told me I could stay with them. My father stayed all night. Early the next morning I drove out to take a look at the schoolhouse, get my bearings, and see what supplies I would need before school started. Well, of all the disappointments that could ever happen to an eighteen-year-old, would-be teacher, I met the biggest one there. Mr. Chigley told me it was an undesirable place, but I didn't get the picture until I actually saw it. The building was a one-room, boxlike house with two windows and a door. It had been partly blown off the foundation by a storm or strong wind and was propped by three long poles on one side to keep it from sliding entirely off. It was located at the edge of a big prairie where hundreds of longhorn steers grazed right up to the very door of the house. On the other side was a woodland that stretched for miles in the opposite direction. The woodland and the prairie were separated by a three-strand barbed-wire fence that barely missed the poles that held the house intact.

While I was looking the situation over, two cowboys rode up, spoke politely, doffed their big broad-brimmed hats, and asked if

I was the teacher. I told them no, but I was thinking about becoming the teacher. Then one of the boys warned, "Don't be caught afoot in this pasture because these longhorn critters will fight; sometimes they even attack us on horseback." After looking the situation over and talking to the cowboys, I started back to where I was to stay while teaching. As I drove along, I came within a few hundred yards of some steers, but they didn't seem to notice me. My father tried to persuade me to go back home with him. But I felt it was a challenge; I could do something to lift those people and set them on a higher plane of living. I stayed. But the great question in my mind was: How could I get to school without coming in contact with those ferocious beasts? The schoolhouse was three miles from where the Byrds lived, and I would have to go the three miles through the pasture where the steers grazed. Mr. and Mrs. Byrd quickly solved the problem. I was to ride horseback and go with their two little boys, who would also ride a horse. I was assigned a beautiful big bay horse. I hadn't been used to riding horseback and had to sit on what was called a side saddle and wear a riding skirt that came down over my feet. Hence I had to lead the horse up to a stump or box or something to enable me to get on. And when I did get on, I had to hold on for dear life to keep from falling off. This method of mounting and riding was quite amusing to the little boys who could jump into the saddle like squirrels. Transportation being solved and some riding practiced, I was ready to begin my first year as a schoolteacher at a school that had a dark and gloomy past.

On September 3, 1899, I started out on my new adventure. I rode horseback up to the schoolhouse and found eight little Indian boys already there. They all seemed to begin talking at the same time, but I couldn't understand a word they said. Later other children came, but I still couldn't understand what they said. It made me feel as if I had suddenly gone to a foreign country and was preparing to teach a seemingly foreign people who spoke a foreign language. I hardly knew how to begin, but I thought the best and first thing was to win their friendship and love. I went out on the playground and played games with them at recess and at noon, and we really had a good time. We soon understood each other much better. I loved those children, and we got along nicely. I let them try to teach me some words in their language, but as I couldn't get the right accent in pronouncing the words, I created much fun for the children. The first word I learned was "chicama" which meant "good morning" or "how are you." That is the way they greeted my every morning. They would wave their hands and say, "Chicama." The words for good-by were "eishi legie." These words were used every evening. We played various games at recess and at noon. We even organized a ball team, and I was chief batter; but I couldn't hit the ball with the bat. I used a piece of a board, but I sure could send that ball flying through the air. I tried to talk their language while on the playground, which pleased the children; and when I would get a word wrong, they enjoyed saying the word over and over until I got it right. I used the blackboard to illustrate words to get English language over to them. A little boy was reading about a pony one day. I asked him if he had ever seen a pony; he said, "No." I then drew the picture of a pony on the blackboard, and he and all the children laughed about it. It took pictures to make a word real to them. They tried to accept my way of living as I tried to accept theirs. We had really built a little haven of love and contentment.

One day, in early December, while the children and I were playing in the yard, a man who had been drinking firewater suddenly appeared, drew a pistol, and began shooting. The children and I took to the woods as fast as our feet could carry us. He followed, still shooting and whooping. After a while, all was still; but we listened for the snap of a bush or some sign that he was still following us. We hid in the woods for hours. All of the children except a fourteen-year-old girl deserted me. Bless her heart. She was my God-sent guardian angel that day. My life was entirely in her hands. I was scared, lost, and unaware of how to get out of those woods or where to go. In desperation, I asked her to go with me back to the schoolhouse so I could get my horse and go home. She said, "No, no, he's there." Then I said, "I can't stay here. Take me somewhere." She then led the way to a white man's house about a mile from where we were standing. The white man went with me to get my horse, but when we got to the schoolhouse, the Indian was still there, as my guardian angel predicted he would be; the white man managed to hold him until I could get my horse and get away. When I rode up to the gate at home, a man came out and took charge of my horse; and I went into the house. Mr. and Mrs. Byrd both met me at the door and inquired about what had happened, as it was then only two o'clock in the afternoon. I was a sight to behold. As I ran through the woods, I had no time to pick the best way to go; so as a result, my dress was torn, my face and hands were scratched and bleeding, and my long hair was loose and hanging down my back and over my shoulders as all of the pins had been snatched out by the limbs that grabbed my hair as I ran beneath them. I related the story of the man shooting up the place and my flight through the woods. As I talked, I illustrated the story by displaying the torn place in my dress, the blood on my hands and face, and my hair hanging loosely over my shoulders. Then in a burst of anger I blurted out, "I'm not going to be run off from this school. I'm going to protect myself and those children. I'm going to be a second Belle Starr. I'm going to prove that I can shoot a pistol straighter than any man who has been drinking firewater." Then I left quickly and went to my room. I went that same evening and got a .32-caliber pistol, and when I showed it to Mr. Byrd, I said, "Let them come now;

I'll not run any more." Mr. Byrd said, "Let me talk to the man who has committed this offense." Armed with my pistol, I went to school the next day wondering what might happen, but I felt like I could handle any situation. To my suprise, about ten o'clock Mr. Byrd brought the offender up to the schoolhouse. He apologized and said that he would tell the other men to stay away. I don't know whether Mr. Byrd had told that Indian that the teacher had a gun, but I wasn't bothered any more.

Opal A. Scales, Muskogee, first attended school in Leader, Indian Territory (Hughes County). She began her teaching career in Allen (Pontotoc County).

We are from a pioneer family who came to the Indian Territory from Texas in a covered wagon in the year 1888. We lived in a log cabin in a settlement known as Leader, named for a famous Indian, Otis Leader. My earliest schooling was in a typical school of that time, a subscription school in Leader. It was the custom then for a parent, often with the help of the teacher, to organize the school by getting the other parents of a community to send their children to the school and to pay a small fee. The teacher, Fannie Holman, and my father secured fifteen pupils, each paying $1.00 per month for the privilege of attending classes. This school was held for three months in the summer under a brush arbor. The teacher boarded around among the patrons. Fannie Holman stayed most of the time at our home.

I began my teaching career in Indian Territory in Allen which was at that time a wild western town. Often "shoot up" occurred on the town square, and the loss of a life was very common. My father expressed his wish that I teach at Gerty, a quiet religious town nearby, rather than the wild Allen. I didn't tell him I had a choice between the two towns, and I chose Allen, where I thought there would be the most excitement; and there was.

I had no teaching certificate, but I obtained my position from a man in McAlester who had charge of employing one teacher in each school in the territory which had Indian pupils. Allen was in the Choctaw Nation. I had just graduated from William Woods College, a junior college in Fulton, Missouri. When I presented my diploma to the man, I was immediately hired. I taught with another teacher, a man, in a one-room school with a partition dividing the room. I had the first six grades, and the man, the other grades. Each month, I received $40 from the Indian agency at McAlester. Ten of the $40 I paid to the school for the privilege of using the building. I taught at Allen for one year. On November 16, 1907, Oklahoma became a state. The new state required me to get a teaching certificate by taking the teacher's examination in Holdenville, Oklahoma, the county seat of Hughes County. I was required to attend a normal school in Holdenville each summer to renew my certificate. My statehood teaching days included one year in Calvin, two years in Francis, one year in Coalgate, and ten years in McAlester, where I was principal of the junior high school. I came to Muskogee in 1924 and taught in West Junior High until 1954, a total of forty-seven teaching years. The highest salary I earned was $2,200, for a one-year contract.

Herbert C. King, president of the Comanche County Retired Teachers Association, contributed the account below, a summary of a black community's attempts to establish a school and of his father's contributions to the effort (Kingfisher County, Oklahoma Territory).

William Clarence King was born March 11, 1867, in Topeka,

Kansas. He attended school and spent the early part of his life there. He was among the first blacks to graduate from high school in Topeka. He came to Oklahoma with his parents in 1887, and they settled in a community seven miles east and one mile south of the county seat in Kingfisher County. The community was later named Pleasant Valley. The community progressed. Pioneers built a church, a school, a lodge hall, and a cemetery. The lodge hall was the first to cease operation. Later, the church was forced to close because the congregation could not find a pastor; but the school lasted until the late 1930's. Today, only one black family lives in the community; but high on the hill stands the cemetery, well kept by the children of those old settlers who have passed on. This community was almost a Utopia. There was no need for law enforcement officers because no vice existed. A few of the people—a very few—smoked, but the community had no crime.

The legislature required the citizens of Pleasant Valley to build separate schools for blacks. A school was built, but they had a difficult time finding a teacher. At this time, the rural facilities were supervised by the county superintendent of schools. To graduate, a person had to take the eighth grade county examination and make a passing grade in all subjects. This test was a grueling two-day affair, administered by a qualified stranger to the students. The testing was done in about eleven subject areas. So many minutes were allowed to complete each test. Schools were only open six months, and this made it very difficult to prepare for the examination, which was administered in early April. If a person missed taking the old county examination, a part of his education was also missed.

Pleasant Valley continued to grow rapidly, but the settlers still found themselves without a teacher. It was suggested that William C. King be employed to teach since he had more education than anyone else and had taught many in the community to read and write and to do simple arithmetic. He had worked in the church and the lodge and was a leader in the community. He had just married Addie May Roger, a young girl with four younger brothers and sisters to raise.

King was hired for the fall term of 1890. Most of the students were related to him as well as each other. King served as a model to the young people in the community. He was noted for his strict discipline, punctuality, clean methods of living, and devotion to others. He was forced to attend summer normal for many years to keep his teaching certificate alive. Most of the time, he drove back and forth in a horse and buggy. He also tried to operate a wheat farm and devoted a large amount of time to the church. He served as secretary of the Western District Baptist Association for forty years.

Geordia Coffey Camp, Oklahoma City, gave this summary of her father's early experiences in Oklahoma Territory (Washita County).

In the year 1893, pioneering in a one-room dugout schoolhouse, with only a dirt floor and no furniture, no books, and no other supplies that might be construed as teaching aids, George Coffey started his first school in the old Cheyenne-Arapaho country. On the beginning day, with a few books of his own, Bibles, almanacs, and old papers brought by some of the fourteen students, he managed to set up a good program of study. The lonely hillside place of learning was located in what is now Washita County. Though largely unsettled, it was here that life in school and out was made colorful by raiding outlaws and Indians. Nine years of teaching in Washita County, and Coffey's duties were doubled. He had been named Washita County Examiner to certify aspiring young men and women who hoped to become teachers themselves. In addition to being superintendent of Sentinel schools, he established what was then known as summer normal school to train new teachers and further the education of those who already had positions as teachers.

Jeryl A. Watson, Okmulgee, described an early subscription school in Indian Territory (McIntosh County).

What were the schools like in the Indian Territory of Oklahoma prior to statehood? This was the question I asked my dad, who came with his family to live in the Indian Territory, near Henryetta, while he was in his early teens. When Dad arrived in 1903, there was no school for white children in the rural community where he lived. There were boarding schools for Indian boys and girls. These were maintained as mission projects by the various denominations. The Indian children who lived near my dad attended a boarding school in Wetumka, about thirty miles away.

During the next year, the white settlers donated lumber and labor to build a schoolhouse near Salem. It was about twelve feet by eighteen feet. It had a cast-iron heater which burned wood. It was furnished with a blackboard and some homemade benches but had no desks. There was a community water bucket and dipper. The older students took turns carrying water from the well at the log house down the road a short distance. The toilets were crude outhouses with open pits and walls made of vertical poles covered with burlap bags. Since grandad had done some teaching before leaving Alabama, he was asked to be the teacher. Reluctantly he agreed, since he had moved West in hopes of improving his ailing health. The times were hard, and he desperately needed the money to support his family. The school was called a subscription school. There was no revenue from state or county; in fact, there was no state or county. The parents paid grandad $1.00 per month for each child he taught. He had about twenty students, four of whom were his own children. This sounds like a very low salary, but at that time, pay was very low for all types of work.

Grandad and his four youngsters started before daylight and walked the four miles to the school building. Upon arrival, they built a fire in the heater, swept the floors, and filled the water bucket. The childrens' clothing was often patched, but they were clean. The boys wore bib overalls, blue work shirts, and long underwear with drop seats. Their headwear was a cap with a bill and earflaps that could be turned down when the weather turned cold. The girls wore long gingham dresses, several petticoats, and high button shoes. They wore their hair in long braids and used no make-up. Most of the girls had a Sunday dress of calico. There were no pencils or writing paper. Each carried his own small slate for working arithmetic and for writing spelling lessons. Each student had his own books, which he carried home at night for safekeeping. Grandad and his four children carried their lunch to school in a big bucket. It consisted of hog meat, cornbread, beans, butter, and sorghum molasses.

Since there was no playground equipment, the students devised their own entertainment for recess periods. The girls brought their dolls and played with them. The boys played "One-Eyed Cat" with a homemade ball and bat. The bat was made by cutting and shaping a young hickory sapling. The ball was made by unraveling an old sock and winding the yarn around a small rock. The boys would often sneak a chew of Erice Greenville chewing tobacco. The students ranged in ages from six to sixteen years. My dad was one of the older students. He had attended about five years of school before coming to Indian

Territory. There were no formal grade levels. Dad remembers studying grammar, arithmetic, geography, and U.S. history. He thinks grandad did a good job teaching him. It must have been true. That was his last year of formal schooling, but now at eighty-three years of age, he is better educated than many college graduates.

Taught to read by her mother, Agness Francis, Erick, first attended school at four years of age (Roger Mills County).

I was born March 15, 1899, near a little post office called Whit, Texas, but six months later my parents moved to a location about fifteen miles northeast of Cheyenne and filed on 160 acres of land in what is now Roger Mills County of Oklahoma. Neighbors were few and far apart, and most of them lived in dugouts. Quanah, Texas, was the nearest town, and, you can be assured, shopping trips were not made very often.

Other families soon came and settled near us, and by the winter of 1903 it was deemed necessary to find a place where a school could be established. A man named Dunbar had settled on a claim about a mile north of our homestead but had died, leaving a little half dugout with the lower walls of native rock and a shingled roof over it. Since there was no one to claim this house, the community appropriated it for a schoolhouse, and a Miss Cloyd was hired to teach the first school. She was paid the fantastic (?) sum of twenty-five cents per month per pupil for a three-month term.

I was only four years old, but mother had taught me to read, and I was thrilled and happy to be allowed to go to class. I don't know how many pupils attended that school, but I do know we were packed in that little house like sardines in a can. Our seats were heavy slabs of cottonwood held up by wooden pegs, had no back rests, and had no padding. I remember we had three pupils in that group who were twenty-five years old and who were enrolled in the third grade. The schoolhouse was located beside a small creek, and not too far up the creek was a spring which was our source of drinking water. The water was carried from this spring in a ten-quart galvanized bucket, and we all drank from a common long-handled dipper. Ugh!

By 1905, our classes had grown so large it was necessary to build a larger schoolhouse. The parents chose a site a few hundred yards from the Dunbar place. A hole was dug back into a hill, and this was roofed. It made a much larger schoolroom, maybe twenty feet wide and forty feet long. Here we were fortunate enough to have real desks, which were roomy enough for three small pupils or two larger ones to each seat.

Ella Draper, Tishomingo, started to school in Indian Territory (Marshall County).

My parents with their first three children came to the Indian Territory in 1892 and established the Sylvan Seminary, the only school for miles around. This was a subscription school, and the tuitions were paid in corn, hogs, or whatever the patrons were able to afford. The men of the community helped haul building material in wagons from Sherman, Texas. Soon they had a two-story building.

Recalling the rugged pioneer days, Edna Alice Cox Simpkins, Elk City, remembers coming to Oklahoma Territory in a covered

wagon and living in an early dugout. She attended her first school in Beckham County.

In autumn of 1899, my grandfather, Isaac N. Johnson, moved to Oklahoma Territory from east of Greenville in Hunt County, North Texas. The wagon was loaded with a sewing machine, cooking utensils, a trunk full of dishes, horse feed, and various other items. One set of bed springs and all bed clothing were carried in the over-jet. A big iron wash pot was placed in front of the spring seat, and in it was a big feather bed in which my Aunt Maud slept one night during a storm near Segar in the Indian Territory. My Uncle Charley Nelson Johnson slept in the horse trough which hung under the wagon. Grandfather, Grandmother, and Uncle Bazil slept on the bed in the over-jet. The next morning, Grandmother was so discouraged that she tried to coax Grandfather to take the road back home; but he was western bound. Weeks later they reached their destination when they came to the free homesteads. They camped nine or ten miles east of the present site of Sayre, in Beckham County, just off the Mobeta Trail, on the banks of a small ravine. They moved farther up this ravine and settled down to hard work.

Grandfather was thoughtful enough to have brought a crowbar, heavy axe, cross-cut saw, hammer, and a square measure. The measurement of their twelve by thirty-foot dugout was taken and digging began. The land was sandy loam, and the dugout was soon finished. It was seven feet deep at the back and opened out on level ground in front as it was dug in a hillside. To provide a roof, willow saplings were cut and laid over cottonwood poles and then covered with two feet of loam on the top. There was a rock fireplace in the dugout, and an old Dutch oven served for cooking meals. We also had a big iron pot in which to boil beans. Dampness arose in the dugout, so the family exchanged places with the horses. It was really a job cleaning and scraping the stable in order to live in it. The next spring (1900), Uncle John and Uncle Charley helped Grandfather build a new two-room house out of rock. Each room was twelve by fourteen feet—a kitchen and a living room with a large fireplace. All overhead (attic) was used for beds. Grandmother divided my Aunt Maud's bedroom from her brothers' by hanging their clothes between; this made a nice partition. They had to wait a while to floor the two rooms downstairs. Lumber was hauled from Weatherford. Expenses were running high.

My parents, J. M. and Mary (Johnson) Cox came in a covered wagon on a visit in August, 1900, but they didn't move from North Texas until December, 1903. My mother and we three children came on the train from Cumby, Texas, to Doxey, Oklahoma Territory. My father came on a freight train with the cattle, horses, and household goods. My father filed on a claim about thirty miles away from Uncle Henry. We were five miles south of Sweetwater, Oklahoma Territory, or eleven miles northwest of Erick, Beckham County, and got our mail at Wingo. We lived in a dugout, two and one-half miles away, on Uncle Henry's place until our half-dugout was built. In November, 1904, I started to school at Friendship School. We lived almost a mile away. We always planned a six-month school, but there was never enough money to finish a term until the year that we moved away in December, 1910. I finished the fourth grade after we moved to Mill Creek. I was the youngest of the three to graduate from the eighth grade. There were fourteen students in the eighth grade class, but only four of us took the state examination. Three of us passed, a boy and two girls. There were fifteen subjects on which you took the examination; part of it was scheduled and the rest of it was offered in May. We didn't get our eighth grade certificate until after school was out that summer.

Arthur C. Brodell, Cleveland, first attended school in the Cherokee Outlet (Pawnee County).

The Cherokee Outlet was opened for settlers September 16, 1893. My parents and I were living in Denver, Colorado. My mother and I went to Nebraska to live with relatives. My father and an uncle drove a team of horses pulling a wagon to Pawnee County. The first stop was at Maramec, where a dugout was home for a few months. My father paid $60 for a man's rights to 160 acres in the east end of Pawnee County where there was more timber. He sent for mother and me. We came by train from Nebraska to Perry, Oklahoma, where father met us in a wagon. We lived in the Maramec dugout until a log cabin was built on the homestead in SE ¼ Section 9 Township 20 N Range 9 E. The first schoolhouse was built of logs as a community project. The promoter for the construction of the building was a Mr. Rigsby—the name given to the district. The log schoolhouse was used until 1907, when a frame building was erected.

Lois McGucken wrote this account of her mother, who began her teaching career in a converted sod smokehouse in Oklahoma Territory (Kay County).

Miss Cora Rowell and William H. Waugh were married a few months before the "run" into the Cherokee Strip. That summer they made frequent trips in the farm wagon to bring food and building supplies. Early in the spring of 1894, they moved into the one-room claim house. Cora and "Old Phipps," her faithful steed of years past, herded livestock while Bill built the pasture fence. One morning she was surprised to see a neighbor, Elroy Criswell, riding her way. Mr. Criswell had received a letter from

A. D. Kersey telling him that he (Mr. Kersey) was appointed county superintendent of Kay County Schools. He was asking Mr. Criswell to help organize a school board and find a teacher. It was necessary to hold a three-month session before funds of $75 were available. Cora agreed to teach the term for the meager amount. Mr. Hugh Hembree lent his sod smokehouse in which to hold school. Seventeen pupils in grades one through eight sat on homemade benches. Slates and textbooks from Kansas schools were used. The March wind blew so much dirt into the schoolroom that the teacher and pupils could not remove their sunbonnets and straw hats. Outside, they played ball. A mother had sewn a string ball. A flat board was their bat. Next year, the little white frame schoolhouse was ready, across the road from the Hembrees'.

Mary Phipps Evans, now deceased, taught at several schools during the territorial days. Here, she recounts her experiences at an Indian school in the Creek Nation (Hughes County).

Just before my fourth year at Antlers, I got a call asking me if I would consider an appointment to teach an Indian school in the Creek Nation. It would pay $50 a month. That was a huge salary for teaching in those days. Besides that, I was to teach in a big, brand-new building. The Indian agent said the school was for the Indians, but there were quite a number of whites there, and their children could attend, too. I took that appointment.

I arrived by train at Spaulding on a Sunday morning at 11:15, and did my heart sink. There was no depot, just a long strip of cinders along a portion of the track. Nobody was there to meet the train except the postmaster who had come for the mail. The conductor shoved me at him and said, "Here is the new teacher," and jumped back on his train. And there I stood. The postmaster wanted to know where I wanted to go, and I had to tell him that I didn't have any place to go. He took me over to his big store, which included the post office, and introduced me as the new Spaulding Indian School teacher to quite a number of men who were there to get their mail. One kindly old gentleman said that I could go to his house and stay with him and his wife until I could find a place to board. His house was near the school. That night the Church of Christ people were holding a service in the schoolhouse. I noticed that they were all taking chairs from their wagons and carrying them into the building. I wondered why, and the next morning I found out why. There wasn't a piece of furnishing in that building except three homemade benches and a big box wood heater with a drum—not a band drum, a heating drum. I tell you, my feathers fell worse than they had when I got off that train. How was I going to teach school with that equipment?

The postmaster had hitched up his buggy and got the railroad overseer to go with him, and they had gone out and told the patrons that the teacher was there and that school would begin Monday. I hunted up the board members responsible for the building to find out about desks. Their problem was just like the problem other areas faced—not enough school money. After paying for the building, they didn't have any money left for desks. We tried to get patrons to donate a desk. Each of the three board members offered to give one, I offered, the postmaster offered, and a young doctor who had his office in the store offered one; but six were all we could get.

The pupils began to come in from the woods by pig trails, since there were not many roads. The three benches were soon filled up with the larger pupils, and the small ones had to sit on the floor and lean back on the wall. I had no table or chair. I had to stand. I just put it up to the children that they were the ones who had to suffer; and if they would co-operate with me, we could get the house seated. We decided to give a box supper. Every girl in school promised to bring a box and to get anyone out of school to do so also. The boys got their fathers to pay them for picking cotton after school and on Saturday, so they could buy a box. We had a cake for the prettiest girl and a pie for the ugliest man. A man from the Church of Christ which met in the school offered to auction off the boxes. He did a good job. Of course, the schoolboys wanted to buy their girl friends' boxes. There were some Texas men there picking cotton, and they would run the boxes up on the schoolboys, then let them go. The Texans did buy boxes, too. The man who sold school furniture gave us most of his commission, which helped a lot. We had enough money to furnish the whole schoolhouse and get a teacher's table and a chair, a global map, and some charts. I had a good turn-out enrollment of 165 pupils with an average of 135 for the nine months. That was the term of 1907 and 1908, the last term a territory school was taught in what was to become the State of Oklahoma.

Cassia Berry, Emporia, Kansas, taught in an integrated school in Oklahoma Territory from 1895 to 1903.

My first teaching job came in 1895 when I was sixteen years old. At that time, teaching remained the best job available for a woman with my qualifications. I taught at three different schools near Okeene, Lahoma, and Meno, Oklahoma. A teacher's responsibilities were far different than those encountered today. Although the number of years required for preparation as a teacher were far less than the requirements of today, they were taught subjects in the eighth grade that are taught as college courses today. In addition to all the other duties, the teacher was expected to act as a janitor.

The schools in which I taught were one-room schools with approximately twenty-five pupils (both black and white) in attendance. Discipline in those years was no problem, even though some of the students were as old as I was and much larger. The parents in those days stood behind the teacher and expected the students to obey. Blackboards were used to great extent and students had their own slates. Paper was used sparingly. In the first school, water had to be carried one-fourth of a mile by the bucketful. There were separate buckets for the white children and the black children. It had been customary for the white children to drink water from the Negro children's bucket if their own bucket was empty and then force the black children to carry more water. One of the first rules I put in force was to see that this practice ceased and that the white children remained responsible for their own water.

Eunice Heizer, Blackwell, tells of her experience in a territorial school (Grant County).

I was born on my father's claim in Grant County during a bad blizzard in January, 1893. Times were hard, but wants were few. And then, too, it was a new land; and the people had not had much time to think of self-improvement and better education. But, as conditions began to improve, they began to yearn for a better way of living which demanded higher education. So they began to build schools and churches.

Of course, I cannot remember the early years; but as soon as I was four and one-half years old, I was trudging two miles to the little new rural school. Then, the next year, I was an enthusiastic pupil. At thirteen, I finished the eighth grade. What could they do with me? But there was an answer. They hired a teacher who was qualified to teach high school, and I took a freshman course from her. Then, probably for want of more to do, I studied and sat with the eighth grade again. The next year, I went to Hunnewell, Kansas, stayed with my grandmother, and studied the second-year work. Professor Clark was a wonderful instructor. He also taught eighth grade, and I attended the classes again. And believe me, I almost learned it by heart; later I found that I had completely mastered the subject matter that I would need in teaching the rural schools. That summer I attended several weeks of special training for teachers at Pond Creek. We called it Teacher's Institute. It was a special cramming school to prepare us for teacher's examination.

Nina May Musgrove Grimes, Walters, first attended a one-room school in Cotton County.

When we came to Oklahoma Territory in 1902, no one had a house. We lived in wagon tops, tents, caves dug back into a hill, shack sod houses, or anything else to try to keep warm and dry. Very few people had milk. There were thousands of cattle in the big pasture, but no one could catch them or milk them. The country was beautiful with green grass, knee high, as far as the eye could see, mingled with beautiful wild flowers of every kind and hue. The creeks and rivers, as you forded the streams, were as clear as crystal. As you sat in your buggy or wagon while the horses drank, you could see the stones on the bottom and see the fish swim between the spokes of the wheels. For food we killed rabbits, frogs, and birds and caught fish. Grapevines ran up the trees. We had plum thickets and plum trees from which we made jelly, butter, and marmalade. Prosperity was rather far away. No one possessed much, but everyone was friendly. No one had anything to brag about; we lived and let live. My education started in an old lime rock schoolhouse in the country. When I came to Oklahoma, I rode a black horse to school. Sometimes as many as four rode him. When I was in the sixth grade, I transferred to Walters School. My teachers passed me over the seventh grade, and I graduated from high school in 1913. My mother always said, "Learn everything you can, you won't know too much to get along in this world!" So I had some art lessons, instrumental music, chorus, china painting, and dramatics.

I entered Normal that summer and fall, taught that winter, and went back again next summer and fall. I graduated from Central State in 1916. I received my life certificate which was sheepskin, the only one ever issued to me.

Ruby Sands, Shawnee, began her career at the end of the territorial years.

I entered the teaching profession at sixteen years of age by taking the county teacher's examination, which was open to anyone who cared to try. Unfortunately for my ego, I failed to pass. After spending a few months memorizing the textbooks, I passed the next examination with flying colors—that is, for a third-grade certificate. It was late in the season, and few schools were not already taken. I hurried down and offered my services to one. After a good bit of discussion, with the school board feeling that I was too young to handle their school and my trying to convince them of my capability, we came to the agreement that if I would put my hair up and my skirts down, the contract was mine at $50 a month for four months.

While in the district, I found a boarding place for $15 a month. I arrived early in December to begin my school. For an enrollment of fifty, the building was small. It must have been rather open, too, for it took two heating stoves to keep it warm. There were bare necessities for teaching equipment—a small blackboard and some chalk. The room was crowded with double desks; and with so many pupils, the small ones had to sit three in a seat. The challenge was great, but I tackled it with vim. I did my best to combine and co-ordinate to get everyone learning something. I began here what I used later, allowing the advanced pupils to help the slower ones. The school had no well. Water was carried from a farmhouse down the road. The bucket of water was passed around and everyone drank from a common dipper. It was a special privilege to go to get a bucket of water. Often, two boys would have a quarrel, then ask to get a bucket of water and have a fight on the way. I might not find it out until later. Our building was too small for much neighborhood enter-

tainment, but a wagonload of us would go to a nearby school for literary on Friday nights. We lost something when we left the literary behind. Perhaps, the 4-H Club has filled in. I enjoyed my school that year, but found a school nearer home the next year.

Mary Kelso Buffington, Stillwater, attended a territorial and later early statehood school built by her grandfather in present-day Lincoln County.

The background for my early education began in the little country school in the northern part of what is now Lincoln County. When the Indian reservations of the Iowa, Sac and Fox, Pottawatomi, and Shawnee tribes were opened to homestead settlement September 22, 1891, my grandfather, Charles A. Kelso, and my father, Ulysses Grant Kelso, took part. This opening, which was called the "second run," did not get as much publicity as the run of 1889, and not as many people took part; but these people were important in Oklahoma history.

In 1894 a petition was circulated for the erection of a schoolhouse in our district. That spring Independence School was built. My grandfather constructed the building. Other men in the community contributed their labor, money, or talents; they were all anxious for their children to have a good education. Independence School building still stands today and is some eighty-four years old. It is old and worn, but the top line of the roof is still erect and very straight. It was a white frame building, with three windows on the north side and three windows on the south side. The door was in the east, and there was a porch on the front. Inside, the walls were finished with wainscotting four feet high all around the room. The wainscotting was painted brown. Above the wainscotting, the walls were painted light green.

There was a slate blackboard on the back wall on the west end. It was in the Independence School that I got my early education through the first eight grades. The year I graduated from the eighth grade, I was the only pupil in the eighth grade, and our teacher could not hold the examination for only one pupil. The teacher at Grand Center School was giving the eighth grade examinations, and I was sent there to take them.

W. A. Franklin, Ponca City, came to Oklahoma in 1898 and had a career as an educator which spanned more than half a century. The following, titled "Reflections of the Ghost of a One-Room Rural Schoolhouse," was originally published in the Oklahoma Teacher *(1954) and is included here with the permission of that journal.*

I am the Ghost of a one-room, rural school. On earth, I was erected in the closing decade of the nineteenth century. My builders were brave and hopeful pioneers in the last great area of free land. These settlers built me even before they had time or means to build comfortable homes for their families. They built me because they believed in giving their children the advantages of education.

I was built of pine lumber, a frame house with windows on each side, a door in the front end, a low platform opposite the door and a blackboard above the platform. In the center of my floor, a coal stove was set in a sandbox. My first desks for pupils were made of pine by men of the community.

I was located so that I would be in walking distance of every home in the district. The land I was built on was deeded to the district to be returned to the owner when I was no longer used for school purposes.

Someone gave me a pretty name, Happy Valley. I had neighbors named Lilyvale and Pleasant Hill. Others were named after schools in Missouri or Kansas like Maple Ridge or Oak Grove. There were others with brave new names like Pioneer, Enterprise, and Liberty.

The first teacher to use me was a settler's daughter who got a county certificate by going to a one-month term of school called a "summer normal" at the county seat. This girl had an eighth grade diploma from a school in Kansas. She was employed by three citizens called a "school board."

On the enrollment day, fifty pupils crowded into my limited space. Some of the pupils were six-year-olds; some were, in size, grown men and women. They came from different states and brought different kinds of textbooks. Most of these pupils had not been in school for one or two years.

The teacher tried to hide her timidity, for she was only eighteen; and several of her pupils were as old. The first day was taken up in trying to group the pupils and make assignments for lessons in the various books. A routine was established, and learning went on satisfactorily for most pupils.

During that year and succeeding years, I became increasingly important to the people of the district. Around me as an institution were built up loyalties that were strong and true. People were proud of their school. I was used as a meeting place. School programs, box suppers on Friday nights, the literary and debating society brought neighbors together. The hearts of parents thrilled as they heard their children "speak their pieces" or take services. On election years, my walls echoed the speeches of candidates for county offices.

Boys and girls grew up in my community. I was the place where they met oftenest. Some of the friendships formed in school ripened into romances that resulted in new homes with a new generation of children to come to me.

Improvements were made in me from time to time as the community prospered. My windows were all moved to one side of me. A circulating heater was placed in one corner. Factory desks were added. But they did not give me complete modernity. Even to my last days, diverging paths led from my front door to two little houses with appropriate signs.

My place as a necessary and permanent part of the community was established—I thought. But times began to change rapidly. Automobiles crowded the horse-drawn vehicles off the roads. They took people faster and farther from home. Roads were improved. Then tractors took the place of the workhorse. Old Dobbin was sold for soap grease and dog food. Farms became larger. Families that were left were smaller. Many people moved to towns and cities.

Teachers' pay increased from $30 a month for six months to $320 a month for ten months. My first teacher had an eighth grade diploma; my last teacher had a degree from a college.

Then came compulsory high school attendance and the school bus. But the final blow was the law that I had to have thirteen children in average daily attendance to keep alive. One year, I did not have that many. Two of my neighbors had the same condition. The people in the three districts decided to make one district out of three. I was left empty and unpainted for two years. Finally a man bought me, tore me apart, and moved my pieces away. The land on which I stood is now a part of a wheat field.

In looking back over it all as a departed spirit, I see little to regret and much to be proud of. I served my community the best I could. Many successful and useful citizens of my state and nation look back to me as their educational mother. As a single building, I am no longer in physical existence. As a representative of a glorious institution, purely American, I will live forever in influence in my country.

"The School at Old Bluff Center" was written by Eunice Elmore Heizer of Blackwell. In the poem, Mrs. Heizer undoubtedly expressed the sentiments of many people who attended or who taught the smaller rural schools.

Nostalgia

We used to go to rural school. We called it old Bluff Center.
Most of us wore ragged clothes, but no one was a renter.
We sat together, two by two, for all the seats were double.
Big boys crowded to the back and usually caused trouble.
We always had a tattle-tale who ran to tell the story.
Always had a bully, too, who strutted in his glory.

There always were some giggly girls, silly little wenches,
Always dared the boys to carve their names upon the benches.
Books and clothing everywhere with everything a clutter.
Hardly room at noon to sit and eat our bread and butter.
Bats and balls and marbles, too, were ever ours to treasure,
With simple games that never failed to give us health and pleasure.

We had a fuss most every day, no matter what was taught us,
And usually we had a fight before the teacher caught us.
A lot of little kids around with dirty hands and faces,
Scampering like a flock of sheep getting in their places.
A bunch of switches standing by that scared a timid creature,
But put there for the boy who bragged that he could whip the teacher.

I went to visit school today. The same that I attended.
I was surprised but must admit it surely did look splendid.
Everything so neat and clean with flowers in all the windows,
A bed of Phlox where used to be a great big pile of cinders.
Children dressed in pretty frills, neat, polite, and pleasant.
Not a discord anywhere, and everyone was present.

I think there's only ten or twelve. They used to come in bunches.
I sat and watched them as they ate their scientific lunches.
Progressive? Sure, but it was fun to be an old-time scholar,
Where one could take things as they came and never even holler.
Sometimes I'm homesick for the days when no one was a renter.
And we could all enjoy a fight in school at old Bluff Center.

Clifford Strozier, Sr., of Tulsa here recounts his experiences in a territorial school (Red Oak), the transition in education which occurred as Oklahoma entered the Union, and his later career as a teacher.

I was born in 1899 on a farm near the little town of Red Oak, some forty-five miles east of McAlester in what is now Latimer County. My Grandfather Strozier came to Indian Territory from

Georgia in 1875, while my Grandfather Elliott came from Mississippi in 1887.

During the territorial days, the schools in all communities were formed by the people and supported by each family which paid tuition for each child attending school. Hence they were known as "tuition schools." Generally the fee was around $2.00 per month per child. In Red Oak a tuition school was held each year; but another type was also conducted there during the school term of 1905–1906. A local businessman was able to persuade the Indian agency at McAlester to pay the teacher's salary out of federal funds, since it was for Indian children; however, white children were allowed to attend. The subscription school was also held at the same time, and parents were allowed to send their children to either or both facilities. Indian academies were organized later in the Indian Territory. They were boarding schools for Indian children only; Jones Academy was located near Hartshorne, and Armstrong Academy was near Durant. These academies were for both boys and girls and any and all Indian children in the areas of the state where they were located. They were free, but the school held at Red Oak was the first free school for Indian and white children.

This first free white school was taught for one term and was held in a vacant store building, with "homemade" benches for seats. There was no blackboard, but the teacher did have an old-fashioned chart; and all pupils who were beginners started with a first reader. There were some twenty-eight pupils in grades one to eight. Most all towns of the early territorial days were tuition schools, with the one exception of the one term of this free school at Red Oak, Indian Territory.

When Oklahoma became a state in 1907, school districts were created in each county, and county superintendents of schools were appointed. The superintendent appointed a school board, or board of education, for each district. Later on when independent districts were organized, they were not under the supervision of county superintendents. They usually were districts that had large enrollments, and were hence justified in having their own superintendents. I recall that my father was one of the first appointed members of the school board at Red Oak in 1907.

The Red Oak school system was not a fully accredited high school when I graduated from it; so I attended the Wilburton (county seat) high school during the 1918–19 term and graduated a second time. I attended the then Oklahoma A. and M. College at Stillwater for the next three years, having to drop out of college because of my father's financial reverses.

During the summer months of 1920 I was able to secure a summer term of teaching near my home town of Red Oak. I secured employment in the Harmony School in Leflore, which was a few miles north of Wister. It was the custom of farm districts to have two terms of school during the year, one in the summer and one during the winter months, so that the children of the family could help cultivate the corn and cotton crops during the spring months and gather the crops during the fall months.

During the summer term, I was the only teacher with some thirty pupils, with one or more children in every grade from one through eight, except the seventh grade. When I reported to teach this school that summer, no outdoor toilets had been provided. However, the woods came right up to the edge of the school grounds, so they had been used for the same purposes. One day a problem arose when one pupil did not go deep enough into the woods for "cover," which resulted in the school having its first outdoor toilets built.

During the summer term of 1921, I taught in Latimer County at the High Bridge North School. This branch school was over in the San Bois Mountains some eight miles from Wilburton, the county seat. The only way to get to this district and to the home of one of the school board members, with whom I roomed and took my meals, was to walk or ride a horse. I did not have a horse, but my landlord did. I rode his horse sometimes. When I walked, I would ride the Rock Island railroad train from Red Oak to Wilburton; then, after some hours' wait, I took the Katy Railroad train, which covered some ten miles per hour. I could save some distance by jumping from the train just as it crossed the high bridge; then I would walk across the mountains to the valley in which the school was located. I was the only teacher and had one or more children in all eight grades except the fourth and sixth. During the months of this term of school, I boarded with one of the school board members who lived some two miles from the school building.

IV

EARLY STATEHOOD

In the years after Oklahoma was admitted to the Union, constant progress was made in the state's educational system. To train teachers, new colleges were founded in old Indian Territory as well as in old Oklahoma; requirements for certification became more stringent; and the consolidation movement began. Yet, most teachers still began their careers in the small, one- or two-room schools. They continued to suffer from a lack of supplies and books, and they continued to serve their schools as janitors, nurses, water carriers, lunch makers, and social direc-

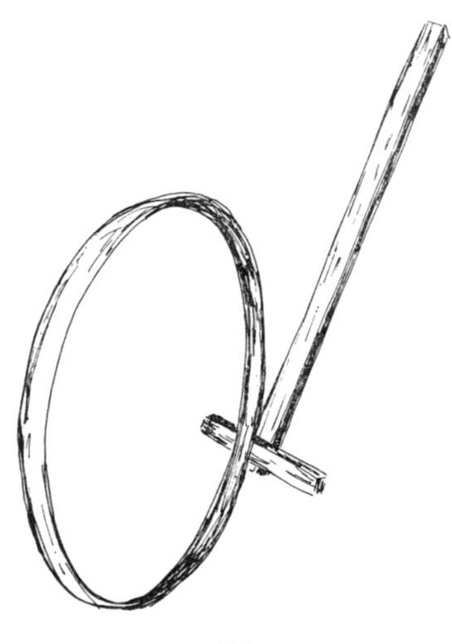

tors. Although salaries remained generally low, teachers still found that they often must spend a part of their pay to purchase supplies or to provide food for needy children. Despite many adversities, however, most teachers had inner qualities which allowed them to triumph over their problems. They provided "their" children with the best education that circumstances allowed. In the following selections, Oklahoma teachers highlight some of their experiences in the early statehood period.

Nettie Belle Howe, Midwest City, taught her first school at Hog Creek, south of Anadarko (Caddo County).

Throughout history education has been of the greatest concern to progressive civilization. In the territorial and early statehood days, Oklahoma was no exception. The territorial government had set aside a section of school land in every township for the purpose of furthering education. One-room schoolhouses sprang up almost as soon as the first settlers arrived. Many schools were made of logs—some even had dirt floors. Sod schoolhouses were common in regions where there were no logs to be had. Before many years passed, however, there were many nice weather-boarded schools, painted white. The need for teachers was very great, and qualifications were not too high. One had only to be sixteen years old, pass the eighth grade county examination, attend a four-week teacher's institute, held at a county seat, and then pass the state examination to receive a third-, second-, or first-grade certificate.

After passing from the eighth grade at Cement, Oklahoma, I expected to take the state teacher's examination at Anadarko, seat of Caddo County, without having to go to the teacher's institute. I was failed. When my school principal remonstrated with the county superintendent for passing others whose grades were not as high, she explained that they allowed points for attending the institute—besides, my size was against me. I was less than five feet tall, weighed about ninety pounds, still wore my hair in curls, and wore size thirteen and a half Buster Brown shoes. Instead of going on into high school, I took the eighth grade over—after all, those were the subjects I would have to teach. The next year I attended the teacher's institute and received my third-grade certificate. I was seventeen that year.

I applied for the Hog Creek School, south of Anadarko, as I was advised to do, and was accepted. It was in such of an "out-of-the way" place and had only six months of school at $35 a month that they had trouble getting an experienced teacher. I signed a contract, and among other stipulations, I agreed to neither dance nor play cards. If the school board had had a glimmer of a lady smoking or using alcohol, they would surely have added that prohibition, too. The schoolhouse was a nice, well-built, frame building, painted white. It was heated with a big, cast-iron stove in the center of the room which held a piece of wood about three feet long. I walked almost two and a half miles to school and did my own janitor work. The director of the school board was an accommodating bachelor who sometimes had the fire going when the weather was bad.

School started in September, and Oklahoma became a state that November. As I remember, we had no particular observance of the occasion. I had from twenty to thirty pupils from the first through the eighth grades, and my consuming concern was to teach them "readin', writin', and 'rithmetic." We did practice for a program for the last day of school. We sang songs, spoke pieces, read stories, had a short dress-up play, and even had a snappy little drill without music. It was the first program of its kind in those "parts" and was enjoyed by pupils and parents alike. After each school term, I would attend Normal School at Weatherford, where I eventually received my first-grade certificate. I taught in two more one-room schools with colorful names—Highview and Buzzard Roost. They were heated the same way. They had no electric lights and no schoolground equipment, although one had an organ. All had large enrollments, and many of my pupils were larger and some older than I was.

That long ago schools were segregated. Blacks had their own school, and Caddo County had an Indian school at Riverside, near Anadarko; thus, I had no experience with minority races. Discipline was a minor problem. School equipment for the playground was nonexistent, and there was no library and no meals. Children were not used to being entertained. They played ball or other games they could think up. I bought my own teaching material from school supply catalogues, such as record cards, flash cards, and incentive awards, as well as all program material. I made my own "mim-e-o-graphs." I worked late into the night grading papers and planning the next day's work.

My second school at Highview was in my own district, which was an acid test for me. But this was one of my most gratifying years. Parents were, for the most part, like my own: they were God-fearing, salt-of-the-earth type of people whose children were taught respect and a high regard for learning.

Transportation was a problem then as it is today. I bought a little bay mustang pony, bridle, saddle with fur pockets, and a blanket—all for $60. Up to that time a sidesaddle was the proper thing. No lady had ever thought of riding astride. I couldn't afford another saddle, so I bought a riding habit. Divided skirts were being advertised in a Sears catalog for the first time, so I ordered one. There were some raised eyebrows, but the divided skirt was much more comfortable in every way than the sidesaddle. In the light of modern styles, I smile at the thought of a divided skirt having been considered risqué. My horse was named Lady, but her actions often belied her name. She had been used as a cattle pony. She had a nice, easy gait, but would stop short or jump sidewise at the least noise or the appearance of a bird, a rabbit, or even a leaf. At times when this occurred, I would go over her head or be left where she was standing. I guess there wasn't enough of me to get hurt. After I closed a gate, Lady would seldom stand still, especially if it was cold, until I could get completely up in the saddle. I often carried supplies that the saddle pockets wouldn't hold. One particular morning, I was carrying a box of chalk. Then it was being packaged in a wooden box four by four by eight inches with a sliding cover top. I got my foot in the stirrup and grabbed for the saddlehorn when Lady took off—she could literally fly. I managed to lean across the saddle and hang on, but I left the hillside scattered with chalk. Lady would always stop after a sprint, giving me time to get organized, and would nuzzle me with her nose as though pleased with her little joke.

My third one-room school was at Buzzard Roost School, southeast of Cement. It was over four miles from my home, and I still had to ride horseback. That was the school year of 1909 and 1910. I had to leave home in the early hours to have the room warm by the time school began. One memorable event that year was sighting Halley's Comet in the northeastern sky. It was visible for several mornings. After the three one-room schools, I taught second grade in the Cement four-room school for one year. After one year at Oklahoma College for Women at Chickasha, I went back to Cement and taught in their new eight-room brick building. There still were no meals, no library, and no playground equipment—we did have supervised play.

My last year of teaching in Oklahoma was at Apache. There I taught fourth grade. This was my most satisfying year. Apache school was rated the highest in the county. The principal was a good administrator. I had reached a point in my teaching career where I could see where I had always wanted to go. Instead, I let a tall rancher, whom I had met a year before, persuade me that South Dakota needed teachers as much as Oklahoma. We were married and went to South Dakota.

Jennie Hays Higgins, Coweta, who began teaching in 1909, recounts her first exposure to a "cotton" school (Wagoner County).

My name was Jennie Hays. I taught my first term of school in 1909. I was sixteen years old. It was a new, one-room school. The district named the school for me, Hays Chapel. That building burned, and a brick structure was erected in the same place. It is used today by the Hays Chapel Demonstration Club. I received $45 a month for a six months' contract. In the next two schools, I received $50 a month.

I think you will be interested in my fourth school. I never heard of one like it nor will I ever forget it. I was to get $60 a month for eight months. But they told me it was a "cotton school." I asked what a cotton school was. My schedule included teaching two months during the summer, July and August, then dismissing for three months and beginning again in December. The school was five miles from my home in Coweta, Wagoner County. It was called the Rothhammer School and was across the Arkansas River.

My father took me over to see the directors and the school in a one-horse buggy. As we came to the school, I said, "That looks more like a church than a schoolhouse." Father replied, "They probably use it for both." In front of the building were three cement steps with banisters at each end a foot wide. There was a small walk leading to a pump at the corner of the house. The doors were open. It had double doors in front. Inside was a double aisle leading to the back of the room. On each side of the door were two cloakrooms. Each had three screened-in shelves on which to put the lunches. Across the walls were three four-inch boards with spike nails in them to hang cloaks and coats. On one side of a cloakroom was a homemade bench with a new tin bucket, dipper, and washpan. In the center of the large aisle was a huge iron stove four or five feet tall and round. It set on a block of cement. In front of the room was a teacher's desk and a straight chair. The blackboard was across the end of the room from one back door to the other. At the bottom of the blackboard was a board to hold the erasers and chalk. There were six old erasers and six new ones. There were four rows of double seats, two on each side of the large aisle. Each row had a small aisle between them and next to the wall. In front of these rows were two homemade benches that reached across two rows of seats.

Monday morning my father took me to school. When we arrived, the yard was full of children and some grown people. I asked, "Why are all these men and women here?" Father thought they had walked with their children for the first time. When I rang the hand bell, all the children and the grown folks came in. Some came in at the front door, and some at the two back doors. The first thing I did was to open the school by singing "My

Country 'Tis of Thee." I said, "The last stanza is like a prayer, and we will bow our heads and sing it softly." I sang a solo. I told them at noon that I would put that song on the blackboard and that from the third grade up we would sing it next Monday. Well, we all sang next Monday. The next thing was seating the pupils by grades. I gave each grade a sheet of paper to write their names, ages, and grades. I began seating the pupils with the eighth grade two to a seat. I found that I had nine grown girls and seven grown boys. When we got to the lower grades, I seated three to a seat. After seating the second grade, I had eighteen or twenty first-graders without seats. I told them to sit on those big benches, when they got tired to sit on the floor, and if they got sleepy to take a nap. When I counted the number that night, I had ninety-six pupils.

After seeing so many pupils, I knew I needed study monitors and supplies for the class. I asked three eighth grade girls to serve as monitors, but they refused. Then two large boys volunteered. From then on, each grade had two or three to volunteer. I selected paper monitors and drink or water monitors. I also had volunteers to sweep the floor. I found that about one-third of the pupils had no books, paper, slates, or pencils. I had twelve pencils and had the boys cut and sharpen them, making twenty-four. I also had a primer, first reader, and second and third readers. The first day was spent organizing and assigning lessons for the next day. I also told the students that school would start at 8:00 and close at 5:00 if we got through our classes. I went to school at 7:30, put the first grade work on the board, and went through several classes' spelling lessons. They were to copy those lessons in the morning, and arithmetic came after recess.

I don't recall our average attendance for the first month, but for the month of August, it was seventy-seven. Some of the larger girls quit when they found they had to obey rules and study. Some smaller children also dropped out. They said it was too hot. At the fall term, only sixty returned. Two new families moved into the district with nine children, but the cotton pickers had gone to other fields and thus reduced my number of students.

After attending rural schools, Adaline Abbott of Shattuck began her teaching career in the late 1920's.

In 1900 and 1901, my father filed on 160 acres in Ellis County, four miles southeast of Gage, Oklahoma. A year later he brought Mother and my three oldest sisters from Chillicothe, Missouri, to live in their new one-room soddy.

In 1903 the settlers of the community gathered to build a one-room school. My two older sisters attended school for three months each winter after fall crops were harvested and before the spring planting would begin. The school was called "Little Wolf" and was located one-half mile east of the creek by the same name. I can still visualize the interior. The vestibule was where we entered after climbing three big wooden steps and where we hung our wraps on hooks in the wall, along with half-gallon syrup pails that held our noon dinner meals. In the south-west corner of the room was a shelflike bench which held a pail of water and the common drinking dipper. It was always the big boys' privilege to go for water from a well one-quarter of a mile away. In the center of the room was the pot-bellied coal stove. On very cold days, we pupils gathered round it to keep warm and recite our lessons. At the front of the room, or the east end, was a rostrum, perhaps ten inches above the floor level, on which sat the teacher's desk. Around the edge of the stage was the blackboard, where we had our daily spelling tests and some-times played "Cat" or "Blocks" or "Going to the Mill" on rainy days. Above the blackboard hung a rack of roller maps.

The first teacher was a Mr. Maxey, who taught two years. He was followed by a Mrs. Emma Huffman, who taught three years. Her salary was $20 a month. We did our reciting of lessons from a backless bench in front of the teacher's desk. No other pupils paid any attention to the class reciting, because they were learning from their books at the same time. Personally, I listened and learned a lot from the older pupils. I attended my first year of school at Little Wolf in 1915. I still remember how Sunday school and church services were held every Sunday morning in the schoolhouse. I can still see how we little ones sat on that recitation bench. Willard always went to sleep during the sermons and fell off the bench. By the time I entered school, we were having a seven- or even eight-month school term. My first teacher was a man, a Mr. Archie Bennett. I was very timid and afraid of men, as I had grown up surrounded by a loving mother, five mischievous sisters, and only one man—my very kind but firm father.

We lived a mile north of the school. On good days, I walked. The road was so sandy, I'd take one step forward and slide back two, it seemed. Since my four older sisters were going to school in town by then, I was lonely, even among other children. On snowy days, the good, big chubby neighbor boy to the north of us came by to see that I'd get to school in good shape. He wore overalls and big galoshes. We played train, and he made a very good engine as he tramped a path through the snow for me to follow. Since I was small, I suppose I made the coal car! A quarter of a mile on our way we were joined by a Ritz boy. A quarter of a mile more, and three McFarlands joined the procession. A quarter of a mile on, the three Cooleys and a Hamilton joined the train for the caboose. What a parade! From the south came the Stewart twins, two Eldringhoffs, two Robinsons, and four Hendersons.

Many times on Fridays, our school would go visiting to a

neighboring school for a spelling bee, a ciphering match, or a geography match. What anticipation as we worked toward those Fridays to spell down or cipher down the opposing side! Then, how we worked before the other school came to play against us. Once in a long while, we would play basketball on our outdoor courts. Sometimes big, little, great, and small had to play to have enough to make a team. But that never mattered to us.

In 1921 I attended the Gage School. I graduated from there with a group of forty students in 1927. The following fall I went to teachers college at Alva, Oklahoma. After attending three years, I taught a year to finance my last year at college. The year after receiving my B.S. degree I taught in a one-room school. What a wonderful, delightful time I had. I drove an old Hudson and took the three children where I roomed and boarded to class with me. Along the way I picked up four cousins before reaching school. In those days a teacher was expected to be her own janitor. But the children were very good; they often built the fire for me and swept the floor.

It was during the depression that I taught in the bend of the South Canadian River for $60 a month. When the wind blew from the south, the air was sandy and hard to breathe. At that time my sister May was superintendent of schools for Ellis County. We had to turn in monthly reports to her. On one line the question asked how our school was ventilated. My answer was "by cracks in the walls." I'd never do that to anyone but her! On windy days we could lean against the brick chimney, which extended from the floor through the rooftop in the middle of the room, and feel it shake.

On April 9, 1947, a terrible tornado ripped through the Texas Panhandle and northwestern Oklahoma. Over one hundred people were killed. After it was all over, we drove over the desolate countryside. All that was left of my Little Wolf School was a broken cement foundation and the bottom cement step, which through the years had replaced the old wooden one. I feel like crying as I pass that spot today. For twenty-one years I've taught from kindergarten through the sixth grade, wherever I was needed, in the Shattuck public schools. I retired in June, 1974.

Helen Weston Snow, Claremore, came from a long line of teachers. Her family moved from Alabama to Indian Territory (Seminole County) shortly before statehood.

I had always sort of taken it for granted that being a Weston meant eventually being a teacher. I knew that early in my life. It looked to me like being born into our family meant you were born to be a teacher. Papa was the first. Beginning about 1883, Papa taught in Alabama until the summer of 1907, when the family moved to the Indian Territory. They settled in the Seminole Nation, near the North Canadian River. Papa was a graduate of a university and had a license both to teach and to preach. For a time, after the move, he farmed and preached. There were no schools in the area except boarding schools for Indians, Mekasukey for boys and Emahaka for girls. Consequently, Mamma taught us at home. The first school for whites that I know about in the area was a subscription school in a little log church, called Sand Creek, which was two miles from our home. But Papa didn't have money to pay for all of us to attend, and none of the five of us of school age went. Mamma just kept on helping us at home.

When "I.T." became a part of the new state of Oklahoma, the state constitution provided for free schools for all children living within the boundaries, I believe. But the fathers in our community were told at Wewoka, the county seat, that no money was yet available for a school, so another year went by. Rebecca

Baker, Indian family name of Kinkahee, had the biggest of all the log houses in our area. She was the widow of Chief Kinkahee, one of the lesser chiefs of the Seminoles. He had been dead about a month when we came to I.T. in the summer of 1907. Rebecca also had several small children, too young to send away from home. It was no problem for the fathers of the community to persuade her to remove the furniture from one room and convert it into a school. The men then sawed big logs in half, put in four pegs in each half for legs, and made tables to serve as desks. They made short benches for each desk, so three students could sit at each. And a teacher was hired. Under such crude conditions, and with so many bootleggers and other gangsters around, Mamma was afraid for us to walk the two miles to Becky's, as everyone called her. So again, we didn't go to class. By this time, Papa was hired to teach his first school at Fair Oaks School, five miles away. He rode horseback every day, and we didn't have enough horses to go around, so we couldn't go to his school. We kept on studying at home.

Probably the most exciting episode in Papa's Oklahoma teaching career happened in a Seminole County rural school, in a community known for its rough teenagers. Big boys had "run off" the two preceding teachers. The school board warned Papa that the boys would try their same tricks with him. One or two swigs of the bootleg stuff from the rum-runners at Keokuk Falls was all it took to make heathens of the young boys, who came to school on occasions to tantalize and intimidate the teacher. The first day, things weren't too bad. The older boys were present and were easily identified by Papa because of their brash behavior, loud talk, and guffaws. The second day was the same, only worse. That night, Papa borrowed a pistol from his landlord, who was also on the school board and who had recommended that Papa be prepared. The third day at noon recess, when the "three musketeers" of the school held a younger boy, took a Christmas gift toy from him, smashed it, and then laughed, it was their undoing with Papa. He rang the bell, called the pupils in, and had three hickory switches in waiting on his desk. After all were seated, he took the pistol from the desk drawer and laid it on top of the desk in plain view. Then one by one, he called the three young men up, used a switch on their behinds to his satisfaction, gave a good warning, and let each go back to his seat. Then he calmly put the pistol back into the desk and sat down beside it. The rest of the afternoon his classes were uninterrupted. And at afternoon recess, the young hoodlums left the schoolground, never to return as long as Papa taught there.

Viva Thacker, Stringtown, described the schools of Atoka County during the early statehood period.

Having been born in Stringtown, Indian Territory, in 1901, I only knew six years of territorial days. We lived on the 640 acres of land allotted to my mother, father, and brother, given by the Choctaw government. Because these allotments adjoined each other, we had a large ranch and farm. Our home was a white one-story frame building with a fireplace in the south end of the house.

We children walked one and one-half miles to and from school, carrying our lunches in dinner buckets. The first year I attended school was in a big one-room schoolhouse which had been built by subscription. A teacher was hired, and each family contributed to her salary. Mrs. Ethel Crews (teacher) enrolled about sixty students with an average attendance of fifty. She taught all eight grades. I shall never forget the long "recitation bench" that stood in the front of the room and the proverbial big pot-bellied stove gracing the approximate center of the room. The drinking water was carried from Sulphur Spring in big cedar buckets by the bigger boys or sometimes by the bigger girls. One long-handled blue-granite dipper was used by the entire school. This old dipper never got scrubbed or sterilized. Later, each child was required to bring his own drinking cup (a few were lucky to own and to display their "folding cups").

Shortly after I started to school, a two-story brick building was erected, and the community hired a staff of three teachers. More instructors were added as the enrollment grew. In 1917 I graduated from Stringtown High School, which only taught through the tenth grade. I roomed and boarded in Atoka and attended the eleventh and the twelfth grades and graduated in 1919. By attending Teachers' Normal State College (now Southeastern State University) at Durant in the summer term of 1919, I received a one-year state certificate and was privileged to teach the school term of 1919–20.

My first teaching was done at Redden, Oklahoma, twelve miles east of Stringtown. I boarded with a family who lived two miles east of the school. My father had bought me a nice, reddish-brown fat pony with long hair hanging just above his hoofs. On week ends, I considered myself a very brave soul to ride horseback all alone the fourteen miles from my school to my home. One week end, I decided to wait until Monday morning to ride to school. On that Monday, ice and snow covered the ground, and I had to saddle and ride. In trying to get to school and get a fire started in the stove before the students got there, I'm afraid I rode my pony much too fast because when we arrived, the pony was all "lathery" and hot. I didn't realize that I should rub him down and cover him with a blanket; thus, he stood all day in the cold and draft. He came down with pneumonia and died. I had to buy another pony.

It goes without saying that the facility was a one-teacher school with an enrollment of thirty students. I was really a greenhorn, afraid some child would ask me a question that I didn't know the answer to. I guess I thought that a teacher should have all the answers. I was janitor, fire-builder, and instructor. It was a custom, there, for the children to invite the teacher to spend one night in their home. One night's lodging I well remember. Two sisters (precious little things) gave me the invitation for a certain night. I went! The parents were cordial; but when I stepped into the house, I was surprised to find dirt floors. They had been swept until hard-packed. I slept with the two little girls on a cornshuck mattress, and the thin sheet we slept on was used as the tablecloth at breakfast the next morning.

B. D. Holbert, Oklahoma City, offers this account of a teacher who attended Langston College in its early years.

I came to Langston University in 1911 from Hillsboro, Texas. The university was then called the "Colored Agricultural and Normal College." They offered courses from the first grade through high school and to a bachelor of science degree. Each student had to take some form of industry along with his academic courses. I chose to take domestic science, the cooking course, because I had practiced cooking at home and had worked in other homes. My mother was a widow, and there were five of us children—myself and four sisters, two older and two younger than I. So I did housework for families and helped my mother keep the family together.

In Hillsboro, Texas, where we lived, the black school only offered the Negro children one year in high school. That is why I went to Langston after completing the eighth grade. After completing high school and domestic science in 1915, I worked five years and entered Prairie View College in Texas. I finished the normal course, which entitled me to a life teaching certificate. I was principal of a grade school for two years in Dallas, Texas, and I was principal of a grade school near Cromwell, Oklahoma, for seven years. During those years, I obtained my B.S. degree from Langston University by working during the summers. I became principal of Dunbar High School in Hobart, and I was there for twenty-one years. During the summers, I obtained my master of education degree from the University of Oklahoma. I became superintendent of a newly created high school in Harris for two years. I then moved to Oklahoma City and substituted in Douglass High School for three years before retiring in 1957.

Fannie Ross Lewis, Stilwell, received her first teaching assignment in 1912 at an Indian school in Adair County.

I began my teaching in 1912 at Fort Still in a little one-room country school, about twenty miles south of Stilwell in Adair County, Oklahoma. My salary was $50 a month; I paid $10 for board and $6 to get there and back by a two-horse buggy. Sometimes, we would get stuck in the mud; and sometimes, water would be up to the bed of the buggy. I went home once a month—pay day. There were twenty-four little fullblood Indian children, and what fun we had—I trying to teach them English and they trying to teach me Cherokee. We had a chart with the alphabet and a few simple words. One boy had a so-called fourth grade reader.

The building was used as a church and meeting house. On Monday mornings I would have to clean it up. For winter heat there was a big old box heater that gave off very little warmth. Big old heavy wooden seats and a long bench or two were in the room, and in front of the class was a raised stagelike affair for the teacher. I soon learned to let the boys out to carry in the wood and the water from a spring in a tin bucket; everyone drank from the same dipper. The term was divided into semesters of three months before Christmas and four months after the holidays. Because of the weather and high water, there always were several days with very few pupils, and once a whole week passed with no attendance. But I rang the bell on schedule. I had signed a contract to teach school. I spent fifty-five years in the classroom as teacher or librarian.

Hazel Allen, Pawnee, comments on the movement to consolidate schools (Payne County).

I was born on January 18, 1906, on a small farm near Yale. My birthplace was a log cabin; however, it had glass windows and a floor made of wood. My parents had come to Oklahoma from Kansas with their families at the time the territory was being opened for settlement. Oklahoma was not a state at that time, and there was not much provision for education under territorial government. On November 16, 1907, Oklahoma became the forty-sixth state, and educational provisions were made in the state constitution.

I was old enough to go to school by 1912. The district in which I lived had voted to consolidate with three adjoining districts and to build a four-room frame school building. This was the first consolidated facility in the state, and it was my first school. The consolidated district was large, and pupils living more than one and one-half miles from the school building had to be transported. Transportation consisted of four covered school wagons drawn by teams of horses. The wagons were owned by the district, but the drivers furnished their own teams and were contracted for the school term.

I rode the wagon to school every day from the first through the eighth grades. The route past my home was about eight miles long over dirt roads which were rough and rocky. Sometimes, we put kerosene heaters in the wagon and covered up with blankets to keep warm. The long seats on either side of the wagon were unpadded benches. This form of transportation continued to be used until sometime in the 1920's. Then, the school wagons were replaced by school buses.

Today, practically all one-room schools in Oklahoma have been consolidated with the independent city schools, and busses go out from the school in every direction to transport the children to the city systems. Some of the routes are twenty-five miles long. Many of the little one-room school buildings were sold; others remained for community use.

After attending the public schools of Stillwater, Maud E. Stimpson of Walters enrolled in the new Oklahoma Agricultural and Mechanical College. She began a teaching career in 1912 in the old Cherokee Nation (Nowata County).

In 1898 my family moved to Oklahoma Territory from Kansas in a covered wagon and settled in the frontier town of Stillwater, home of the Oklahoma Agricultural and Mechanical College. The only building on the campus was Old Central, completed in 1894, now the oldest college building in the state. Four others were under construction at the time. Our home was just across the street from the campus. In the fall, my schooling began in first grade, and as it continued through elementary grades, high school, and college, I feel that I really grew up with the town and the college—now Oklahoma State University.

During those early days Stillwater had no public utilities. Kerosene lamps furnished light, and coal or wood was used for heating and cooking. Ice was delivered daily by horse-drawn vehicle. Our family, like many others, drew water from a well drilled within the house. The first electric lights were single incandescent bulbs, hung by a cord from the ceiling; there were no wall switches. Telephones were mounted on the wall with a hand-operated bell—the type now sought by antique collectors. A "hack" which made two trips daily to the nearest railroad, twenty miles away, remained the only link with the outside world.

The only public school was a new three-story brick structure—the Alcott—which housed both elementary and high school classes. Here I attended my first three years, walking the nine blocks and carrying a sack lunch. The janitor was a benign Civil War veteran, with snow white hair and long white beard; to me, he was the veritable image of Santa Claus. During the noon hour he entertained us children with war stories. When time came to ring the iron bell, which hung in the belfry, he would let us take turns clinging to the bell rope as it moved up and down, and this was quite a thrill. My fourth grade was spent in the newly constructed Jefferson School. It and the new Lincoln School in the south part of town each accommodated grades one to four and relieved the congestion in the main building—proof of the increasing population. The next year I returned to Alcott and continued attendance there until ready for college.

There were few high school graduates in those early days, and to bolster attendance, A. and M. instituted a sub-freshman course to prepare high school undergraduates for college entrance. The college was founded in 1890. The first classes were held in the Congregational church on December 14, 1891. Accounts differ as to the number of students; one says not more than a dozen with three instructors while another gives the number as forty-five and counts a faculty of four. The first graduation in the "Territory" took place in 1896 in Old Central, when six young men received B.S. degrees. Enrollment increased steadily. In my class of 1912, fifty-two men and nineteen women were graduated. In 1974 there were more than three thousand graduates, from nine colleges with 132 divisions, including advanced degrees and including those finishing from the Technical Institute in Oklahoma City. Every state in the Union was represented, as were many foreign countries. The faculty numbered just under one thousand. The campus has changed unbelievably with its fine modern buildings, increased acreage, and beautiful landscaping. Old Central, once condemned and destined for demolition, has been restored and given to the Oklahoma Historical Society for use as a museum.

In territorial days and early statehood, teachers were somewhat scarce in Oklahoma, and qualifications were minimal. To teach a one-room country school, grades one to eight, all that was required was an eighth grade diploma and a satisfactory score on a county examination. There were numerous rural schools, since many families lived in remote areas with no means of transportation. For a salary of $30 to $35 per month the teacher was also janitor and sole director of all activities of the school. The schoolhouse was sort of community center where many social and political events took place, such as pie or box suppers, spelling bees, literary programs, political gatherings, and even Sunday school. A county superintendent had jurisdiction over all the schools in his county, the hiring and paying of teachers, and all records of grades.

During my school years the town grew in population and in improvements, as did the schools. The state, too, had grown, and teacher qualifications were more demanding. Application for a position included, besides the usual inquiries as to education, experience, and church affiliation, such questions as "Do you dance? Do you play cards? Do you play a musical instrument?

Do you sing?" Special talents seemed to be an asset, and it was implied that cards and dancing were taboo. A college degree carried with it a lifetime teaching certificate, provided certain required courses in education had been completed. The day after my graduation was my twentieth birthday. The summer was spent attending classes to fulfill those requirements. Thus, equipped with a B.S. degree, my life certificate, and a nine-month contract at $70 per month to teach four years of high school Latin and two years of German, I awaited the opening of school with anxious anticipation.

Practice teaching was not included in training until many years later. Experience came with the actual process of teaching. Mine began in Nowata, in the heart of the Cherokee Indian Nation. It was also a throbbing oil town—all new and strange to me. I fell in love at once with the town and its wonderful people. The school superintendent was a fine Christian gentleman and a great help to me with his understanding and advice. Some of my pupils were as old as I and probably more sophisticated. It didn't take long to realize that friction existed between the superintendent and the school board. The result was that at the close of the year, the superintendent and the entire high school faculty were dismissed. What a disappointment to be fired after my first year! Others would surely regard me as a failure, and it might be impossible to get another school. I appealed to the president of the board, asking that they allow me to resign. The board did send a letter informing me of re-election, but the wording left no doubt that an immediate resignation was expected.

Within a few weeks, my application was accepted for a similar position at the same salary in a mining district in the northeast corner of the state. Here the people were just as gracious and friendly as those I had left behind. I completed that year and had signed a contract for the ensuing year when a call came from Nowata, from the new superintendent, whom I had met before leaving, asking me to return to my former position at a salary of $80, at that time considered top pay. I was pleasantly surprised to be met by a bevy of former students who gave me a heart-warming welcome.

Zoe Calvert Crutchfield, Elk City, summarizes the experiences of her first year of teaching (1914) in Washita County.

I began my teaching career of forty-five years at Friendship School in Washita County in the year 1914. In a two-room rural school I taught the first four grades for the term of six months. Classes began in December after the cotton crop had been gathered and ended in May. At this time children picked the cotton by hand. Several years later they began pulling the boll with the cotton. As was the custom at this time, I was not only teacher but janitor and playground supervisor, for which I received the sum of $40 per month. Fortunately, I had learned to build fires at home and soon learned to arrange for kindling and coal before leaving school in the evening, which was a lifesaver on a cold winter morning after walking through field and pasture to reach school. The schoolhouse door was never locked at this time, so if any child reached class before the teacher, he could get inside the building out of the cold.

The equipment in this school consisted of double desks and seats which were not fastened to the floor, blackboard, chalk, and erasers. Erasers then were made of wood on which felt strips of different colors were glued. When dropped on the bare wooden floor, they were quite noisy. The blackboard was fastened to the wall at a height convenient for adults, which small children could barely reach. The well-remembered pot-bellied stove had been removed from the center of the room to one corner.

The schoolhouse was the center of community interest and activities. Church services and Sunday school were held in the building on Sundays, not only in this school but in schools of other communities where there was no church. Literary clubs and Farmers-Union meetings also met in the schoolhouse. On Monday morning it was not unusual to find the kindling and coal that the teacher had left beside the stove used, and no one had thought to replace it. Also, it remained necessary to sweep the floor again on the morning following any meeting in the school over the week end or on the previous night. At these meetings small children were kept quiet and entertained by playing with things found in the children's desks. Naturally, it required some time on the following morning to get books and pencils back to the rightful owners.

My warrant was never sent to me in those early years of teaching, even though the clerk of the school board had a child in school who could have brought it. So I had to drive by horse and buggy three or four miles to the clerk's home to get my warrant at the end of the month. Quite often, he would not be at home, and I would have to make a second trip. I'm not writing these things in the form of complaint but am stating things as they were. This was the community where I was born and where I grew up. I was working among and with people whom I loved and had known most of my life. Also, I was thankful to have a job where I could stay at home with my mother, Mrs. H. E. Neill, who had been a widow for several years.

There was no playground equipment on the school grounds at this time; and the children played games called blackman, stealing rocks, dare base, and ante-over. The last mentioned was played with a ball brought to school by one of the pupils. The ball was usually homemade and was also used to play baseball. The bat used was a flat board; and sometimes one of the larger boys would use his pocketknife to whittle off the sides at one end to make it easier to hold when batting. Some children would bring a rope to school which was used for jumping rope. You may be assured that whichever child brought it, the rope was very popular, and some children would offer to do special favors in order to get the use of it. Also, with the owner's permission, the rope would be used for a game called tug-of-war. Another game played quite often but rather dangerous was whip-crack. It was especially dangerous for the small children who were placed at the end of the line. Small boys would bring tops or marbles, which provided entertainment for those who couldn't compete in other games. The last period of Friday afternoon was quite often used for a ciphering or spelling match. Parents would sometimes visit school at this time in hopes of seeing their child excel in one of these.

All children brought their lunches to school at this time, as I can only remember one family who lived close enough to school for their children to go home for lunch and return within one hour. No fancy lunch pails were in use at that time, so most of the children brought their lunches in a gallon or half-gallon syrup pail with a tight-fitting lid, depending on the number for which the lunch had been prepared. The lunch pails were set on the floor at the back of the room, where the children's wraps were hung on a nail. On extremely cold days, it sometimes happened that the sandwiches were frozen by lunch time.

The school building was equipped with a belfry and a large bell which was rung by pulling a rope that extended through a hole in the ceiling to the floor. This bell, when rung, could be heard throughout the district most of the time, depending on the direction and intensity of the wind. It was the custom for the teacher to ring the bell at 8:30 in the morning to remind parents that children should be on their way to school or they were likely to be tardy. The children were not permitted to ring the bell without permission, which was frequently given as a favor for having a lesson well prepared or for unusually good behavior.

Double desks were in use, occupied by two children usually in the same grade, but not always, as some wanted to sit with their brother or sister. The girls occupied seats on one side of the room; the boys took seats on the other side. These desks were more comfortable for older children, as the smaller children could not reach the floor with their feet. Long recitation benches were placed in the front of the room near the teacher's desk, where the children were called by grades for their recitation period. For instance, second grade children would occupy these benches for their reading lesson; and fourth grade would be called to occupy these benches for their arithmetic. A cistern with a pump provided drinking water. Most of the children had their own drinking cups, as this was about the time the common drinking pail and dipper had disappeared. However, if someone forgot or lost his cup, someone else would lend him one. Everyone looked forward to a box supper in early December, which not only provided money for treats and the Christmas tree, but was also an enjoyable social event for old and young alike.

Only a teenager when her career began, Chloe H. Glessner of Oklahoma City taught her first one-room school in Cedar Vale, near Hinton (Caddo County).

My first school term is really vivid to me. The first day I stood before twenty-two children ranging in age from six to seventeen years, in grades one through eight. I felt more afraid and inadequate than I have ever felt in my life. I was nineteen years old. It was October, 1916. I had graduated from high school the previous May. I was beginning a long teaching career in this one-room school, Cedar Vale, which was three and one-half miles from my home town of Hinton. I felt lucky to have secured this work. There were those who depended on me. My mother, a widow, needed what help I could give her. My sister was still in high school, and my brothers were still in grade school. We were not paupers, but we had to manage to stave the wolf from the door. We owned our home and an eighty-acre farm. The rent from the farm was indeed meager to support the family.

When I tell you my first salary, you may laugh. And I'm sure you will wonder, as I do, how I could have helped anyone at $60 a month. Besides this, the term of school was only six months in length. Out of my salary, I paid $3.50 for my board and room. From the farm home where I stayed, I walked one and one-fourth miles to school. It seemed a long distance as I walked against a strong north wind. I never got away from school until at least 4:30 in the evening. Sometimes there was snow on the ground. Again there was a muddy country road to slosh through, and many times it was almost dark when I arrived home.

I was superintendent, principal, teacher, and custodian. When school was dismissed at 4:00 P.M., I began my janitorial duties. I swept the room, and I assure you there was nothing to lay the dust. I sputtered and coughed as the dust rose in clouds around me. The next morning I was there by 7:30 to start the fire in the large pot-bellied stove. With the help of some sticks soaked in kerosene, I became adept as a fire-builder. A few times, I forgot to put my sticks in to soak the night before and had real trouble. What can be more exasperating than a fire that won't start? You may be sure I needed a fire by the time I'd walked that far so early in the morning. In January we had a deep snow. The sturdy farm youths never appeared to tire of snowballing. One day they had a terrible snowball fight. I had been watching them from the window. One boy seemed to be getting the worst of it and ran toward the schoolhouse. Just as I opened the door to intercede, a hard snowball hit the left side of my forehead. By the next morning, the bruise was very noticeable, and as the blue-green settled around my eye, I was a sight! I had a hard time that week end explaining my black eye to family and friends.

One of my most embarrassing moments came when I was hearing a second grade reading class. They were lined up in the front of the room—three little girls. Pretty soon I heard a trickle of water. It wasn't long until there was quite a puddle standing on the floor around the little girl in the middle. The girl had not asked to be excused, and it was too late to excuse her now. I asked myself, "What is the thing to do?" All the time, I fervently prayed that the older children wouldn't laugh. I felt I could not stand it if they did. That pretty child was already humiliated. It was written on her face. When the class finished reading, I excused them as usual to go to their seats. I acted as though nothing had happened. At recess time, which happily came right then, they all filed outside. You can be sure I made haste to do a mopping job!

One evening I arrived at my adopted home; my landlady, Mrs. Boston, was quite perturbed. The Bostons had no children, and they had sort of adopted me. She had been eavesdropping on the rural telephone that day. She couldn't wait to tell me what she had heard. The conversation went something like this: Mrs. Gore had commented, "What is that little new teacher doing? Dess says she hain't any bigger than him. I hear she looks just like a kid!" Now, the woman's son was fifteen years old and in the fourth grade. During the geography class the week before I had asked, "Dess, in what country do you live?" His reply was, "I live in Caddo County." Whereupon I said, "No, Dess, I don't mean the county or state—I mean what country like England or Germany or the United States do you live in?" But this boy, a man in size, still maintained that he lived in Caddo County, which he did. I don't know what became of him, but I've often wondered if he finally learned that he lived in the United States.

In those days, almost every rural school felt the term was incomplete unless there was a pie supper and a performance given by the pupils. I worked hard preparing a program for this affair. As the teacher I was expected to give a short introductory speech. Mr. Boston, my landlord, was anxious for me to succeed and offered to help me with my speech. He was a good critic, too. The night came for the pie supper. Every child was there with his parents. Each was dressed in the best he had. In some cases the best was pretty poor, but they were all clean. Parents were no different then than now. How proud they were to watch their offspring perform. And perform these youngsters did. They did better than the teacher! I got up before the audience to introduce the program. My speech left me! However, I managed to say a few sentences and apparently didn't appear too flustered. But, afterward, I had no idea what I had said.

Viola Martin Barton, Enid, started teaching in 1917 in Harper County.

I lived in Harper County, Oklahoma—county seat, Buffalo. This county was taken from part of Woodward and Woods counties. My father filed on a claim, proved it up, and received a title to 160 acres. He built a sod shack, as he was a blacksmith. Our first home was a hole dug in the ground and sodded up about two feet with a tent over it. When it rained, it filled up with some water. I remember one instance when father had been to town and brought a letter from a friend in Ohio. She "wished we were comfortably situated in our new home." We were sitting with our feet on the rounds of the chairs to keep them out of the water.

When mother finished reading, the mush bowl was full of water, as there was a greased spot over the bowl.

I attended my first school in a sod building with dirt floors. After finishing the eighth grade, I went to a Friends Academy at Gate, Oklahoma, in Beaver County. There were no high schools in our county at that time. The following summer, I attended normal school and then took the teacher's examination and received a third-grade certificate. I began teaching at seventeen years of age in 1917. At this time, there were eighty-four one-room districts in the county. At present, there are three grade schools and three high schools. The children now must be bussed thirty and forty miles one way. This seems to be rather hard on the small children.

I was late starting my first term, as a windstorm had twisted the building off the foundation and the insurance company had not settled. A young man in the district offered his house, which was a dugout, to start school. It only had windows in front, which were boarded. For a blackboard, three foot boards were nailed together and painted black. There was a topsy stove for heat; we used cowchips and wood for fuel. One child put in the chips, and another took out the ashes. The drinking water was carried in a jug. The children rode in wagons, in buggies, and on horseback or came on foot. My salary was $50 a month. I paid $20 for room and board for myself and board for my saddle pony. We were given warrants which had to be discounted to get them cashed. I know of some teachers who had to take out an insurance policy in order to get cash. Our early entertainments were programs, literary society meetings, and spelling and ciphering matches. The last day of school, parents would bring well-filled baskets of food, and everyone enjoyed a good time at a community picnic. Many schools were judged model schools, where a good program was carried out and a building kept in good repair. When a project was to be carried out to raise funds, a box supper, pie supper, ice cream supper, or noodle soup supper was held. One winter we put on "Ten Nights in a Bar Room" with the young people of the community. This play was taken to several communities to help raise money for our school.

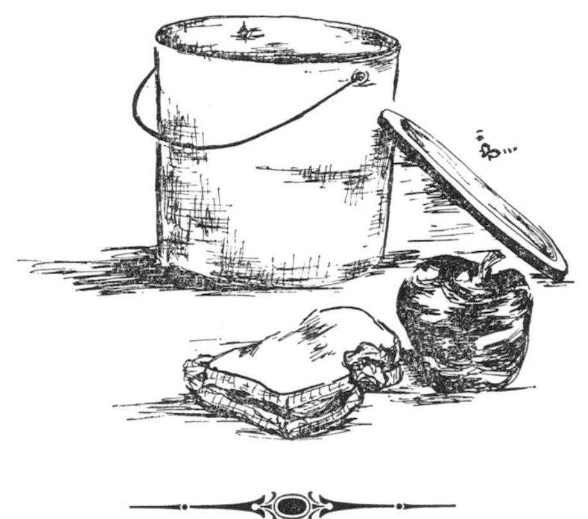

A. D. Hefley of McAlester had not even attended school before he was fourteen years old. By the time he was twenty-five, he had many years of teaching experience. Here, he tells of his early "schoolin'" and the quest for his first job.

As I trudged my way over the hot trail home that afternoon in 1910 after my first day of school, I was on cloud nine. "I like school and I like my teacher, Mr. John Banks," I blurted out as I entered the little log cabin we had rented as a place to live. My father was pleased. I attended the two-month session and continued for four more summers, attending two months in the winter before time to plant the crops in the spring. My mother had taught me to read a little before I entered Mr. Banks's school, and my ambitions ran high. Some day after I learned enough to be a teacher, I wouldn't have to eat corn pone and blackstrap for breakfast. I studied hard, and I learned quickly under Mr.

Banks's guidance and watchful eye. Four years later, I found myself in the fifth grade. I read everything in sight from borrowed newspapers and books to United States history and civics. Learning was a pleasure with Mr. Banks standing by. I kept diligently at my schoolwork, four summers and four winters. I was eighteen years of age but unwilling to give up and quit school. I was fully determined to continue my education.

One morning in mid-January as the classes were marching in to pursue their studies for the day, Mr. Banks tapped me on the shoulder and motioned me aside. I was frightened at this and thought I had fractured the rules. My fears were unfounded, however; and Mr. Banks told me that the citizens of the Nale community had just finished building a new school. It was a one-room pine box structure, and the people of the community were looking for a teacher. "I want you to teach that school, and I'm going to get it for you," he further confided to me. "But I can't do that," I protested, "I don't know enough to teach." "I know that," Mr. Banks replied, "but I'm going to help you. We are going to McAlester in the morning and ask Mr. T. T. Lewis to grant you a temporary certificate." I was shocked! I didn't know what to say. Mr. Banks had already talked to the school board, and the new school was to be a branch of the Indianola school system. The Indianola board of education agreed for me to have the school if I could get a certificate and get the signatures of every patron in the new district. Mr. Lewis, the county superintendent, was to set an examination the following day. I was dumbfounded. I knew I couldn't pass that examination, but Mr. Banks was going to recommend me to the county superintendent. The next day, we caught the early morning train to McAlester. "I want you to meet my young friend who is an up-and-coming young man," my teacher told the county superintendent, "and I want you to set him an examination." Mr. Lewis retired to his private office and in a few minutes came out with a handful of papers. "Write on these," he said, and turned and went back to his private office. In a few minutes he returned, picked up the papers and laid a temporary permit on the desk before me. "That will be two dollars," he said. I turned every color of the rainbow; I was covered with embarrassment. I didn't have a cent and didn't know that examinations cost money. I looked up and saw Mr. Banks standing a few feet away. He sensed my embarrassment, took two silver dollars from his pocket, and handed them to Mr. Lewis. "Let's go," he said, motioning me to follow him.

When we were outside the office, I told my teacher that Mr. Lewis would no doubt take the certificate away from me once he had read my examination papers, for I knew I had not answered a single question on the test. "Mr. Lewis will not read your papers," my teacher assured me. Our train was standing on the tracks, ready to pull out when we arrived at the depot. The next day, Mr. Banks hitched his team of horses to the buckboard, and we were off to secure the signatures of patrons asking the school board to hire me. We worked all day, going from one patron to another, asking for signatures. We secured everyone in the neighborhood except one, John Drake, who refused to add his name to our list. The next day, we drove to Indianola where we presented the petition to S. M. Gold, clerk of the board. "Did you get them all," he inquired of me. "No," I said, "I got them all but one." "Who was that?" he inquired. When I told him that Mr. Drake had turned me down, he said, "We won't count that one because he is unable to read or write. He could not write his name. I know because I hold a mortgage on his property."

I was making progress, and my next move was the signing of a contract. Then came the hitch. Mr. Gold offered me $20 per month for a term of four months. I countered with the assertion that Mr. Banks was getting $60 a month, and I thought I ought to have at least $50. "But you must remember," Mr. Gold informed me, "that you have had no experience. Go see Jim

Bynum," he said. "Meanwhile, I will be writing out your contract." Mr. Bynum was a wealthy merchant and cotton buyer. I told him what Mr. Gold had offered for teaching. "That sounds just like old Stephen," he said. "Come with me and I'll talk with him for you." "Why do you have the gall to offer this young man the measley sum of $20 per month for his work?" Mr. Bynum asked. "Because that's all the money we have in the treasury," Mr. Gold said. "If that's what's bothering you," Mr. Bynum said, "draw up a contract for a decent wage; and if at the end of the term you run out of money, I will give you my personal check for the difference." We compromised for $40 per month, provided I would cut the wood and keep the fires going. I took the job at that price. I was glad to get it.

Beth Ball, Enid, began her teaching in a one-room rural school in 1918 in Kingfisher County. Particularly interesting is an account of her first "meeting" with the Ku Klux Klan.

Way back in 1918–19 I taught my first school in a small rural school only three miles from my home in Kingfisher. There was never a dull moment! I hadn't planned on teaching that year, but rather I'd planned on going back to Kingfisher College for my sophomore year. However, the college didn't have enough enrollment to maintain a full staff; and since I was asked to apply for the rural teacher's position, I did—and I was hired.

It was the "law" of my school district that the teacher should reside in the district during the school week. I rented a room close to my teacher friends' home. My salary was $65 a month, and I paid $3 a week for an upstairs room (no bathroom); I had kitchen privileges. My landlord and his wife were very strict Protestants, and he used to read the "Menace" out loud every night. If I crossed him and objected to some of the statements, he would only read louder than ever; and I had a hard time getting to sleep at night, since the stairwell was open and there was no door to my one big room upstairs. I remember that I finally stuffed my ears with cotton every night!

My school was a mile away from my rooming house, and I had to start early in order to build the fire, dust the furniture, fill the lamps with oil, bring in water and wood and coal, and repair any damage that had occurred after I had locked up the night before. My school was on the banks of a creek where a small rickety bridge crossed. Many trees grew around the school; and I would have been afraid to walk there alone had I not had the companionship of Lyrton, who was the eighth grade brother of my two teacher friends. We met at the corner each morning and arrived at the school building promptly at 8:00 A.M. Sometimes, the building was locked just as I had left it—and sometimes, it was open! When I would look closer, I could see that someone had shot the padlock open and had broken into the building. Obscene things would be on the blackboard, and my coal basket would be full of tobacco juice and spit. Lyrton and I soon learned to dump it out in the yard and take it to the pump for a good cleaning before refilling. I also learned that my school was used for Ku Klux Klan meetings, by other secret groups, and even for lovers' rendezvous. Once, I found some coins and a woman's ruby ring.

One night "Big Mac," the president of the school board, took his daughters and me down to the school, where we hid the car behind a group of trees. We didn't wait long until the KKK's began to arrive. They were all covered with sheets (even their horses), but we recognized a polio victim who lived in the community by the way one arm and one foot protruded straight out under his sheet. After quite a group had gathered, they forced open the door to the school and had a meeting. Later, we heard that someone had stolen horses and cows that very evening, and, of course, we wondered who did it. The "night visitors" weren't satisfied with the havoc they wrought inside my schoolhouse, but they also pushed over the outside toilets nearly every time. Then I would have to send the boys out to the woods on one side of the building and take the girls for a long walk the other way. Finally, "Big Mac" and the county superintendent of schools notified the school patrons that they would no longer tolerate such actions, and the outhouses were disturbed no more.

To top off all my troubles, a hive of bees located on the north wall of my building and buzzed and swarmed until we were afraid to go on that side of the building. One morning, when Lyrton and I arrived at school, we found the doorknob all sticky. When we went inside, honey and dead bees were smeared all over the room. I "lost my cool" and sent all the children home. Lyrton and I walked back home, and his father called the county superintendent out there. I refused to go back to the school until they hired someone to come out and clean up the place and remove the bees.

The crowning blow of the year came towards the close of school. Someone had told the polio victim that the teacher was "sweet on him." He used to ride up on his horse at recess time and stare at every move I made. I played ball and other games with the children. I felt very self-conscious but never said anything to him. Finally, one day when we were going in from recess, he tied up his horse and walked in the door. To my horror, I saw that he had a gun in his hand! He sat toward the rear of the room and shot toward the ceiling! One big overgrown boy knew him and finally talked him into leaving. That night, the sheriff went to his home and arrested him. His folks had to promise that he would never come near the school again before the sheriff would release him from jail.

For enjoyment we had spelling bees and "literary meetings,"

box suppers, pie socials, and exchange meetings with other rural schools. I had pupils in every grade, and I was very proud of all their accomplishments. We started the hot lunch program, and I learned to make good soup. I played the old pump organ, and we all sang with gusto. We had a wonderful Christmas program, complete with costumes and Santa Claus.

Bessie McBroom Watson of Ada also comments on the Klan's activities. She taught in Ahloso (Pontotoc County).

The schoolhouse in Ahloso was used for church services often. Once a revival was in session in back of the room. One night, the preacher was near closing his sermon when fifty white pointed caps and white capes with faces covered came filing in across the front of the audience. One put a ten-dollar bill on the preacher's stand. In all my years I have never seen more excitement. Young children were scared and crying; objectors hurried to their wagons, buggies, and horses to leave. Many were expressing their feelings and beliefs against the Ku Klux Klan. One man and his wife disagreed. He wanted to leave because he was against the KKK; she wanted to stay longer because she thought they were doing a good deed. He got into their buggy and left for home. She had to catch a ride with a neighbor. A group later organized the "Anti-Ku Klux Klan," thus ending the public appearance of the Klan in Egypt district.

Mabel Baldwin Couch, Chelsea, began her teaching in 1918 in a two-room school (Nowata County).

I began my teaching at Salt Creek, a school in Nowata County, which was considered one of the best, since it was two-roomed. That was progress. I was hired without much ado and told to begin work January 2, 1918. The ground was covered with snow, and it didn't look very encouraging to me, but I was determined to make a go of it. I got a place to board about two miles from school with a Mrs. Hendrickson. I walked to school. I met the other teacher, Miss Josephine Phillips, and the forty-eight youngsters I was to teach. I was the primary teacher and would teach the first four grades.

I must describe our school. It was a rectangular frame building, with a long entry hall across the front. A door led to either room. Across the sides were coat hooks and nails to hang wraps. On either end were shelves on which to set the dinner pails. There was a thin partition dividing the two rooms that connected with a door. We considered the furniture nice. They had done away with the old homemade benches and replaced them with the now old-fashioned desks that seated two pupils. They were fastened to the pine floor. The teacher was expected to keep the floor oiled to keep down dust. The windows once had shades, but most of them were gone or in very bad shape. A hand-painted blackboard extended across the front and one side of the room. An old cannonball-type stove provided heat, and a few pokes with an iron would make that old stove get red-hot once the coal was burning. The youngsters by the stove sweated, while others were still cold. Before I left, we were the proud owners of a jacketed sove, with more evenly distributed heat. I had my desk, which had replaced the homemade table.

Each room boasted a "library." That library was really no more than a glass-front bookcase which held about 250 books. The collection represented a standard set for the times, I'm sure; I had read every book before I started teaching—from *Aunt Martha's Corner Cupboard* to *Vanity Fair*. Some of those books were good, but some were there surely just to fill space. Pupils brought their own books, paper, pens and ink, pencils, and slates. We also had some standard maps, very much dilapidated, and a reading chart. I know the reading chart was standard because my own first reading lesson in school was taught from one just like it. We didn't have any of the teaching devices primary teachers now think they must have. Neither did we have busy work, workbooks, or so many other things schools now possess. We worked with the barest necessities; and, speaking for all pioneer teachers, we must have been fairly successful, judging from the success of many well-known men and women we helped to educate in one- and two-room schools.

I am not going to say I was rapturously happy that first year. No. In fact, far from it—I was terrified, homesick, and dreaded each day. I felt so inadequate for my responsibility. I couldn't see the results of my labor fast enough. If I could have gone home, I would have ended my teaching career shortly. But that snow lingered and lingered. Roads were not cleared in those days. I had to stay. Was I getting rich? Far from it. I was teaching for $65 a month. I paid $15 a month for board and room. I completed that year, and we celebrated the occasion with a basket dinner.

I didn't reapply. I secretly felt that I was a failure and that my teaching days were over. So, imagine my surprise when I received a letter from the county superintendent urging me to come to his office and sign a contract with a $10 raise in salary and the promise of new teaching equipment. But I politely declined. The board was not so easily shaken off. They came to my home and begged me to return, assuring me over and over how very pleased they were with my teaching. Finally, they prevailed upon me to teach one more year. I tried—and that "one more year" stretched into forty-four years of public school teaching, followed by two summers of the new Head Start program and some private teaching to help bolster some youngsters that had fallen behind.

In 1916 at fifteen years of age, Okla Gunter Mitchell began her teaching career in Sequoyah County. Destined to serve Oklahoma as a teacher and administrator for over fifty years, she continued a family tradition begun by her mother, who had taught subscription schools in Indian Territory. Here, Mrs. Mitchell highlights her career, especially her experiences in Indian schools.

When I began my career, I was just a bit over fifteen years of age. At that time (1916), the county superintendent of schools could issue a teaching certificate if the applicant had completed the eighth grade. I was granted a certificate and went to teach in a two-teacher rural school which was located back in the hills about eighteen miles from my home in Sequoyah County. The principal, Walter Fox, was a Cherokee. A neighbor of ours, he would leave for his boarding place every Sunday afternoon and come back home each Friday after school; and he provided my transportation—driving two sleek black horses drawing a buggy over the rough roads in the county.

The family in the community with whom we boarded were fullblood Cherokees who spoke their language fluently, but who did not bother to speak much English. To communicate with them posed a bigger problem for me than going to the classroom my first day to teach; however, I did pretty well pointing and grunting and making signs. They were people of means—the "Mrs." received oil royalties and always had good country "grub." I was still somewhat handicapped because I did not speak nor could I understand the Cherokee language. My father was one-quarter Cherokee and could speak and understand quite a bit, but we children seldom heard him use the language. I realized now that I needed to learn more of the language—at least the words for the food being served in order to ask for whatever I wished to have. Soon, I learned to enunciate and accent their words properly. Since there were so many little Cherokee children enrolled in my school, I could communicate with them—at least until they became acquainted with me and learned more English.

All my teaching career was in Sequoyah County with the exception of two years. Many of the rural schools where I taught are no longer in existence, but there were many of them still operating when I succeeded in being elected as Sequoyah County school superintendent in 1947. I was the first woman elected to that office. I served for four years and managed to visit every rural facility and the dependent high schools in the county at least three or more times during each semester. I kept busy trying to improve the buildings, secure qualified teachers, and eliminate fire hazards. I also introduced lunch programs in some of the schools, improved sanitation in and around the facilities, and acquired new textbooks and teaching aids.

Another who taught in the early statehood era was Maynee E. Reavis, Shawnee.

My first experience in teaching was in a one-room building about four miles north of Seminole. I started in the fall of 1914, before oil was discovered in that vicinity. I was eighteen and had just graduated from high school. I had a two-year temporary state certificate. As it seems is always the case, the three-man school board for that district was dominated by one member. He said I was too young and inexperienced, but he finally agreed to sign my contract for a six months' term at $35 a month. If I proved to be a satisfactory teacher, the term was to be extended by one more month in the spring. I had to sweep, dust, and make the fires in the winter, as well as teach. My pupils ranged from a five-year-old in the primer class to a girl nineteen years old in the eighth grade. I also had three eighteen-year-olds in the seventh. Of course I never let the pupils know that I was only eighteen years old myself.

My grandfather had friends living two and one-half miles from the school. He arranged for me to room and board with them for $15 a month. He also let me have his old bay mare and a buggy for transportation. I drove to school early, taking a lunch, and stayed until after 5:00 P.M. to plan work for the next day and sweep and clean the building. Often some pupils stayed to help, but, being farmers' children, they had evening chores to do at home.

Of course our drinking water came from a well, and there were two outside toilets, one for the girls and one for the boys. There was no playground equipment, and there were not enough boys for a baseball team. The highest number enrolled was nineteen, and often several were absent because of home chores or illness. We played blackman, hide-and-seek, one-eyed-cat, and anything else we could think of during the lunch hour or the play periods.

At the end of the six months the school board extended the term another month. The only criticism the dominating member made was that I didn't wield the paddle. He was a strong believer in the theory that when one spares the rod, one spoils the child. He asked me to come back to teach the next year, but I went to a new school where I was paid twice the salary.

Ruby Wallace Sherrick of Ramona taught in early schools in Washington County. She contrasts conditions as they evolved from 1914 to the mid-1920's.

I finished the eighth grade at Ramona and went through high school there, graduating in 1914. In those days, Ramona School was the wealthiest district in the state and had everything that money could buy. We had music, art, band (with school-owned instruments), and a home economics department. The large gymnasium was a separate building, and the downstairs housed showers and dressing rooms, a swimming pool, manual training rooms, and shop and mechanical drawing classrooms. Ramona's income was received from the huge oil tank farms north of town. In 1914 we were still carrying our lunches and riding horses to school, but the board soon purchased five school buses and later began serving hot lunches to the pupils.

After graduation from Ramona High School, I attended out-of-state colleges and returned to Ramona in 1916 to teach at East Side, which was a rural facility two miles east of town. My first school was a two-room building, but I was the only teacher. I had about twenty pupils from grades one through eight. Many of the pupils were larger than I, and some were almost as old. We had no water and no playground equipment. There were the usual wood-burning stove, outdoor privies, and a horse barn. I either rode a horse to school or walked. I felt that I was never a good math student, but in those days a teacher had to *know* all the answers. There was no, "Let's look it up." Those seventh and eighth grade math problems were hard, and I had our banker work my problems in advance for me.

By the mid-1920's many advancements had been made in school equipment. We had good maps, a planetarium, a piano, art paper, paste, scissors, and many other supplies. We began serving a hot dish at noon. We had no indoor plumbing or restrooms. These were still outside but were much more sanitary because they had large, dug pits. Our water was from a cistern; we had a good cellar; and we had swings, basketballs and goals, a merry-go-round, and teeter-totters. We had installed a huge coal-burning stove to warm the classroom. After several years the tank farms were removed, the oil taxes failed to come to our district, and we became hard-pressed for funds. Salaries were cut, the number of teachers decreased, and many changes had to be made; but we always kept a fine school and had an excellent lunch program.

Mary Buffington, Stillwater, spent her first years teaching in Lincoln and Osage counties.

The first year of my teaching was in Spring Hill in Lincoln County. In the spring of 1922, about six weeks before the end of the term, the clerk of the Spring Hill school board called me, asking if I would come and finish the term of school for them. Their teacher had had a heart attack and had passed away. As I was to graduate from high school at the end of the term, I felt that I should not leave school at that time, but two weeks before I was to graduate, I decided I would go and apply for the teaching job at Spring Hill for the coming year. The next day my sister took me in her buggy to see the school board members. I was hired to teach the coming semester of school, a six months' term, at $80 per month.

I shall never forget that little schoolhouse. Time and weather had really been hard on it. The tin which covered the sides of the building had been painted red. It was coming loose in some places; and when the wind blew, it was very noisy. When the wind was not blowing, a woodpecker used to get in where the tin was loose and hunt for worms in the wood. The window panes were put in with tacks, and the cold wind came in. The furniture had been there a long time, but it was usable. The tall, round heating stove stood in the center of the room and was very good at heating the room. There weren't enough books, and there were no other supplies. I provided extra paper and pencils at my own expense. The children brought their own lunches.

A teacher was not only required to teach in those early days, but had to build fires and do the janitor work as well. If you have ever burned dead sumac, you will know that it catches fire readily and makes very good kindling for starting fires. There was a patch of dead sumac across the road from the schoolhouse; and every evening, after I had swept the floor and had the room neat again, I would slip across the road and get some sumac to start my fire the next morning. Then I filled the coal scuttle and set my small jar of kerosene nearby so that I could soon have a fire the next day. The following morning the weather was usually much colder than it had been the night before; and I hurried along so that I could have the house warm before my pupils arrived. I was surprised and dismayed when I found no kindling, no kerosene, and no coal. The coal scuttle had tobacco juice about three inches deep in it. A civic meeting had been held the night before, and the group had used everything I had readied for building the fire. I looked at the coal scuttle in disgust and silently asked, "if all this goes with teaching, do I want to continue?" I decided that I wouldn't let the incident discourage me. From that time on, when a meeting was to be held, I had my kindling and kerosene "stashed away."

In 1923 I hunted for a school which had a longer term and, perhaps, higher wages. It was the rule then that if you applied to a district out of your own county, you had to have at least a second-grade certificate. The teacher's tests were not held in Lincoln County at Chandler until after school was out in May. I took the test for a second-grade certificate, passed it, and received my certificate; but the school boards had hired right after their March meetings. So I decided to attend A. and M. College and work for a state certificate. At the end of the year at A. and M. (1923–24), I received my two-year state certificate. A member of the Indian Camp school board sent me word that they would need a teacher at their school in Osage County and that they would like for me to apply for the position. I made an appointment with them and applied in person. I was hired for a nine-month term at $125 per month. At Indian Camp School, I had a new look at teaching. The parents were interested and were wonderful in helping with the school activities and 4-H Club work.

Pearl Wickham, McAlester, began her career in a one-room school (Pittsburg County).

Why did I teach? My first contract came by accident. In 1920, fresh out of high school, I entered teachers' college in Emporia, Kansas. At mid-term I happened to get sick and had to come home. The 1920 census had been taken, and it revealed that small children in our community were not attending school because of the three miles they had to walk to class. They could not keep up with the larger students. The bigger children would be late if they lagged behind with the smaller ones. The parents appealed to the school board for a neighborhood primary school, but the cost of such a school had not been included in the budget. The neighborhood then offered the church for the school if the board would hire a teacher, and my friends in the community recommended me. My qualifications, although nil, were acceptable to the community, most of whom were illiterate, and were tolerated by the board because of lack of funds, and employment was contingent on my agreeing to attend summer school. My salary was $50 per month. To me that was a windfall!

The day that school opened I was in a trauma. I didn't know the first thing to do or say. All the children were my neighbors. I had gone to school just the year before with their sisters and brothers. They had always known me as Pearl. What would they call me today? How could I look mature overnight? The parents took care of the name. They had instructed the little ones to call me "Miss Pearl." Maturity was my problem, and that was solved by high-heeled shoes, my hair fixed atop my head, some "specs," and a stern look. The little ones were afraid and timid but anxious to learn.

We had no desks. Children sat in church chairs, and writing was difficult because they had to hold slates on their laps. Some children knelt on their knees and used the seat of their chair as a desk or table. The superintendent came to visit us. He had collected some obsolete, discarded desks from other schools and brought them to us. The children were jubilant. The enthusiasm prodded them into trying harder. We worked together for two years; then the first group was promoted to the third grade and were ready for the fourth by mid-term. Being in one room with only a chart, some flash cards, and one small blackboard, plus a few discarded textbooks, left one compelled to improvise in every possible way to meet current and anticipated needs. This disadvantage became an asset. We learned to be resourceful and self-reliant.

Claude C. Harris, Muskogee, attended and later taught his first classes in Riverside School (Seminole County).

I was born May 1, 1901, near Francis in the Chickasaw Nation and reared north of Little in the Seminole Nation. My first school experience was in an old log building used by the Methodist brethren and made available for a subscription school. The building had no floor as we think of floors—the furniture consisted of rough lumber that served for pews of the church group and seats for the older children, while the primary folks rested their bottoms on hewed-down logs. There were no toilets; a plum bush thicket across the trail of a road served the toilet needs. The water was sledded into the building in a fifty-five gallon stave barrel. Every student had the equal opportunity of using the same tin cups attached to the barrel with a heavy cord.

Seminole County was platted into fifty-six school districts at statehood. I shall never forget the experience of enrolling in the Riverside School, District forty-three, in December, 1908, and being ushered to a Montgomery double desk with a shiny inkwell, which I thought was a new dollar as my inducement to sit down. The teacher was only a young lady who had finished the eighth grade. The students ranged in age from five to twenty-one. Little real learning took place, but a lot of other happenings which required the attention of the school board every few days kept the motley group together. As I look back, the home jobs—cutting wood, clearing the land, ploughing, planting, tending, and gathering the crops—were the strongest incentives for attending school.

I began my career as a teacher in the same school in the summer of 1921, a term that ended after five months for the lack of funds. The first direct state aid came to the school near the end of March after the school had closed at the end of February. Every youngster was retained because of the short term, but the 1922–23 term went for seven months, and the students' progress was very satisfactory.

I moved to Justice, south of Wewoka, in 1923 to a one-room school. As many as sixty-six pupils were in school on the same day. Did they learn? The interaction of the pupils, the older helping the younger, those who could helping those who could not—yes, they learned more than their lessons: they learned self-direction, co-operation, to search out for themselves, and to apply themselves to the learning chore; many learned to think, to interpret rules and formulas, and especially to get along—and, by the way, the teacher thinks that it was there that he learned to teach, even though he had been exposed to Bagley and other writers of pedagogy.

Nineteen twenty-three was the year that the state Department of Education came out with the model school program, a plan designed to improve the physical plant and the aesthetic environment of the schools. Yes, Justice achieved a rating that classified it as a model school. The state Department of Education came out with the elementary school accrediting program in 1927–28. A school could receive an accredited rating if it achieved a superior model school rating and if the students made or exceeded the state norm on a general academic test given the seventh and eighth grades; later the age limit was lowered to include grades three through eight. Justice, my school, was one of the two to receive the accredited rating the first year the program was instituted.

Until recently, separation of the white and black races remained the predominant pattern in Oklahoma, as in other states. Azalee Hart, Bristow, comments on early "separatism" in society and in education.

Remember the old days of separatism? We went to school separately. We had separate county teachers' meetings. We ate separately.

I grew up on the farm. There were several Negro men living to the west of us. They worked for my father sometimes. When the threshing crew arrived, the beds were removed from a bedroom, and a long table was set up for the noon meal of the white men. The Negro part of the crew sat around the table on the screened back porch, where our family ordinarily dined in summer. When there were no more than two black men working for my father on ordinary days, when we had not yet moved to the porch, they ate at a separate small table in the same room with the family. If there were too many of them, they just waited until we ate. One day when there was reason to hurry the group of black men back to work, they were allowed to eat first while the family waited.

In school districts where the Negroes were in the minority, they attended classes in a smaller building called the separate, or the minority, school. My first teaching in 1923 was done in a separate school! No, my pupils were not black. In this case, the blacks were in the majority, and they had the larger facility. In my school on the bank of the Arkansas River in Wagoner County, there were a dozen whites in grades one through five. Up on the hill was a two-room, two-teacher facility for the blacks in all eight grades. On a few occasions, when this school for some reason dismissed before we did, they just stared quietly as they passed if our pupils were on the playground. Ours did likewise.

Edna Martin Ray, Fairview, recounts her first day of teaching at Elm Grove School (Major County).

It was nearing the end of the early statehood period when I began teaching school as Miss Edna Martin. I was barely eighteen years of age when I arrived the morning of September 10, 1923, at the Elm Grove School. It was in Major County and was located about two and one-half miles north of Isabella. I drove the seven and one-half miles from the home of my parents, Ed and Flora Martin, in their Model "T" touring car, which I had only recently learned to drive. By living at home, I was able to save the board and room money to help me finish my high school education. Family doctor bills had forced me to postpone going, after finishing my freshman year at Fairview High School; and I was teaching the eight-month term for $85 per month, which would make it possible for me to attend Northwestern State Teachers College at Alva in summers and finish Fairview High in two more years.

Eighteen years of age was the youngest age one could teach school at that time, and one could do so by passing a teacher's examination. I was still seventeen when I took the examination given by our county superintendent. The subjects over which the tests were given were agriculture, arithmetic, civics, composition, domestic science, geography, grammar, Oklahoma history, United States history, music, physiology and hygiene, reading, spelling, theory and practice, and writing. I passed this examination and was issued a third-grade teaching certificate which qualified me to teach for one year. I had had no formal training in teaching methods, so I made up my own schedule in all eight grades for the twelve subjects I was required to teach. This was done from memory of the way classes were held in the country school which I had attended.

Elm Grove's schoolhouse was typical of those of the communities of that period—an oblong wooden building painted white, with rows of tall windows on both sides and a large bell in a belfry on top of the building. The school was located on a flat piece of land, fenced on three sides. There were no trees or shrubs. At the back of the yard was a coalhouse which separated the boys' and girls' toilets some distance apart. In the schoolhouse there was an entrance hall across the end of the building, with rows of hooks for hanging coats and caps, and there were shelves for the lunch pails. In the classroom the teacher's desk and chair were on a low stage at the opposite end of the room from the entrance. On the wall back of the desk was a blackboard, and above it was the United States flag. There was a long recitation seat in front of the desk to which each class would come when the teacher called for it to recite. Most of the rows of desks were double desks allowing for the seating of two persons. A large potbellied stove remained in the center of the room and was to be used in the winter to burn coal to heat the room. It was part of my job to build the fires and keep coal in the building to keep the fire going.

At 8:30 A.M. I went to the hall and rang the big bell by pulling up and down on the long rope that hung down from the bell through the ceiling. The sounds of the bell pealed out across the countryside to let the community know that it was one-half hour until time for school to begin for the day. This ringing was kept up for three or four minutes to distinguish it from the short ringing periods at 8:55 and the final ringing at 9:00. At the ringing of the last bell, the pupils gathered at the front entrance into two lines, as was their custom. Those having seats on the north side of the room joined the north line, and those who sat on the south side got into the south line. After I saw that both lines were in straight formation, I gave them the permission to pass into the room and to hang their caps up in the hall as they passed through it. Then they each stopped beside the desk he had chosen and remained standing until given my signal to be seated. I was following the procedure I had been taught in grade school, and it seemed to be the same that the children were accustomed to.

I was a very shy, young girl, having had very little experience in standing before a group. I am sure I must have been half scared to death that morning when I faced twenty-two new faces. Thirteen of the pupils were boys, with eight of them teenagers—some as big as I was. Of the nine girls, three were teenagers. We made it through the day just fine, but I have no memory of how. At the two fifteen-minute recess periods and the noon hour, I played on the school ground with the children, as I had always been sportsminded. But of the traditional games played throughout the year—work-up (a ball game), blackman, dare-base, run-for-supper, and drop-the-handkerchief—I do not recall the ones played that day. When school let out at 4:00 P.M., we used the formation marching out of "books away, hands folded, turn, arise, pass," the same formation that my own grade school days had taught. After the pupils had marched out, they stayed quietly in their lines until I dismissed them as I stood in the doorway. After the children had gone from the schoolhouse and I had my own desk work completed, I did my own janitor work of sweeping the

wooden floors, re-straightening the desks that had to be moved to sweep under them, and dusting the furniture. The day had certainly been a new experience.

Bernice Cox Martin, who in 1970 concluded a career that spanned half a century, recalls her first Oklahoma home in Alva (Woods County) and her schooling in the early statehood period.

Impressions of childhood are permanent. I vividly recall the time my father left us in Indiana to come to Alva, Oklahoma, to buy a farm to which we were to move in April of 1908. Memories of the sale in Indiana, farewell to friends who thought we were moving to a wild country, a farewell visit to relatives in southern Indiana, and crossing the Mississippi River on the Rock Island train are vivid.

In my first view of Alva I saw it as a town with very wide dirt streets. The city square was surrounded by hitching posts for teams of horses and on three sides were watering troughs so the horses could be given a drink before the drive home. Two things that enticed my parents to this location were the Friends church here and the college where we could get an education. My father and brother had left two weeks earlier in a boxcar with two horses, some tools, our furniture, and other possessions. These had been unloaded, and we were ready to spend the summer in the three-room house that was on the place. About two weeks after our arrival we saw our first tornado. Dad saw it coming and yelled, "get to the cave." We did. It passed over us, but some people were killed east of Alva.

That summer we built a new seven-room house that fitted our needs very well. My brother and sister still live there. The storm cave was attached, so never again did we have to rush through rain and hail to reach shelter. In 1908 there was no electricity and no running water (there was a cistern on the back porch). Coal or wood had to be carried in for the kitchen range and the heating stove, and the ashes had to be carried out. The outdoor toilet was located some distance from the house. This gave us exercise, and the air-conditioning discouraged loitering on cold days.

On the corner of our farm, one-half mile from our house, was a one-room country school, North Eagle. Many such schools had been built three miles apart to provide for the education of rural children in this state. My father had attended Earlham College at Richmond, Indiana, and had taught country schools in Indiana. Mother, too, was a graduate of Indiana State Normal and had taught. They were the source of my inspiration to become a teacher. Dad was employed to teach North Eagle School. The school term lasted seven months, and he received $50 per month (nothing was withheld for social security or income tax). This cash income meant a great deal to a family in those early years. Four years later he began teaching at Friendship School west of Hopeton. He drove the six miles in a two-wheeled cart because he had to ford the Eagle Chief Creek. This original building has since been moved to Hopeton and is now the community center there.

I liked books, and when my older brother and sisters would have their books, I had mine. In the fall of 1908 I recall my mother's saying that if I must always have a book, I might as well go to school and learn something. In September I started to school while still a four-year-old, trudging along with dad and the other pupils from that direction, some of whom had already walked two miles before they reached our place. This walk was a delight in the fall when the weather was good, but rain and snow in winter made it horrible.

One acre of ground was set aside for the schoolgrounds. The

building was located near one side. This provided for a large playground. The building had one door on the west, and four windows on each side provided light and ventilation. A large coal-burning stove in the center provided heat in winter. Across the front was a blackboard and above it hung a huge American flag with forty-six stars. The last star had been added the year before when Oklahoma became a state. Across the front was a raised platform on which was the teacher's desk and chair. In the rear was the stand with the water bucket on it, and in the bucket was the long-handled dipper from which everyone drank. We must not have known about germs then. The coat room was a long line of hooks across the back wall of the building. There was always a variety of odors in winter when these wet coats were drying in the warm room, and twenty or more pairs of muddy overshoes were scattered on the floor, convenient for the older boys to kick or stumble over when they went outside to the toilet or to get a drink. There were large double desks. Sometimes these were convenient, but it was easy to talk to your neighbors, and books were always mixed. These were soon replaced with single desks. These were a variety of sizes and each pupil chose the size where he could sit with his feet on the floor. Each pupil provided his own books and equipment. There were few books in the school library. Lunch always came from home. Some pupils had dinner buckets; others used paper sacks. Some had sandwiches and an apple or cookies; others had cold biscuits left over from breakfast. Playground? There was no equipment, but there was always something to do. Usually there were running games such as hide-and-seek, follow-the-leader (whenever snow was on the ground), three-deep, and run, sheep, run.

There were about twenty-five pupils enrolled in my first year in all eight grades. We learned to work independently because there was no time for supervised study. We knew a lesson must be prepared so that we could recite that lesson when we were called to the recitation bench, which was in the front of the room directly in front of the teacher's desk. There was nothing more humiliating than to be told before a whole class to "take a lesson over." Eighth graders felt that they had to study because they had to pass the eighth grade examination given by the county superintendent of schools. A diploma signed by him was required for entrance to high school. Eighth grade pupils in Woods County went to a normal which provided four years of high school and two years of college. Graduation from the normal provided a life certificate entitling the holder to teach in any public school in Oklahoma.

I went to school at North Eagle for five years. In the seventh grade, I drove with my older sister three and one-half miles to Alva. She was graduating from Northwestern that year, and I enrolled in the seventh grade at the training school there. After two months I was promoted to the eighth grade. In 1915 I entered my first year at Northwestern, receiving my life certificate in 1921. This was the year the normal became Northwestern State Teachers College, and the first degrees were granted. It is interesting to note that when I retired from teaching in 1970, I was still teaching on the life certificate I had received fifty years before. Times have changed. The one-room country school is a thing of the past. It filled a definite place in education. We learned in that school to think and work independently and to co-operate with others.

Beginning her career in 1927, Cecile Peterson of Watonga taught her first school on the Cheyenne-Arapaho reservation (Dewey County).

In September, 1927, I walked three miles to my first school

expecting to be greeted by thirty-five excited children. Instead, I found waiting at the door of Tin Top School seven Indian braves. This school was in the heart of the Cheyenne-Arapaho reservation, and approximately half of the students were Indians. Upon seeing these men, my first impulse was to turn and run; but, remembering that my brother had many Indian friends in this area, I braced myself, squared my shoulders, and faced them. Upon hearing one ask, "are you Eagle Boy's sister?" my fears disappeared; I knew in these men I had friends. Eagle Boy was my brother who had supplied them with eagle feathers for their costumes for many years.

And, indeed, they were friends, for not once in the school term of seven months did the Indian children fail to get to school. These parents saw that they were there and that they stayed. Before, when the Indian agent from Concho came with a doctor to give the children their vaccinations, the children would run away, going out through the windows since the only outside door would be barred by the agent. When they took off this year, they came right back because those same Indian men were just outside to see that they did. It was a most interesting year, despite the inconveniences of having to build fires (blackjack wood really makes a good, warm fire), of bringing water fifty yards from a well whose pump continually lost its prime and would freeze in the winter time, and of trying to sweep a rough splintered floor made from the flat side of split logs with no finish.

The Indian children were very courteous and wanted to share. At Christmas they came bearing their beaded gifts—bookmarks, headbands, and even a beaded pair of garters. Everything they brought represented something of their handiwork or from their heritage. These gifts were quite a contrast to the store-purchased gifts of the white children.

It was most difficult to say "no," when I was asked to return the next year. Even an offer of a $5 per month raise over the $75 per month salary I had been receiving for a seven-month school was not sufficient for me to remain and decline a most lucrative offer that I had been given. In this latest offer, I would receive $90 per month plus an additional month of school. Also, the distance I would have to walk would be only one mile instead of the three, and I would be ten miles closer to my home.

The Indian children, however, convinced me that I wanted to make teaching my life's work. I loved them dearly. Yet I could never quite bring myself to eat those bits of food which they wanted to share with me, for I was never sure what it was—maybe puppy. I could not hurt their feelings by refusing, and I would skillfully manage to get it into my lunch basket to be disposed of later.

Perhaps the most interesting or amusing event was the day we stood in the school yard watching the federal officers, or "revenuers" as we called them, as they destroyed a still and seven hundred gallons of mash. The still was being operated by the father of one of my school board members and grandfather of six of my white students. A little six-year-old boy very casually said, "Yep! They've got Grandpa again."

Although I have taught thirty-six more terms of school, thirty-four of them in Watonga, I think none have been more fruitful, enjoyable, or rewarding than that seven-month term I taught at Tin Top School, which is now submerged in the Canton Lake.

Edith Koons Thiessen, Alva, started teaching in 1927 in a one-room school (Major County).

My teaching career started in a little red schoolhouse, out in the blackjack country west of Fairview, more commonly known as the "sticks." Out on Highway 60, back in the fall of 1927, I began teaching on a special permit because I was only seventeen years old. The term was eight months, and the pay was $60 per month. In October, I found myself in a new tile building which had most of the standard equipment with the exception of the blackboard. That I was unprepared for many of the situations that arose was a mild understatement. To begin with, the opening day I found myself surrounded by boys and girls, many of them taller than I and some nearly as old. Then one exclaimed, "How are we going to know whether we mean you or Edith Cole, when we say 'Edith'?" That was my introduction to the informality that prevailed in this small community where nearly everyone was related to someone else.

Then came the day when a young man, son of the woman who was clerk of the school board, came to install the blackboard (it wasn't known as chalkboard then, and it was real slate—a quality that I have longed for since). I didn't try to keep the children really quiet—it was a little too exciting to remain silent with all the noise and pounding and confusion. Imagine my surprise to hear that I couldn't keep order, a very severe charge in those days! However, before long Mrs. Patterson, the board member, came to visit school; to my relief, she went away saying that my discipline was satisfactory.

Many things I learned in the two years that I taught there. I spent the first winter there, saving and scrimping so that I might go to school a winter and get a state certificate, and with it, I could qualify for much better wages. I rented an attic room in an old, old house. I could stand erect in the center, but the slanting roof reached the floor at the sides of the room. I think that I paid $5 a month to live there. I bought a little two-burner wickless kerosene stove to cook on and heated water to wash the dishes. One cannot properly appreciate a stove like that unless one has used the unpredictable, smelly, smoky things. All water and slop had to be carried up and down narrow, rickety steps. But all this did not compare to the cold and dreariness of the attic—and even that discomfort faded into the background when I found that the house was infested with rats! Real, big, live rats! How they scampered about at night—and the noise they made as they dragged my shoes around!

One school experience that I especially remember had to do with Cecil, a little dark-haired, velvety-eyed fellow who was just barely five. What a time I had, for he often had a puddle at his feet. He was too shy to ask to leave the room, even after I tried to explain to him that it was quite all right; in fact, I insisted that he go to the outdoor facility without stopping to ask for my permission. When this did not solve the problem, I told him that if he made one more puddle, I was going to spank him. He made the puddle, and I gave him the spanking. How badly I felt that I had allowed myself to be pushed into such a situation! I taught many years before I spanked or whipped anyone again.

Rural teachers in that day were expected to do the janitor work—most contracts had that duty included, and there was no doubt about whose responsibility it was. We had a big pot-bellied coal stove that should have provided ample heat for the building, but there was just one catch—the patrons were not about to spend money for coal with all the blackjacks at their doorsteps. So there was the woodpile—green wood, at that. If you have never had the experience of building a fire, especially with green wood, you probably can't appreciate the problems that I had. I had asked the school board for some kindling to warm up the wood a little, and their response was to give me a little axe, or I guess you could call it a hatchet, to cut my own! Fridays, I would lay in a supply of wood and kindling for Monday's fire; but I soon learned that I might not have any. Church congregations held services in the schoolhouse every Saturday and Sunday and usually exhausted any wood I had collected. I don't know who did what, but I could be quite sure that my fuel supply would be depleted when Monday came.

Occasionally, spelling and ciphering matches were held in the evenings for neighborhood entertainment. It was my job to pronounce the words, and I never had to disclose my ability (or lack of it) in spelling. I do remember being challenged in a ciphering match and was just barely able to uphold my standing in the community by "putting down" a man who was good and went from match to match for the pleasure of the competition.

The years taught in the Leslie district, north of Fairview, were memorable in many ways; and in thinking back over those years, much of what happened now seems incredible. To begin with, I had a heavy teaching load—thirty-some-odd children in all eight grades. One of the boys had such a low IQ that I spent two years trying to teach him to count. He finally learned to count to thirteen, but he always left out the number seven. Most of the children here were of German background. Some came to school unable to speak English and were very shy. One little fellow remained so frightened that he lay under a row of desks all day. Some of the older boys tried to embarrass me by using the German language, which I could not understand. To add to the difficulty of the job here was the fact that the parents expected to have a program once a month. The teacher was expected to plan the program that young people in the district would participate in. Nothing less than an hour and a half was considered acceptable. Pie and box suppers were important social events in many districts. Often, the proceeds went for playground equipment, or, in some areas, they made possible Christmas treats for everyone in the district as well as all who brought or bought pies or boxes. And the rivalry was great. Boxes went for the outlandish sums of $8 and $10. "There ought to be a law again' it," clacked some of the grannies.

After being taught at home by her parents, Loy Pollan Tullis of Miami, Oklahoma, began her formal education in a small school near Cayuga in Delaware County. Later, she taught her first classes in that same school.

In 1909, though only four years old, I trudged eagerly to school through the "big, dark woods." I lost my cloth *ABC Book* on the way home; I cried myself to sleep because I thought I would never learn to read. The next morning mamma and I plodded through mud, down the fence row, until we found my book. Rain had washed all the letters away. I was heartbroken.

Soon after the *ABC Book* episode, on January 1, 1910, we moved to Delaware County, near Cayuga. There I did my next reading. I did it by spelling out the headlines from the newspapers that graced the walls of our native lumber home. Mamma told me the words as I spelled them out. On my seventh birthday, daddy taught me, "to the tune of a hickory stick," to count to one hundred. In the autumn of 1912, I began regular school. Class was held in the Roman Catholic church on the edge of Cayuga Village. I went to school in Cayuga District for seven years.

In 1912 we built a new house of pine, painted it white, and moved into it by Christmas. It was the second white house outside of Cayuga Village. The village burned early in 1913. Only the five-story carriage shop, the priest's house, and the Catholic church were left standing. The fire destroyed a hotel, general store, post office, blacksmith shop, and eight or ten dwellings. Now the Catholic church house is the only building left. It is used only occasionally for religious services.

School was held in that church for three or four years, but in the spring of 1913 the new schoolhouse was built. We went to school in the new building in the last month of school in 1913. We had lovely red cherrywood double seats, a blackboard, chalk tray, erasers and chalk, a regular teacher's desk and chair, and a metal bookcase with reference books and a large *Webster's Dictionary.* We also had wall coal-oil lamps with mirror reflectors. The room was heated by a large wood-burning box stove. The eight tall windows let in light and air to make our new school an up-to-date school indeed.

My first year of teaching began in August, 1925, at Cayuga, the very same school where I had begun to "read, write, spell, and cipher" in the autumn of 1912. The first day of school I had eight grades, thirty-nine pupils, and thirty-nine classes. I realized that those were too many classes for one day. But by alternating and combining, I went to school the next morning with only seventeen classes each day.

Cayuga was a "Model A" school, and I kept it that way. We posted our daily schedule on the wall and had music every morning which ended with a prayer by me or one of the pupils. We had our own drilled well with a hand pump to supply our water. Each pupil brought his own drinking cup, and we had two water buckets with a dipper. We had a wash basin and a clean towel each day. We also had a medicine chest supplied with first aid materials. We kept the schoolyard clean; the outdoor toilets were scrubbed and had a mail-order catalog in each. We needed all of these facilities for we had broken arms, faintings, upset stomachs, cuts, bruises, splinters from well-oiled floors, and alarms from drinking listerine and peroxide from the medicine chest.

I was the sole ruler over all. I taught, praised, punished, advised, loved, and doctored. One day Clyde broke his arm; I carried him into the house and took him to the doctor. Lucille fainted on the basketball court outside, and I revived her. John Mark ran a three-inch splinter into his foot, and I cut a slit with Dick's pocketknife and removed the splinter with a pair of pliers. My first year the average daily attendance numbered over thirty all year; everyone passed; and we all went home happy.

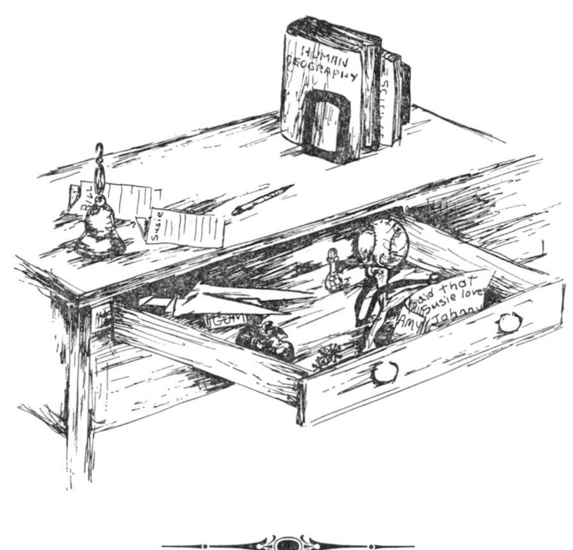

Mabel Couch, who contributed another narrative to this section, here points out that early schools served many social functions.

Schools were the center of the social life in the early days. The teacher played an important part. She, or he, was expected to sponsor a Christmas tree with treats for everyone; to raise money for the annual Christmas party there was usually a pie supper or box supper. The ladies and girls brought decorated boxes to the supper. An auctioneer sold the meals to the highest bidders. Sometimes a program, prepared by the teacher and pupils, preceded the auction. Believe me, those boxes often sold high—when two or more jealous suitors began to bid on their lady love's pie. Another money-raising scheme was to sponsor a cake sale for the "Most Popular Lady" in the house. Then money flowed freely; but we had to handle the sale with care, for sometimes anger flowed freer than money, and a fist fight or fights might ensue if some girl was edged out by a competitor. If things began to get out of hand, time was called, and the "lady" having the most money to her credit was declared the winner. The collected money was then used to buy treats for everyone who helped raise it. Then the teacher and pupils made ready the Christmas program. Recitations, songs, and dialogues were all performed by the pupils. I sometimes wonder how many "stars" made their first appearance in the one-room school. It was all very exciting (and nerve-wracking) to the teacher, I know. I was always glad when the Christmas tree program was over. Then we settled down to real work. Now, I wouldn't lead you to believe that school teaching was all work and no fun or pleasure. There were many tangible things to give pleasure and some intangible ones that only teachers may understand.

V

THE DEPRESSION ERA

During the 1930's, people in almost all occupations suffered, but the depression was particularly hard on those who chose teaching as a profession. Oklahoma educators found that money for supplies and equipment remained almost impossible to acquire, as the tax revenue of local and county governments declined. Teachers found that their pay warrants were often not worth stated face value and were cashable only at heavy discounts. Far more serious, teachers day-in and day-out had to face poorly clad, poorly fed children whose parents likewise suffered the ill effects of the depression. But earlier frontier conditions in Oklahoma had forged a hearty breed. Communities, helped by the state and the federal governments, united to overcome hard times. As many of the following selections demonstrate, teachers did their part. They worked without supplies and equipment when necessary; they accepted, with little protest, the meager salary that came after their warrants were discounted; and they—on many occasions—shared what they had with their school children and with the impoverished families of their district. They continued the tradition of professionalism and concern for community begun by their forefathers.

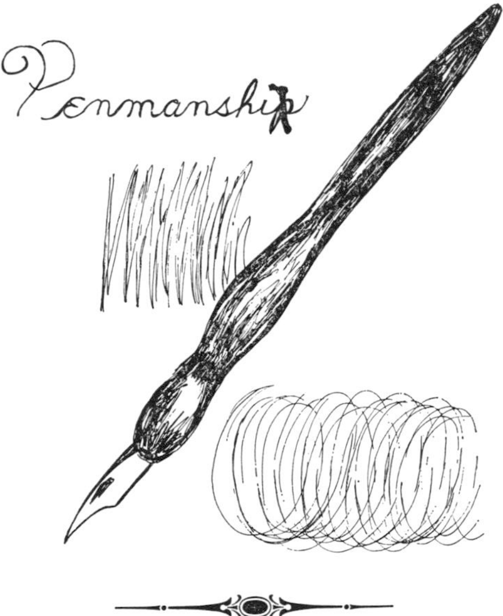

During the depression, teachers often put the welfare of their students above their own interests. Livonia Jones of Stillwater remembers a makeshift hot lunch program that teachers organized for pupils and remembers the months she went without pay in order for class to continue.

During the depression years we offered our children a hot lunch program of sorts. A small building, which had housed a shoe repair shop and which was located about a block from our building, was converted into a lunchroom. In weather fair or foul, we marched the children to lunch—a large number of them often barefoot and in overalls. Lunch consisted of soup and crackers, at first served in pint tin cups. Later we did get bowls. Many years later, good hot lunches were served at the lunchroom in the high school, which was five blocks from the grade school building. Usually we walked the children to and from lunch, but if weather were too disagreeable, a school bus transported the children. At one time during the 1930's it was learned there was no money for teachers' salaries the last six weeks of school. Our school board put the facts before us. If we chose not to continue teaching, the high school students would lose one year's credit. The decision was ours. Every teacher agreed to complete the year. We never got our pay, but the students did get their year's credit. I don't believe any of us ever regretted it.

Elizabeth Howard, Sapulpa, began her teaching career in Sapulpa in the middle of the depression. She remembers discounted warrants, early hot lunch programs, and the many times that part of her pay went to unfortunate children.

My teaching experience began in 1931. The depression was upon us. I had a beginning salary of $50 per month. During the depression, before the federal- or state-sponsored lunch programs were started, mothers would bring vegetables and meat to the school to prepare soup for those children whom the principal found to be in need of food. There were those who fainted in school and who came without lunches. I remember that many children would go home after school, get a bucket or other container, and trudge down to the place where soup was being dispensed. Teachers bought shoes, mittens, and other articles of clothing, as well as extra sandwiches for lunches. They did this at a time when their warrants were being discounted 50 to 60 per cent. Many of these students grew up, married, lived in the same neighborhood, enrolled their children in the same school, and saw the children in the same classrooms with the same teachers who had taught them. There was a closeness in this relationship not to be found among some of the other schools, especially the more affluent ones.

Jessie May Hines, Chickasha, recalls the uncertainty of employment and the irregular paychecks during the depression—and an unusual switch: this time the husband lost his job because his wife was employed.

Those of us who have taught many years in Oklahoma remember well the depression. I lost my little savings in a bank failure. I took a 10 per cent discount to get any money at all on my warrants, as paychecks were then called. I received six months' pay for nine months of teaching. Twice I received eight months' pay for nine months of teaching. I married in the 1930's, and my husband lost his job soon after our marriage because I was receiving an income and someone else could benefit from his job. I was afraid to quit teaching because we might not have any income. Finally I did quit full-time teaching for a year and had that year's experience as a substitute teacher in Oklahoma City. I disliked the irregularities of that kind of teaching, but I did have some invaluable training. I attended teaching conferences under the leadership of some very fine supervisors in music and other subjects. Teaching in the various schools was an education from which I tried to benefit fully. I have used many of the methods since.

Also having experience with discounted warrants, Genevieve L. Kysar, Sayre, taught in Washita County during the depression.

I remember very clearly an incident which happened when

the banks closed during the depression in March, 1933. What a shock it was when I realized that the bank would not cash checks and that the stores were afraid to charge. I was at home near Hinton getting ready to return to my teaching job near Colony. I had no money. My entire family helped me search every drawer and pocket. We found less than $1.00 in change. Our farm home was a haven. I took food from the cellar and kitchen. I drove the twenty-five miles to the house where I had a light-housekeeping room rented upstairs.

That winter was one of my worst. My room was furnished with the bare necessities, a monkey stove, a bed, and a table. I walked one and one-half miles to school every morning, built the fire, and did the janitorial work, in addition to teaching from 9:00 to 4:00 every day.

Ellen Watson Wood, Watonga, taught in Lawton during the great depression. She was assigned a school in a poor section of town and can now offer insight regarding the problems of migrants during the 1930's.

After graduating from Oklahoma State University (then A. and M.) in 1936, I was hired to teach third and fourth grades in Jefferson Grade School at Lawton. Lawton was my place of birth and was where I had received most of my public schooling. I had already had one year of teaching experience in a rural school, but when I learned I was assigned to teach in the low-income section of the town, I realized that I would have many new experiences. The area of town where I was to teach was one block from the railroad tracks and power plant. Most of the families in this ward were Mexican and Anglo transients who had built tiny one-room houses out of scrap tin and wood. These flat-top houses were scattered up and down the railroad tracks for about one mile. About three-fourths of the fathers were working on the W.P.A. projects in Comanche County. The average monthly wage for the W.P.A. workers was $28. There wasn't enough money to spend on furniture, and the families often slept on straw-filled mattresses. If they couldn't find a used wood stove for both heating and cooking, they used metal barrels or pieces of bent tin with a grate on top. Boxes were used for seating and all storage. There was no welfare department in 1936, but the county commissioners sometimes issued grocery orders in case of emergencies.

My classroom would have seated thirty-five pupils comfortably, but I had fifty-seven, and sometimes there were a few more. Extra desks and chairs were brought from the other four grade schools, and four chairs were placed at my desk for the overflow. I needed a desk, but there was no sitting-down time because there was so much remedial work to be done. The ages of my third and fourth graders varied from eleven years old to seventeen years old. There were no pupils who could do the fourth grade work at the beginning of the school term, and most were only capable of doing first and second grade levels of work. Some had attended only a few months of school. It was necessary to borrow books from the first grade teacher.

With the wonderful help and encouragement of my principal, Miss Jennie Schwarte, and with the help of Mrs. Rozella Becker, first and second grade teacher, we planned what needed to be done. We weighed and measured every child in school. We felt that the slow learning was partly due to poor nourishment and home conditions. We kept a weekly chart on every child. Home studies were made on each family. We learned that most children had no breakfast and sometimes only had one meal a day. The children's hair was stiff and strawlike. After every child received a medical check-up from a doctor, the reports were given to the teacher; and a county health nurse visited the school regularly. From the reports, we learned that the children needed more food. There remained no lunchroom program, so we called on the manager of the Lawton mission house. Through the aid of the mission house, it was possible for a noon meal of soup or stew, bread, and milk to be brought to the school every day. Often the Salvation Army supplied sacks of fruit. Also, we had an understanding that any child who had no breakfast was to have milk and a roll of some sort, if he or she would only tell us, before classes began in the morning.

In about a month we noticed a difference in the children's skin coloring and hair texture. Too, the children had gained weight. Within two months, we noticed progress being made in their schoolwork. The playground activities improved, and the older children were able to hit a volleyball over the net. Throughout the remainder of the school term, there was improvement. The boys and girls did well in the school programs and were outstanding in the all-city-school May festival, which was held on the high school football field. We three teachers were proud when all three of our maypoles were done perfectly along with about twenty others winding in unison.

The teachers helped the W.P.A. workers' wives sign for employment in the county sewing room and in library book-mending projects. Some were hired to make corduroy pants and jackets for boys and skirts and jackets for the girls. The blue-and wine-colored material was furnished by the state. Workshops were begun all over the state to help the indigent pupils in every county. Nearly all of our pupils were dressed alike, but no one made an issue of it, as far as I can remember. One thing I do remember is that the pupils got along very well together. All seemed to work harder to better themselves in everything they did. A fourteen-year-old Mexican boy who started the third grade in September had been promoted to the other classroom to do fifth grade work by mid-term and finished the sixth grade near the top of his class. Many reached their grade levels during the year.

I recall that we did not have many visual aids unless we made them because money was so scarce; but we surely used the hectograph for duplicating materials for regular assignments, tests, and remedial work.

I taught in the Jefferson School for three years. The experiences and rewards received were many. There was love and understanding given the pupils, and respect and love were returned. We noticed a group of happier, healthier, and better students at the end of each term. Some families found better employment and moved from their squatters' dwelling. Some families moved away from Lawton. We teachers did not get rich money-wise, but we were rich in experiences such as seeing the child reach his grade level after many hours of hard work and seeing his eyes light up when he was issued a new corduroy jacket and pants—or the girl being pleased with her jacket and skirt. Sometimes, it was the joy of a satisfying meal or a pat on the back to let the student know he was doing all right. For my efforts, I received $97 a month when the warrants were good. Sometimes we held them several months; or if we had a good banker, he held them and loaned us money on them until they could be cashed.

Vera Smith Cornelius, Oklahoma City, taught in western Oklahoma during the depression. She began a hot lunch program for her students at Mound Valley, Canadian County.

After graduating from high school in the spring of 1927, I took the third-grade teacher's examination. Immediately, I began teaching in the rural schools of Oklahoma for $85 a month. Six years later, during the deep depression, the salaries were considerably lower everywhere. I moved to a one-room school in Canadian County known as Mound Valley, which was often called the "Cracker Box." I taught there for a salary of $60 per month.

The Canadian County school was situated close to an Indian mound in the midst of a mesquite flat where prickly pear cactus grew rampant. The cacti had invaded the school ground, and to keep the thorns from piercing our shoes, the children brought hoes and shovels one Friday afternoon, and we cleared the school ground of the menace. The average daily attendance was about twenty-five, and there was little money. Books, pencils, chalk, paper, and other supplies were at a premium and were used sparingly. Because of the drought, the children brought their own drinking water in a fruit jar from home. The cisterns were all dry, and water had to be hauled from a great distance. Many children had very scanty lunches or no lunches at all, and great was the day when the surplus commodities were issued to the schools. These included canned brown beans, canned meat (beef), soy flour, rice, and powdered milk.

One of the patrons furnished a two-burner oil stove. On this, we would prepare the noon-day meal. All children were very eager to help. The parents would send whatever vegetables, noodles, cocoa, sugar, or seasonings that they might have. We sometimes had beef with noodles, vegetable stew, beans, chili with beans, rice and milk sprinkled with cinnamon, hot cocoa, or meat pie. The cooking meant a lot of planning and extra work for the teacher, who was already custodian and swept and oiled the floors, who built the fires, and who had many other chores—not to mention the regular routine of the school. But the smiles that the hot meal program brought to those eager little faces made it all worthwhile and was something never to be forgotten.

During the winter and spring months, the dust storms were so severe that when the children started home from school (and all walked), they would have to stay within the section lines. During one particular storm, it was so dark at 2:00 P.M. that we couldn't see to read. So we just sat there and began telling stories and singing, just hoping the parents would come to take the children home. On this particular day, everyone had a ride home. There were times not only at Mound Valley but at other schools when there was no money available to pay teachers' salaries. The common law of the day was that if a district were short of funds, any teacher who was a teacher would finish the school year. Teachers followed this rule; and in our area, no schools were closed.

During the depression neighbors often banded together to help each other. And the more fortunate people often helped those who suffered from hard times. Julia B. Smith vividly recalls the effects of the depression.

My husband, a successful public school administrator for many years, had been notified his salary would be cut. In 1929 depression clouds were gathering, and teachers were the first to feel its effects. A dedicated group, they had not yet learned to demand their just due. They took what they could get and gave and gave and gave. We pondered our situation, feeling the urge to escape the crowded city and return to more familiar surroundings in our home state—to familiar faces and the wide open spaces we loved. But even in Oklahoma the appropriations were being cut. Teachers were a dime a dozen, taking anything and using up meager savings to survive.

It was difficult for a proud man to start down the scale when he had been at the top, but it became necessary for my husband to take the superintendency of a small inland school. It was the fall of 1932. We had been warned that warrants, teachers' paychecks, might not be cashed after January, 1933. Therefore, we hoarded our $200 checks more carefully than ever. January arrived and, sure enough, the banks remained closed and when they opened, officers refused to cash warrants. The school board broke up our warrants into small denominations, $10, $25, or $50. Now, the squeeze began! We moved into an older home, the owner of which had faith and would take warrants at face value—$10 per month for a good five-room house. Local merchants refused to take the warrants for their merchandise *but* continued to send their children to school. Yet only one teacher resigned. Some were married, with husbands to support them. Of course, it was most difficult for those of us who were new in the state, having no one to stand behind us.

Times became more difficult. The city water hydrant on the back porch cost $2.00 per month, too much during the depression. We had it cut off and used water from a deep well, drawn by hand, usually by the two children; it was very cold and good. There was no bathroom, but a tub in the kitchen sufficed quite well for baths. Electricity and gas for cooking and heating were greatly appreciated. A bountiful garden the year before and kind neighbors to show me how to can had supplied us with much food that helped us. A friend lent us a cow and taught my young son how to milk. We had great times trying to get milk from that little cow. In the fall the children and I, with a neighbor and her children, walked to the woods, making a picnic of gathering wild grapes and persimmons. They made wonderful jelly as well as grape juice for the winter. On all social occasions, women in that community served grape juice, hot or cold.

Wheat was 35 cents a bushel, but I paid 50 cents for a very clean bushel. It was ground at a local mill into flour. We enjoyed whole wheat bread of every kind and also cereal made from it for several years. It was carefully stored. Seventy-five baby chicks were bought, too, early in the spring. We had no place to keep them except an empty room. I spread papers down on the floor during the day, then caught them, putting them in boxes with jars of hot water to keep them warm at night. Being a mother hen proved quite tiresome before warm weather permitted them to be taken out to the old barn and henhouse. Chickens like to be petted, and I had to push them away, for I knew what must be done later. The children cried, "No, don't kill them," but one night we had fried chicken with cream gravy and hot biscuits, and they forgot where the chickens came from.

These were dust bowl days in Oklahoma. There was little rain, and wind literally blew the plants right of the garden. One summer, storm clouds came, and a hard downpour followed. I forgot the chickens, thinking that they were safe under the shed. At the height of the storm, I glanced out; to my horror, dozens of my poor chicks were huddled in the corner of the fence, nearest the house, limp as wet dish rags, frightened of the first storm they had known. We saved a few by wrapping them in towels and drying them on the oven door. I sold eggs that winter for ten cents a dozen. The peach trees in our yard were loaded with fruit; but with no rain, they had shriveled in the hot sun. Now, rain came just in time, and they began ripening. No peach had a chance to hit the ground—not one was wasted. We were so hungry for fruit that we had peach cobbler for breakfast, dinner, and supper; and the neighbors who had no fruit received a bucket full. Peaches were canned, preserved, pickled, and dried for futurc use.

Neighbors were wonderful, sharing and helping each other. We never asked for or received help, but when the government paid the ranchers to kill beef they could not feed, if the animal was in a condition to use, they might share a part of the beef. My husband came in one morning with a quarter of beef that a student had brought him. With no refrigerator or ice, I had to work fast. Again, an experienced neighbor came to my aid. He brought a pressure cooker, cut up the meat, and told me how to can it. I remembered, as a child, in the early days, seeing a woman use a bucket of water that sat on a rack with a white cloth dipped in the water. Then the cloth was draped around some small shelves that held milk and butter. The whole contraption sat in a tub; thus the wet cloth, breeze blowing through it, lowered the temperature several degrees. Our well water was quite cold, and this worked fine to keep milk.

Many folks were moving. They became desperate, not knowing what to do. Families with peaked-faced children camped by the side of the road where they had picked cotton. Old cars, loaded down, chugged past and often stopped. I always shared what I could. One morning, my family had just left for school when a timid knock brought me from the kitchen. Two scrawny, dust-covered little boys stood there holding out a can. "Will you give us some coffee for our Grandma?" they asked. I hurried to add a bit of water to what would have been my last cup of coffee. Never a day passed that someone did not come to our door asking for help. Long lines of freight cars teemed with literally hundreds of people who were going south or just going, looking for they knew not what. People lived in the side of hills, in caves—with nothing.

There are those who scoff at government work projects. Perhaps some programs have continued too long, but those who survived the trying times of the depression regarded the projects as manna from Heaven. Professional folks were given needed work. Writers went to work collecting local history. The university sent my husband out to do rehabilitation work among those who had gone down too far to help themselves. Artists began art projects. Best of all, men were put to work reclaiming the dust bowl. Trees were planted and formed shelter belts, terraces held rain where it fell, and hillsides were planted to grass. C.C.C. boys built roads through virgin forests and did work in parks, much of which can still be seen.

Finally, our warrants were cashed by the bank, and we returned to a larger field of endeavor. Perhaps a generous government has allowed some people to remain dependent on its bounty too long. It may take time to build back the pioneer spirit of independence.

After beginning her career in 1930 at the age of sixteen, Kate J. Lewis, Purcell, remembers sharing her first salary with students whose families were less fortunate.

It still seems like a miracle when I think how I procured my first teaching position. The depression was beginning. Jobs were scarce, and I was not quite seventeen. By fibbing a little, I had secured a two-year state teaching certificate. My age necessitated the misrepresentation, and at the time, it seemed of vital importance that I start earning my own livelihood.

Feet dangling from the side of a flatbed truck, I rode twenty miles into the poorest county of southeastern Oklahoma, seeking employment. My only reference was the county superintendent who recommended me because we were members of the same singing class. He would have been more reluctant to recommend me had he stood nearer so that he could hear me sing. Contract held securely in one hand, I pulled off my shoes and waded the creek to put in my application to the school board clerk who was plowing in a nearby field. Without much hesitation, he gave me a stamp of approval; then he directed me to the homes of the other two board members. They, too, signed my contract. None of the school board members told me that after Christmas my warrants could not be cashed without a discount because the county was out of funds. I sold one warrant at 50 per cent of its face value. Needless to say, these circumstances didn't help me pay off debts or help my standard of living.

These were trying times for my patrons, too. Many of them relied on making a living from the sale of "moonshine whisky." Children came to school barefooted all winter, bringing very poor rations for their noon meal. Many of the children's parents came down with pellagra because of poor diets. Then the big blow came. Federal officers raided the whisky stills and took the brewers to the Muskogee jail. After that, the mothers and children became desperate for the necessities of life. These conditions stopped many of the children from attending school.

My $90 a month warrant would have seemed like a fortune had I gotten full value. Still, I couldn't help sharing the discounted remainder with the poorer children. Some of them were staying away from school because they had no coats to wear. At one time, I bought a second-hand Mackinaw for a ten-year-old boy. Another time, I bought six pairs of canvas shoes from a Sears-Roebuck sale catalog for my team to wear to the county basketball tournament. The children shared with me, too, often giving me a baked sweet potato from a lunch pail. Once, a small boy gave me some roasted possum. That was too much! My stomach rebelled. So that the child would not be offended, I took it home with me.

Somehow, I managed to stay at this school for four years, after which conditions became better. With the Franklin D. Roosevelt administration, many relief agencies were created. Then I moved on to a better-funded county where the warrants were good throughout the whole year.

Ethel L. Snodgrass, Nowata, remembers the austere life teachers faced in the 1930's.

My first three years of teaching were in the rural schools beginning in 1932–33. Those were hard times because of the great depression. Salaries were low—mine was $75 a month for a nine-month term. Allocations for instructional materials were practically nonexistent. To have the necessary tools with which to work, it was necessary to buy them out of my small salary. And to make the situation worse, I had to pay back money I had borrowed for my education. Teaching positions remained scarce, and there were numerous restrictions placed on a teacher's personal life.

During the first two years of my employment, I lived at home, which was a little over two miles from school. The first year, I rode a horse to school because I couldn't afford a car. The third year I changed schools. That year, I rented a room and had kitchen privileges. I shall never forget that winter. The gas lines would freeze up, and the house would be without heat. One morning, I awoke to find my bed covered with snow which had blown in through the cracks around the window.

Recalling a story of near-starvation during the depression, Lucille Jenkins of Meeker recounts that she did all she could for the three children of one impoverished family.

The tremendous amount of food wasted in our present school cafeterias recalls like magic the stark realities of the depression years when people farmed the dry, barren sand hills; and the government didn't have welfare programs and food stamps. My mind refuses to erase the sad, pale look of three little brothers who would say that they didn't like to eat lunch or that they weren't hungry when the school children and the teacher opened their lunches. In those days, most of the children's lunches consisted of bread, butter, and jelly, with an occasional piece of side meat. The more affluent would have some peanut butter on Monday after the family shopping had been done on Saturday; and the lucky ones might have a piece of cake which was left from the Sunday dinner.

My three lovable, dependable little brothers sometimes had a biscuit with syrup or butter and sugar on a piece of bread; but most of the time they had nothing and just did without. The proud way they stood before me, with backs straight, heads high, and hands at their side refusing any offer I made of food lingers in my memories. Their gaunt look and pleading blue eyes made it impossible for me to eat; I spent endless hours figuring ways to feed my little brothers without seemingly meaning to do so. I remember the pleased, happy look that was achieved by a handful of raisins in their coat pocket, or pecans, peanuts, popcorn, or a piece of candy. It was easy for the teacher to fumble in the cloakroom straightening their coats. The government's surplus fruit was available for schools if the teacher would haul, load, and disburse. Well, the teacher didn't have a car, but the school bus driver was a local farm boy who acted as delivery boy and brought apples, oranges, and raisins on the school bus. This fruit was a real treat to the children. The happy thought of this memory is that those three little brothers are now nice-looking men and have accepted roles of responsibilities in society; in fact, none of those bread-and-jelly lunch eaters became delinquents.

Yna Vey Hatchett, another Meeker resident, also recalls the hunger that was prevalent during the 1930's.

When I reflect back to the many memories of my teaching years, I recall the days of the depression. These were the years when real poverty was evident. My husband and I taught in a small rural town. Most of our pupils came from the surrounding countryside where the schools were beginning to consolidate. My husband was superintendent, and I was hired as principal of the high school. This was an unusual situation during these times, but it worked very nicely in this particular community.

During the terrible days of the depression at least half of the parents became unemployed. Banks were failing, and it was difficult to pay the teachers their salaries for the last two months of the term. The pupils had to bring sack lunches to school or go home at noon if their homes were within walking distance. Many times, I made sandwiches and pots of stew for students who had very little to eat or had no lunches at all. I prepared the food before coming to school in the morning. Some of the students' lunches consisted only of potato peelings or a piece of dry bread.

Now in our retirement days, we often have some of these students visit us in our home. We cannot help having a feeling of pride to know that so many of them have become successful and useful citizens as they scattered to the different parts of our country.

Mabel Baldwin Couch, Chelsea, also began a hot lunch program.

During the depression of the 1930's, in addition to teaching, I cooked lunch and served it. Old-timers will recall that the government furnished staple food to schools. It was up to the teacher to get it delivered and to be responsible for its safety. That responsibility was not taken lightly. Many people remained out of work, and families went hungry. But people were generally honest, and I never lost any food. My husband hauled the food to the school, and we locked it in one of the cloakrooms. I cooked in big, big kettles atop a pot-bellied coal stove. Pupils brought a cup, spoon, and a bowl from home to use at lunch, and they carried them home each night to wash. I've cooked and served hundreds of pounds of brown beans, dozens of cases of canned tomatoes, gallons and gallons of cocoa, hundreds of boxes of crackers, and pounds and pounds of creamery butter. The food I dished out to hungry children meant extra work and no extra pay for me. But I enjoyed staying after school to pick the rocks from the beans, to wash them, and to put them on to soak for the next day's lunch. I was repaid by seeing hungry little children fed and their minds expand and by seeing their happy expressions and words.

Not only did families and communities suffer during the depression, but also some districts became so pressed for funds that they could not afford the upkeep on their schools. Pearl Laxson, Temple, faced this type of hardship in Roger Mills County.

I proudly received my Leedey High School diploma in 1928 at the age of seventeen. After that memorable May event, I immediately enrolled in an all-girl school, the College of Industrial Arts at Denton, Texas. My father believed that because of my age, it would be better for me to attend a non-coeducational institution. One year later, with a temporary teaching certificate under my arm, I applied for and received a teaching position, embarking upon a career which terminated in Temple, Oklahoma, after the 1971–72 term.

There is little chance that young teachers, entering the profession during the past decade, will ever be able to imagine conditions endured by teachers forty years ago in one- and two-room rural schools. My first school, located almost on the south bank of the Canadian River north of Elk City, was built for a proposed secondary school, but those hopes never materialized. One of the three rooms served as living space for the other teacher and myself. How many of today's teachers would live twelve miles from the nearest community and one-half mile from the nearest neighbor in a building so poorly constructed that blowing snow sifted through the cracks and covered our belongings? Because I had no teaching experience, the school board offered me $65 a month. My teaching partner received $75 for helping build fires, carry in coal and wood, and get our younger students on and off horses, in addition to classroom work. We went home each week mainly to enjoy mother's cooking and to bring back milk, eggs, and another week's supply of odds and ends. Our staple groceries averaged near $2.50 per week. We were fortunate to have sympathetic patrons who shared pork and beef when they butchered.

After working in a school that had various teaching aids, I seriously doubt if I would try to get along with the meager supplies my first school possessed. A jacket stove in each room was the source of warmth in cold weather. They were void of thermostats, causing temperature fluctuations in proportion to the amount of fuel shoveled through the cast-iron doors and to the amount of the ashes accumulated before a teacher or an older student would remove them. My room had twelve desks, four of which were double. One small blackboard, one-half box of chalk, six erasers, a few ragged charts, and some dog-eared books I had scrounged made up my supply of visual aid materials. One water bucket and a bent-handled dipper served as a drinking fountain minus the cold water we received later in larger schools. Our water supply was a pump at the back door. The pump also served as a motivating device. Young students who did good work were permitted to fill the drinking-water bucket. My homemade desk was an example of how a teacher's desk should not be designed. It served the purpose for which it was intended, but it did no more.

Hot lunches for schools did not exist for children in rural areas during the questionable "good old days." Lunches were brought to school in paper sacks and gallon buckets, void of thermos bottles but containing solid foods like boiled eggs, bacon-egg sandwiches, an apple or an orange, jam and bologna sandwiches, and large homemade biscuits with holes punched in the side and filled with black molasses, all packed by doting mothers.

Recess activities varied among tossing a basketball at the one goal, using the two swings and four see-saws, and playing tag, ante-over, pop-the-whip, jacks, and other games. Two relief stations for boys and girls were located on opposite corners of the school plot, offering a degree of privacy. A long shed separated the two toilets and was used to shelter animals that transported our children to and from school. The horses were fed corn, which served two purposes—namely, as nourishment and as a source of ammunition for corncob fights.

My teaching companion and I became accustomed to our teaching conditions with little complaining, but one duty was silently resented by us. As much as we liked our school board members, all tobacco chewers, we had a number of occasions to observe their lack of marksmanship in hitting strategically placed gallon buckets. If they met in my room, it was my problem to clean up the mess, and the duty was shifted to the other teacher if the group met in her room.

My most memorable experience during my first school year had much more than a cool reception. Our eight-month school term had only two weeks left when the coal supply became exhausted. The board elected not to buy more coal; this would have been acceptable had not a late blizzard swept down, covering all roads with drifts of snow which blocked all roads to town. Something beyond the call of duty had to happen soon. Our living-room quarters provided the answer. Enough desks were moved into and arranged on each side of our room. I taught my classes on one side, and my friend used the other side. A stove in the middle of the room provided adequate heat. We burned all available loose combustible material, and a patron contributed a little coal so that we could complete the year's classroom teaching.

Another teacher who had to start a career in the middle of the depression was Pauline Thompson Sharpe of Edmond.

I started teaching in the fall of 1933 in a one-room school in Lincoln County for $45 a month. My first contract had an Oklahoma Education Association membership paper at the bottom of my contract, and the dues were $1.00. School board members wanted to know if I would join the OEA, and I said yes. They told me if I had not been willing to join, they would have refused me a contract.

I was expected to ring a large bell thirty minutes before school started to let the students and parents know I was on the job; some would stop working and come to school when they heard the bell. I swept the schoolroom after class or early in the morning before the students arrived. In the winter I built the fire in the stove and had the room warm in time for class. Some of my early stoves burned wood or coal. The schools had very few supplies, usually a large dictionary and a few old library books. Each child brought his own textbooks, workbooks, tablets, and pencils. The father usually sharpened the child's pencil with his pocketknife. The pupil was told to make the pencil last a long time. We didn't have a sharpener in our first school. Other supplies were a water bucket and a dipper. There was little else.

Lack of experience caused me to do a lot of foolish things, like tossing powdered coal on a fire and not stirring it, causing the stove to explode black smoke in the room. On that occasion, the teacher and students all had to flee outside until the smoke subsided. Also at this same school, I once allowed five boys to go after a Christmas tree with an ax. After they left, I began to worry about all the things that could happen to them. Finally, some of the boys returned; they had cut a tree too large to bring back to school. They had tried and had pulled it through a creek. A neighbor took his wagon and horses to bring the tree to school. The students and I tried to wash the mud off of the tree. We were told to let the mud dry, and then brush it off. We certainly had a dirty Christmas tree on the back side.

A new chore was added during the depression. We cooked lunch for the students. We had potatoes, bacon or hog jowl, butter, canned tomatoes, canned milk, and cocoa. For lunch, we had soup and hot chocolate or cocoa. Before school started the older girls and I would peel potatoes and put the meat, water, and potatoes on to cook all morning on the heating stove. Later, we would add tomatoes and seasoning. In another large cooker, we would heat water, cocoa, and canned milk. Each child brought a cup, dish, and a spoon from home. We also had to heat water on the stove to wash our dishes with the students' help.

Later, I taught in a country school in Payne County near Perkins, where I had the Iowa Indian students. I learned a lot from them about their customs. The Indian students always liked to tease me by talking in their native language.

Goldie Lemon Coffey, Muskogee, offers the following comment about hard times.

Some of the greatest hardships of the early teachers were monetary as a result of low salaries, double standards for men and women, depressions, and insufficient funds. For three years, from 1928 to 1931, I frequently left Muskogee High in tears because money was withheld or was not to be had on payday. Regardless of money, we worked on and worked hard. The only adverse words I have to repeat came from a board member who was slow in recognizing teaching as a profession. He said: "You knew when you chose teaching that you were going into missionary work."

Eva Mae Young, Crawford, comments on the "dust bowl" days in Roger Mills County.

I will remember the 1930's as the dust bowl days. One day, an approaching cloud of dust made my students so uneasy that we dropped all pretense of classes. I read an interesting book to the children while the superintendent was trying to decide if we should send the buses on home. The children all put handkerchiefs over their mouths as the schoolroom grew dark with dust.

There were no lights. Later, my eyes and throat were sore, but no one panicked. On the way home to my boarding place, my new black lunch bucket became so pockmarked by sand and pebbles that it never looked new any more. I was glad I lived nearby because that sandstorm was awful.

Marguerite Isbell Smith, Oklahoma City, recalls several "dusters" that swept through Woodward County during the 1930's.

I remember well the dust storms in western Oklahoma, especially during the springs of 1937 and 1938. I was teaching at a consolidated high school called Richmond in Woodward County. It had been months since we had had a rain, and most water wells were dry. I can still see that big black cloud as it came moving in our direction, from the north, on that sultry afternoon. It looked like doomsday; it appeared black as night as it rolled in. We dismissed school for the day, and the students rushed home. Although it was only mid-afternoon, it became totally dark outside. Even the chickens went to roost. All windows and doors were tightly closed. We wet bed sheets and towels and placed them over the cracks in the windows and doors. We also dampened our handkerchiefs and washcloths and placed them over our noses. Even then we could hardly breathe. Looking out the window, we could not even see the fence post just a few feet from the house. We lit a kerosene lamp and waited for the dust storm to go away. It was well into the next day before it was over. This was only one of several dust storms I survived in the mid–1930's. Those dark clouds of rich topsoil continued to roll across Oklahoma for several years, until the government finally stepped in and taught the farmers to plant trees, terrace the contours of the fields, and plant grass and cover crops to break the wind.

"Black blizzards" also struck Texas County, as Effie Nagel remembers.

When I began teaching in the fall of 1928, salaries were very low. We had to take warrants that we were never sure of getting our amount of money. Many times we needed to register them. As I remember, the banks usually cashed them for us. During my first year of teaching, I taught for $80 a month.

This was during the dust bowl days. "Black blizzards," as these hazardous dust storms were called, visited us frequently. Many of them were very severe. By the time they reached us, everything was so dark that we could not see our hands in front of us. These frightening, rolling clouds would come from the north and sometimes lasted for hours. We could see them coming from miles away. Many of these dark storms appeared while I was teaching in the schoolroom. They were so dark that we had to stop classwork. This was very exciting for the students, especially because they could play "hide-and-seek" in the room and never be seen. Usually, when the storms occurred, the parents came (if possible) and took the children home. I would remain at school until the storm subsided well enough for me to drive home. These storms usually ended at sundown or soon thereafter. If I drove home during the storm, I must travel seven miles on the main highway, and this was very dangerous at times. Talk about spooky times—I endured them, especially when I had to stay at school after all the children had gone home. The noises in the room created by high winds were not pleasant. At night, before I left for home, I would scatter sweeping compound over the entire floor. The next morning, I went to school a little early and swept the floor before the children arrived.

Not all of the teachers' experiences during the depression were unpleasant. Although times remained hard, Addie Pettit of Hartshorne recalls with joy her year spent teaching in a one-room school on Buffalo Mountain (Pittsburg County).

After I secured my third-grade certificate, the Pittsburg County superintendent told me that the teacher on Buffalo Mountain, north of Adamson, had married and planned to move to Texas. Here was my chance to teach. My oldest sister, Nellie McBee, and her husband, Pete, took me to see the school board and to submit my application for the job. The road leading from Adamson over the mountain was no more than a cowpath. Both hands had to be used to "hold on." The car, a 1929 "Chevy," literally climbed huge boulders. I found out later that had this been a rainy spring, we could not have crossed the mountain streams. Each time it rained, the streams quickly overflowed, and the only way off the mountain was to crawl the gas pipeline. This feat I mastered. I would hold the sack that contained my belongings in my mouth, put my dress down inside my undergarments, close my eyes, and scamper across these swift mountain streams. These circumstances would have turned most girls of my age and ignorance back to civilization—and this sometimes impossible road was only one aspect of the trouble I would face. The road, swift mountain streams, and the uninhabited wilderness were frightening; but the dire poverty of the people of the mountain remained almost incredulous. I knew in my mind that I could survive, and this would be a start.

The first contract to teach school was the most precious document I have ever signed. It was for a split nine-month term—six weeks beginning in June and the remainder of the term beginning in the fall. My salary was to be $75 a month for teaching and $5 a month for janitorial work, which including sweeping the floors and building a fire in the huge coal heater in the winter months. I was to board with Mr. and Mrs. Blake Mendenhall. Mr. Mendenhall was the clerk of the school board. Their home, which was a dingy two-room frame structure with a lean-to kitchen, stood shakily in the middle of a thickly wooded area four miles from the school. The house faced the east with a full-width porch across the front. The north bedroom, which served as a combination living room and bedroom, had a huge fireplace in the north end. In addition to this fireplace, the room had two double beds, several cane-bottom chairs, and a sewing machine. Only the bare necessities were available here—bare, that is, as far as physical needs were concerned.

The daily rations were slim or maybe I should say repetitious. Our meals consisted mostly of beans, potatoes, eggs, squirrel, and water biscuits. Even though the family lived on a farm, they had no milk cow; therefore, no milk or butter was available. It was squirrel, squirrel, squirrel every day. Our lunch sack was stuffed with biscuits and squirrel. But you'd be surprised how well you could consume this fare after the four-mile walk from the Mendenhalls' home to the school and the physical exercise that made the morning recess so enjoyable.

My stay in this home made me much more appreciative of my own humble beginnings. An unusual thing that I have wondered about through the years is the fact that there was no outside toilet and, of course, no inside toilet either. Now you'd never dream just how the absence of this one facility could influence your whole life. Even though the house was located in a wooded area, one always remained skeptical about the choice of a spot. One couldn't decide which would be safer—behind the barn or out in the woods. To say the least, it was never a relaxed situation.

I shall never, never forget that first Monday morning in class. The Mendenhall children and I walked up the hot, dusty road to the schoolhouse. When we arrived, the seventeen pupils were already there, waiting to see the new teacher. They were typical mountain youngsters—shy and timid. The teacher could be placed in this same category also because, underneath my calm exterior, butterflies were fluttering all inside me. I think I was afraid of the big boys, in spite of the fact that they were well behaved. Two of the students were older than I—one boy and one girl. At nine o'clock, I rang the bell; and the students dutifully lined up in front of the small one-room school to march inside. The line formed with the primer boy first in line and graduated to the oldest boy, an eighth grader.

The inside of the school was typical of all those of this period in history, the only difference being that it was unusually small. A six-inch platform was built across the east end of the building. On this stage was the teacher's desk, chair, the "black" board, and a bench for the students to sit on during recitation. In the middle of the room stood a huge coal-burning heater. It appeared too large for the room, and indeed it was. In the southwest corner was a homemade stand that held the water bucket and community dipper. Since class was in session during the hot summer months of July and August, I know that there must have been torrid days and an abundance of flies and other insects, but I can't remember any of these discomforts. It was probably because I was still on "cloud nine" and experienced only the glory of being in full control. As I reminisce, I can truthfully say that the year 1930–31 that I spent on Buffalo Mountain is the most precious memory I have of my life-long teaching career.

Eva Lee Fobes, Sapulpa, adds:

I started teaching in 1933. America was just beginning to pull out of the years of depression. My checks were not always honored at the bank because there was no money in the treasury. My first contract was for $480 for eight months. My last contract was for $10,650 for twelve months, and checks were always honored.

Early rural schools were far from modern. It was not until electricity came to the country that there was any improvement. I always carried matches to start the fire at school. Then, in the evening, I swept the floor before I went home. I took all the papers and graded them at night. There were no teachers' aides in those days. For a number of years, I drove a pickup truck with a cab on the back and picked up the children and took them to school. I was the only school bus driver the students had.

The early schools were centers for community entertainment. We always had to have a Christmas program and a last-day-of-school program. People came from miles around to see our productions. One time, we decided to have a supper at the school for the last-night program. Everybody came with their lunches, and it began to rain. It came down so hard and fast that when it was time to go home, all roads were flooded, and there remained nothing to do but spend the night in the schoolhouse. Some bridges were washed out and had to be repaired before we could get home the next day.

There was very little equipment in those early buildings. We had maps and a globe but little else. The only duplicating equipment was a hectograph pan which could only be used every other day. Such inefficient equipment forced students to improvise. Children traced a lot to develop their own maps and charts. They took pride in their school, helping with decorating the room. We also had a 4-H Club which the children enjoyed. They entered the Creek County Fair and won several prizes.

Edna Mason, Bethany, taught in Kay County during the depression.

The "great depression" was beginning, and I felt the financial need to teach in order to continue my college education. I earned additional college hours by attending summer sessions, extension classes at night, correspondence courses, and Saturday classes on campus at Edmond and Stillwater. In the summer of 1955, I received my B.S. degree in education from Central State College.

For five years I taught at Union District sixty-one. My third and fourth years, I received $125 a month for the eight-month term. Because of the depression, salaries began to go down, and I taught the last two years for $95 and $90 a month; and I felt fortunate to get that salary. It was during these years that teachers had to take a discount in order to cash their warrants. Again, I was fortunate to have a friend who cashed my warrants without discounting them.

The schoolhouse was relatively new and was well equipped for a rural school at that time. I was excited at my good fortune even though I was expected to be the janitor who built the fires. I oiled the floors and did the sweeping and cleaning. We had gas lights, a water fountain with a spigot for drinking, filled as needed from a well, and a two-burner gas hot plate on which I prepared hot lunches during the cold months. Not all children cared to participate in the hot lunch program and were not required to do so. The parents of those who did want the hot lunch took turns furnishing food. The desks were on runners in rows arranged according to size. They were easily moved for sweeping. There was the traditional "recitation bench," which served as a cot for a child who didn't feel well. We also had a reading table and chairs for the primary reading classes. A wall clock, a piano, and a storage cabinet for supplies completed the furnishings.

There was a barn for the horses, as many of the children rode ponies to school. A place for the teacher's car was added at one end of the barn. Baseball bats and balls, a basketball and outdoor ball court, swings, and teeter-totters comprised the playground equipment. We utilized everything we had, and we remained happy with what was available. My enrollment varied from twenty-four to thirty-eight, including grades one through eight.

Much improvement was taking place in the schools, as each district was striving to become a superior model with an accredited rating according to standard requirements set up by the state department. Each year we were visited by the county superintendent and a state inspector who rated the school and made recommendations for further improvements. Eighth grade students were required to take the county examination.

The school was also the community center. The PTA, Mother's Study Group, 4-H Club, poultry shows, community Christmas tree, school picnics, and last-day-of-school program all contributed to the association of teacher, pupils, and parents. There were county academic contests, track meets, basketball tournaments, and fair exhibits for all districts. We participated in all events. A county commencement for eighth graders was a special occasion.

I recall vividly the snowstorm of 1932. I was living in Tonkawa and driving to class. I attempted to get to school and did get as far as the driveway. My model "A" Ford just couldn't make it. I was forced to leave it in the snowdrift. On entering my room, I found that the fire had gone out, the fish had frozen, and their bowl had broken. On the table was a cake of ice with gold fish in it. All the potted house plants had frozen, too; and the room was unbearably cold. One little boy who lived a short distance from the school came. We waited a short while and decided to walk to his home. We were so cold that we fell in the yard and had to be helped into the house. The walls of the house were covered with ice. The mother and I made comforters so we could keep warm at night. Country roads were impassable, and we were snowbound. Finally, on the fourth day, one of my patrons managed to get through the drifts with on oil field truck, pulled my car out of the drift, got it started for me, and managed to get me started home. It was another week before we could have school.

In a "homemade classroom" in 1935, Ray Claiborne of Lawton demonstrated the resourcefulness of our teachers. Still innovative, he now teaches at Cameron University.

In the heart of the depression (1935) we moved to Blair, Oklahoma, where I had been selected as high school principal and coach. At this time, I had been in school work eight years—two as a principal of a grade school in Cotton County and six years as superintendent of a two-year high school in Beckham County.

After taking the position at Blair, I was asked to teach typing. This was a new subject at the school, and I was the only teacher with any college hours in typing (I had only three). It was a great surprise to me to be asked to teach something completely new and one that I was really not prepared to handle. But in 1935 a job was most appreciated and difficult to come by. To make plans for this assignment was not easy. I asked about the typing room and typewriters. Well, there was no space and no machines, but the board wanted to start a class in typing. A room had to be found, and each student was to furnish his own machine.

During the summer the janitor cleaned out a storage room located just over the boiler in the basement. The room had few windows, the floor was uneven (that didn't matter), and we had several leaks in the roof. Typing tables remained unavailable, and the janitor took twelve inch boards and placed them at the right height around the room. This gave table space for the students. For chairs we took nail kegs secured from the lumber yard and placed nice smooth boards on top of the kegs. This put us in the typing business. During this time I made a trip to Walters to visit my high school typing teacher, and she gave me some wonderful help. I also remembered how I had been taught in high school and the eight weeks period in college.

In my class of twenty-five students, we were ready to start the first typing class. To get this class moving, I was faced with every type of machine available in 1935. I had portable and upright typewriters. We had Underwood, Remington, L. C. Smith, and Woodstock. I had students eager to learn; and because the desire was present, the class was fun. We used the counting method to learn the key board, and in short time we were on our way.

This experience was proof to me that fancy new equipment is not necessary to bring about learning. The real need is desire. We had that.

Robert H. Wood, Watonga, was one "country boy" who never forgot his roots. Reared on a farm in Okmulgee County, Wood became a vocational agriculture teacher and herein recounts some of his experiences in Indian schools.

Schools and education have been a part of my life ever since I was born. My father taught in Indian Territory and Oklahoma Territory before statehood. When I was born, he was superintendent of schools at Dewar. Though mother was not a teacher, she was a very staunch believer in education. She helped by keeping four teachers, who roomed and boarded in our home. One of the earliest pictures I have of me is one when I was three years old sitting astride of a large sow. It was captioned, "Robert riding 'College'." "College" was a swine my mother had bought as a small pig and raised to be a large sow. The profit from the sale of this swine was to go into a fund for my college education. There was never any thought even in the dark days of the depression that I would not go to college.

There were four boys and four girls in our family. Dad found it necessary to supplement his income in many ways, including working on pipelines and in hayfields during the summer months and in department stores on Saturdays. We also had a small farming operation most of the years I was in public schools. Dad was a firm believer that growing boys needed work and chores to do to keep them out of mischief. We always had milk cows, chickens, some hogs, and a large truck garden. Most of the time, our operations were large enough to include two or three teams of horses and mules. We grew feed, cotton, and peanuts as well as the truck garden. The earliest income that I had was from selling farm produce (butter, buttermilk, eggs, vegetables, watermelons, cantaloupes). I learned to love agriculture and had a dream of farming some day. I found that I could combine my desire to teach and the desire to be connected with agriculture by majoring in agricultural education and teaching vocational agriculture in college.

My first job when I graduated from O.S.U. (then A. and M.) in 1937 involved the founding of a vocational agriculture department at Indiahoma High School in Comanche County. The trough of depression was still pretty deep, but we had a banker who was willing to lend the boys money to pay a reasonable amount for livestock projects. Vo-ag teachers did many things in those days. Besides classes with high school boys, we had classes for adult farmers; and we also had "out-of-school" youth groups. Among other things, my FFA boys and I ran many miles of terrace lines and helped the farmers build their terraces with turning plows. We did much of the veterinary work in the community, especially castration, shots, and control of insects projects. The satisfaction realized from my job was the close fellowship I had with the boys and their families as we developed good livestock, dairy products, and crops. We also went to fairs, went to give talks and demonstrations, and did community service work.

After nearly five years in public schools, I received an appointment as an agriculture instructor in a Bureau of Indian Affairs school. First, I went to Zuni, New Mexico, and then to Albuquerque. Both were interesting and rewarding, and we enjoyed life and work there. However, things were a little unsettled in that agency; and by 1943 we were back in Oklahoma at Jones Academy near Hartshorne, where I stayed for five years. The agriculture instructors in the BIA schools were also the farm managers. At Jones Academy we had a farm of about 1,600 acres. Of this, approximately 350 acres were in cultivation, including ten acres of irrigated garden. There was an average of 250 boys living in the dormitory. They ranged in age from five to eighteen years and attended grades one through ten. Juniors then went to Chilocco, Haskell, or Sequoyah. I had agriculture classes with boys in the seventh through tenth grades, and we had an active 4-H Club. I also developed a Homestead Club fashioned after the FFA. These boys had an eighty-acre "homestead" farm assigned to them. On their farms they developed a subsistence type of farming program with cattle, a team of horses, small laying flock, turkeys, and some milk goats. They shared in the money made from the farm. They shared according to the work they contributed.

It was the philosophy of the bureau schools that all students should have chores and housekeeping responsibilities and learn to work and develop useful marketable skills as well. As agriculture instructor I was to develop an agriculture program that would help to produce the food needed for this large "family," and I was to help the boys develop useful skills and responsibility.

We had a herd of forty Holstein cows, twenty-five Hereford cows, twenty brood sows, four hundred hens, and six draft horses and mules. We also had a tractor, a combine, and power equipment, as well as horse-drawn implements. Each boy was assigned to specific jobs or chores on the farm, in the dairy, in the kitchen, in the bakery, in the maintenance department, or in the powerhouse. They were rotated in these assignments so that each boy might develop a variety of skills. The older boys were assigned to various farm and vocational activities for one-half day for a semester and were graded on their work and skills developed during that semester. I had several helpers who were in charge of these boys: a dairyman, a farm foreman, a farm laborer, and a yard maintenance man. Each of these was to teach the boys working with him how to do these jobs and develop skill and responsibility for them. Our dairy had milking machines, a pasteurizer, a separator, and other modern equipment. We produced most of the meat, milk, eggs, butter, and even vegetables used by the students, and most of the feed and hay for the livestock.

Most all of my boys were from broken homes. Some were court cases paroled to the school. Jones Academy was their home for most of the year, and for some it was their only home. Many very rewarding experiences were outside the field of agriculture. I was boxing coach all the years, and I also coached the football and basketball teams some of the seasons. Ellen, my wife, and I organized a Sunday school; and some of the other teachers helped. We were able to get some of the preachers from Hartshorne to come out to talk to the boys, too. We organized a Cub Scout pack. I was pack master, and Ellen had one of the dens as den mother. I also showed a movie for the boys each Saturday night.

This was a full and rewarding work as we participated in the whole life of this community. It was more than just classwork in a schoolroom.

A leading Oklahoma educator and a past-president of the Oklahoma Retired Teachers' Association, J. C. Fitzgerald of Stillwater is one teacher who, in the midst of the depression, planned and executed an innovative plan designed to broaden the perspective of his Cushing students (Payne County). With the help of his wife, Elizabeth, who is also a teacher with many years' experience, J. C. succeeded in organizing several out-of-state trips for his students.

Having grown up in small, rural communities, neither my wife nor I had ever been more than one hundred miles from home; but in the mid-thirties, we made a trip to Carlsbad Caverns and were so impressed that we thought of how great it would be to take our school children to see this natural wonder. We were told by park officials that children and teachers would be admitted free. Upon returning home, we discussed with our school board the possibility of using the school bus to take the older pupils to Carlsbad. The board was agreeable; so after some studying and figuring, we decided we could take twenty-six children and four teachers for $5.00 each. Plans were completed; and in the spring after the close of school, we left for Carlsbad.

As many people will remember, these were dust bowl days. We stopped at a state park in Hereford, Texas, for a night's camp. The park ranger invited us to spend the night in the ballroom of the park if we would remove our shoes and walk on the floor only in our sock feet. The dust was so bad that the park ranger and his wife kept their small baby in a basket under the table with a sheet draped over the top to protect the baby. The sheet was kept moist to stop the dust.

On our first evening in New Mexico, we camped out near the caverns at Carlsbad and watched the bats come out of the caves that evening, and the next morning we made a tour through the cave. That evening, after cooking our steak, fried potatoes, and fruit for supper, we invoiced our funds and decided we had enough money to go on to Juarez, Old Mexico. Of course, no one dissented. The principal, who was also bus driver, drove into Juarez, where we picked up a local Mexican guide who showed us the city. Of course, by this time, the children had spent all of the change that they had brought with them, so we pulled enough from our treasury to give each child twenty-five cents to spend in Juarez. Each of them sent a postcard home and spent the rest quite foolishly as children will do. We camped out each night and cooked our breakfast and supper. For lunch, we usually made sandwiches and had plenty of fresh fruit.

On our return, we again checked our finances and decided we had enough money to have an ice cream and cake party at White Rock Lake Park in Dallas, Texas, which we enjoyed. Upon returning to Cushing after the six-day trip, we divided the remaining funds in the kitty and refunded $1.79 to each pupil. Some man in the community accused us of making money on the trip. When told that was impossible, he said, "Well, I don't know how, but they did. They didn't do it for nothing." True, we did not "do it for nothing." We executed the project for our students.

The following year we developed our seventh and eighth grade curriculum around another proposed trip, this one to the Gulf Coast area. A large five-by-seven-foot map of the United States was mounted on the wall, and the pupils and teacher planned the trip. In English, the students wrote letters to chambers of commerce in cities along our proposed route, which, after being checked by teachers and rewritten, were mailed. Chambers of commerce responded by inquiring how many were to be in the party, what kinds of facilities would be needed, and how long the visit would be. This resulted in several two-way communications. In mathematics, we figured the number of miles to be traveled, miles per gallon for gas, cost of the fuel, and even the number of times the wheels would turn round per mile on the trip. We set up books for a savings and accounting system whereby students could deposit any change any time during the year. Prior to the trip in the spring, each child's deposits were returned for his use on the tour, with the exception of fifty cents per month. This $6 was the pupil's share of expenses for the tour. With all the correspondence with chambers of commerce, we had to set up a reading corner in the room where all of the folders and brochures were placed for perusal by the students. There was no problem getting students to read. No problems existed in motivating them. This was probably the best teaching we ever did.

The second tour was quite successful; and in the meantime, the Hillside Travel Club had accumulated a one-wheel trailer to haul camping equipment and supplies. A baggage rack was built by a local blacksmith and bolted on top of the bus where all bedding and luggage was packed, was covered by waterproof canvas, and was securely tied with ropes. We also carried two eight-by-ten-foot tents—one for boys and one for girls for dressing. By this time, in most areas chambers of commerce had arranged housing for us in park buildings, but many nights we camped out.

In 1939, our project was to attend the World's Fair (Golden Gate International Exposition) in San Francisco. No one in the party had ever been to California. We did have a family of friends who lived in Oakland who agreed to help us with camping facilities. This was quite an extensive three weeks tour, and many people said, "You can't do it—it's impossible, especially to take both boys and girls like this." Luckily, everything went off quite well. The young teachers hadn't learned yet that it couldn't be done; with reluctant approval of parents, they did it. One parent told the local banker that if we wired back and needed money, to be sure to let us have it. We had already arranged a secret code word with the banker if we wired for money. Fortunately, we returned with a surplus, which was deposited as seed money for a 1940 trip to Washington, D. C., and the New York City World's Fair.

In 1940, with money previously collected and a new school bus, the travel club was ready for the New York trip; but early in the spring, the state attorney general ruled that it was illegal to take a school bus out of the state. Imagine the trauma when, after a year's preparation, it looked as if everything was off. The four teachers at the school got their heads together and agreed to pool their funds and buy an old bus from a used car dealer. After returning from the trip, they would sell the vehicle and share the loss. The bus was purchased for $187.50, serviced, and put in shape. The lady teachers and girls reupholstered the seats while the boys touched up the paint and replaced the luggage rack—and the trip was on!

It was a four-week trip with six days spent camped, with tents, in Washington, D. C., at a tourist facility on the banks of the Potomac. The trip was a great learning experience for twenty-six country kids. Through courtesy of our congressman, we were provided with special-priced tickets to the New York World's Fair. Can you imagine this country teacher driving an old 1936 Ford school bus through the Holland Tunnel into New York City? We camped for five days in the Bronx, and the Bronx police were so fascinated with our group that we had perfect police protection at all times. We rode the electric trains to and from the fair each day and returned to our tents at night. We rode the elevated train down to Times Square one night. (Who would be crazy enough to try such a stunt in the 1970's?)

We left the New York World's Fair and went up into the mountains at the Chemung County aerial glider area and camped in beautiful cottages with swimming pools and with nurse and lifeguard services provided free. We were associated with a group of underprivileged children from New York City at what was known as a fresh-air summer camp. It was difficult for the children at the camp to understand how a group of children from Oklahoma (they thought all Oklahomans were Indians) could get to New York World's Fair when even they had not been there.

One evening at the camp, our group was invited to a big pavillion to meet with the fresh-air kids from New York. Here each group sang songs and told about themselves. And finally at the close of the session, each told what nationality he or she was. We closed the party by agreeing that we were all Americans and joined in singing "God Bless America." An experience such as this, thousands of miles from home, sent a tingle down one's spine that became unforgettable. Some of the New York children asked many questions about the Indians, the cowboys, and the wild animals in Oklahoma. One of our boys said a girl asked what he would do if he met a wildcat in the fields or road. He said that he told her he would choke it to death.

We could write a book about these trip experiences. This was the last extensive trip for the Hillside School, as the teachers sold the old bus for $450, and I resigned as principal at Cushing to become county superintendent of schools.

VI

THE MODERN ERA

"The Times, They Are a-Changin," is a phrase which divulges a major trend in the modern era of Oklahoma education. Certainly, many teachers whose thoughts are recorded in this chapter would agree. Many of the reminiscences selected for this section deal with innovations since World War II. The decline of the one- and two-teacher schools, progressive learning techniques, integration, increased monies made available for supplies, growth of libraries, adaptation of new technology—such as television—to

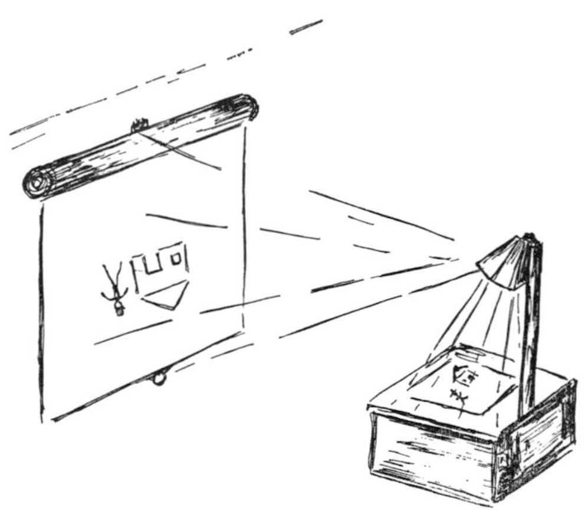

the classroom, the rise of vocational education, the increasing professionalism of teachers, innovative programs designed to take children out of the classroom and to let them experience the "real" world—these topics are but a few of the highlights of this chapter. Yet for all the wonders of the modern age, some teachers wonder if all the changes are for the better. It could be pointed out that nothing can replace a good instructor; especially irreplaceable are the strong-willed, inspiring, and caring people who were Oklahoma's pioneering teachers.

Lucile Danner Claiborne of Lawton, who—like her husband, Ray—still teaches at Cameron University, contrasts the past with the present in Oklahoma education and suggests that today's teachers might well examine the philosophy of early-day instruction.

I started teaching in 1924, just out of high school with a two-year state certificate, in a small two-room country school. My salary was $100 per month. Ten girls from my high school attended Central State Teachers College that summer after graduation, and we all had schools that fall. I took nine hours in educational courses mostly geared on "how to teach." I still think that the training we got then better prepared us for teaching than the training the young teachers are receiving today. Knowledge of subject matter to be taught is one thing, but knowing how to impart that information is equally important.

My first year would be a nightmare to the young teacher today. I taught the first four grades in a two-room country school in Cotton County. I boarded with the upper grade teacher and principal, Ira Lee Jones. She was a wonderfully capable and dedicated teacher, and I learned much from her—and from the pupils

—that first year. We built the fires, did our own janitor work, planned programs for the monthly community meetings, organized the Christmas program, and bought and sacked treats for everyone in the school to be placed under the Christmas tree, which we put up and decorated with the help of the students. We coached two basketball teams, boys and girls, on an outside court, sponsored 4-H Clubs, and trained track entries and academic contestants for the annual spring county meets. We entered in everything, too. On top of all that, we taught school from 9:00 to 4:00. What did we do in our spare time, you might ask. Wouldn't teachers howl today, 1975, if they had to do all that? By the way, we had to grade all the papers ourselves, and we didn't have notebooks to check plus or minus. Yes, there has been a great change!

The amazing thing is that the pupils achieved much in those days and came out well grounded in the fundamentals in spite of the fact that we had no visual aids or teaching equipment other than that which we made or collected or drew on the board. We had never heard of an opaque projection, a movie machine, or a television. In the 1960's, I had an experience with a mathematics class taught by television in one of the high schools in Oklahoma City. The achievement in that class didn't compare favorably with the other four math classes I taught in which I had to do all preparation for presentation myself. What I'm trying to say is that all the teaching aids in the world, all the fine buildings, all the money for equipment, and all the high salaries for teachers cannot replace the initiative of a dedicated teacher and the motivation for a desire to learn.

Teachers today have many problems and pressures which we did not have, and they deserve higher salaries; but they should be more appreciative of the efforts made to improve their image as deserving public servants and should really assume a greater responsibility in training our children and youth of today.

I remember the subject for discussion on the agenda of a state and district teachers' meeting one time was "Are instructors responsible for teaching moral and spiritual values?" A breakdown came when we ceased to accept that responsibility, which we did; and we are paying for it today in a decay of these values in our society. I recommend that we return to some of the old principles upon which our great nation was founded and on this our "bicentennial year" rededicate ourselves to save our country from total collapse.

Although progress in education came rapidly after World War II, Nettie Doughty, Fairview, reminds us that the one-room rural school had a long existence (Nowata County).

I taught school for twenty years, and I remember the first year almost as well as the last. The year was in 1944, and I had a job at a one-room rural school named Ruby, near Nowata. I had a brother and family and an aunt and uncle living at Nowata, and they told me of the vacancy.

The school had only eight pupils and was to be closed the next year, but I was told if I wanted to teach there on those conditions, they would hire me. I accepted because I wanted the experience, and vacancies were few. I roomed and boarded with an eighth grade girl's family. It was a mile and a half to the school. Most of the time I walked, but sometimes the girl and I rode an old mare. The schoolhouse was typical of the one-room facilities at that time, with the old-fashioned desks, a long bench in front, and a pot-bellied stove. No visual aids were available, and we had to carry sack lunches. Of course, I was the janitor—building the fire on cold mornings, carrying in the fuel, and sweeping the floor.

There was very little supervision and few reports. I think I had a couple of visits from the county superintendent, but I wasn't kept very busy. I did some homework on the eighth grade math to keep ahead of my pupil, and I usually spent the week ends with the relatives in Nowata.

Interestingly, Fleta M. Hill of Mangum contrasts her first (1931) and last (1974) years of teaching and capsules many significant changes that have taken place.

What changes I have witnessed in the field of education in the forty-three years since I started teaching! My first year in 1931 was in a one-room rural school, Emerson, in Roger Mills County, located about twelve miles southwest of Cheyenne. My last year of teaching in 1974 was in an independent school in southwest Oklahoma City, Crooked Oak. I taught in nine different schools, mostly in southwestern Oklahoma.

My first building was a one-room frame schoolhouse, furnished with double desks, a large wood- or coal-burning stove, a teacher's desk, a cloakroom near the back door, and a worn wooden floor. We had outside toilets, and we pumped water from a well located on the sandy school ground which was surrounded by sagebrush and a few low trees. The last building I taught in was a low sprawling brick one with fourteen classrooms, a cafeteria, offices, and inside restrooms. We had a sink and water fountain in each room, with two movable coat closets, which doubled on the front as a bulletin board or as display space. The floors were tile; and at the beginning of each new season, the floors and woodwork were freshly painted or polished. There was a large playground, black-topped with paved tennis courts and a large grass-covered play area. This doubled as a park and picnic area in the summer.

I do not remember that we had any playground equipment in my first school. We played many games and had fun. We played a lot of baseball, but the older boys brought their equipment from home. The district had no money with which to buy playground equipment. In my last school, each room had several different types of balls, such as softballs, basketballs, kick balls, and footballs. We also had bats and some gloves. On the playground, there were about five swings, two basketball goals, a merry-go-round, two tennis courts, and a baseball diamond.

According to standards today, my first salary was low at $85 per month for nine months. This was in the midst of the depression; I had worked my way through college and had no funds left. I was tickled to death to have the job at that salary. Sometimes, during this period, it was necessary to discount the warrants to get them cashed. People of the district were just unable to pay their ad valorem tax. In 1974, during my last year of teaching, my monthly salary on a ten-month basis was $841.50. With tax deductions, insurance, and retirement, I still drew about $600. Of course, living expenses had increased greatly, as I remember paying $15 per month for my first light-housekeeping room; and after arriving at my destination, I walked wherever I went or rode with someone else. I did not mind walking, even through the deep sand, because others walked, too; and all the students walked to school because there was no public transportation there. In 1931 every county had many small schools; but it was not long until the trend of people leaving the farms began, and the schools began to consolidate and centralize. By 1960 most of the rural schools had been closed. In Greer County, where I now live, there were twenty-seven schools in 1930. Today in 1975 there remain only two schools in the county. This is very typical of what has happened all over the state. We have also lost something of the personal contact with the students and the parents.

Teachers of today have more personal freedom, as not so much is expected of them as community participants. When I first started my career, teachers were expected to set high moral standards. Whether you could play or sing for church or provide some entertainment in the community was a criterion in your being hired. In my first job, I was not only teacher but also janitor, doctor, and playground supervisor. My day started early, especially in winter, when I went to school early enough to start a fire in the stove and to get coal from an outside bin. At the end of the day, I swept the schoolhouse or got help from the older students. I do not remember that the building was ever locked, and it was used for church on the week ends and for other community affairs during the week. Nothing was ever bothered that I know of or remember.

All students brought their lunches from home in 1931; and each ate at his own desk, making quick work of that so he could get to the playground. In 1974 most everyone had a hot meal in the cafeteria. Those who could paid for their lunches, but those who could not had their lunches paid by the U.S. government. A lot of food was wasted because so many children would not eat some of the foods that the cooks were required to serve as a balanced meal.

As for available materials to be used in the schoolroom, in my first class we did not have any encyclopedias, library books, or resource materials of any kind. Whatever paper, construction paper, crayolas, or other material that we had was supplied either by the pupils or by the teacher. In 1974 I had an abundance of resource material, maps, library books, paper, film strips, and all needed supplies. Each year we had an allocation for supplies and library books. Some of the funds were supplied through the government title programs. Most of the pupils supplied their own paper and pencils, but often the poorer students had to have these supplied. I saw a lot of waste and carelessness in the use of paper.

School life in 1931 was not all drudgery. About once each month we either visited or were visited by a neighboring school, Dempsey, which was about four miles west. We traveled in a borrowed broomcorn wagon. We would spend the day, having ciphering, spelling, and geography contests. We would usually end the day with a baseball game, and everyone went home tired but happy whether we won or lost. Also, in the spring, we always took part in the county contests. In the fall, we always had a pie supper to raise money for a Christmas tree. This was the highlight of the year, when the whole community came together for program and Christmas tree with treats for all.

I do not remember having any real discipline problems in my first school. Most of the pupils understood the rules for behavior; and when a rule was broken, they expected to be punished. I'm sure I made some mistakes in judgment; but when punishment was given, it was administered quickly and soon forgotten. About 1940 I went back to college to finish my work for my B.S. degree. I especially noticed that in the education courses the idea was being taught that if you were a good teacher, you could let the pupils have self-discipline. A philosophy prevailed that pupils should have more freedom to express themselves. Perhaps we needed some direction in this line, but it seems that this pendulum has swung too far and that we have been seeing some results of this problem in the student rebellions and of the "doing of their own thing." At any rate, with the coming of integration and its subsequent problems, we punished a child only after every alternative had been tried. In most cases, a student could get by with a lot of poor behavior before he got anything beyond counseling, begging, pleading, and threatening before he might be paddled. If it became necessary to paddle a child, the teacher did it in the office with a supervisor or another witness teacher. Sometimes it seemed to me that a child had probably forgotten why he was punished by the time it happened.

Since I began teaching, there have been many changes in curriculum. We have added some subjects such as art, music, and physical education. There was not so much stress on the fundamentals or the "three R's." We have gone from the self-contained classroom to departmental teaching and back again several times in grade schools, and still controversy remains. There is a trend back to the "open classroom" type of teaching, and I wonder if we're headed for the one-room school again.

Ruby R. Barber, Midwest City, also contrasts "then and now," focusing on the 1950's and the troubled 1960's.

Education in Oklahoma from the Sputnik era through the

troubled sixties into the traumatic seventies was a kaleidoscope of change which resulted in new and better ways of teaching and improved schools to meet the needs of the pupils. I began teaching in Oklahoma in 1952, the pre-Sputnik era, and taught for twenty-one years through some of the most rapidly changing, but the most challenging and interesting, times. In the year 1952 I found schools with traditional teaching methods and low salaries. I started my Oklahoma teaching career with a bachelor's degree and three years' teaching experience in a suburban high school at a grand salary of $2,825 a year.

The first few years continued to reflect the traditional pattern; but with the launching of Sputnik I in 1957, a sudden stress on quality teaching became apparent. For example, ability grouping with the accent on the exceptional child was an innovation for quality education. We had let Russia outstrip us in space; therefore, we must train our mathematicians, scientists, and engineers with the objective of outstripping the Soviets as quickly as possible. Scholastic excellence for the student was emphasized, along with improved teacher training. Our school board required that we go back to school for work on advanced degrees and for specialized training in workshops and seminars. By 1963 I had earned my master's degree and had participated in many a special training session on methods of promoting scholastic excellence.

The emphasis on scholastic excellence continued until we moved into the era of rebellion and dissension which started in the late 1960's and carried over into the early 1970's. We began to throw out the old and to search for the new, impelled by mounting rebellion and resentment of authority among both the students and the faculty. There was rebellion not only against the Vietnam war but also against the establishment in general. Tradition and traditional methods were attacked with a vengeance. Free school advocates arose. Many authorities through the various media were urging alternatives to school, even to the point of deschooling our culture. In our high school, we sought and initiated new methods of teaching and alternatives to traditional patterns. We emphasized inductive teaching; we experimented with team-teaching and informal classroom procedures. We offered more variety and freedom of choice in the curriculum and class schedules. The emphasis shifted from excellence in scholastic achievement to student interests, rights, and freedoms. Student committees often visited the administration offices and demanded their rights.

Dissident groups from nearby colleges and universities infiltrated the high schools, drawing younger students into their meetings and training them for disruption and demonstration. When it became apparent that drugs were being sold in the high school parking lots during breaks, narcotics agents were called in to help. A student, suspected of selling narcotics, was actually picked up from my creative writing class by two narcotics agents one morning. The boy was released later, but he was picked up again in a narcotics raid on a hippie hangout in the nearby city on the very night that he was to have graduated from high school. One new teacher, under the guise of student rights, brought a militant speaker to his classes who advocated the use of marijuana and other drugs and urged rebellion against authority.

Also during this time, I had the unique experience of having a former member of the "Hell's Angels" group as a practice teacher. He was supposed to have been a reformed "Hell's Angel," but somehow he hadn't been able to shed their radical philosophy. He carried it into the classroom and proselytized the high school students for his cause. He was subsequently relieved of his role as a practice teacher by his supervising professor from his sponsoring university.

Teachers during that time were rebelling, too. They were demonstrating and threatening to strike through their professional organizations for a living wage. Their first breakthrough came in 1964–65 when they got their first really good raise from the state. The adjusted basic beginning salary tripled the amount that had been paid at the time when I first began to teach. Thus Oklahoma teachers' wages began to come out of the cellar of salaries in the nation.

Another sign of the times and of the rise in status and authority of the students was revealed in our yearbook. The faculty pictures were moved from the front of the yearbook to the back. Their position of status was pre-empted by student activities, athletic prowess, and candid shots of the students.

What did all the rebellion and change do to teaching? Despite all the trauma and turbulence, much good came from it. In the first place, we moved from rigidity to creativity and variety; this was a much-needed change. More emphasis was placed on teaching critical thinking and problem-solving. The atmosphere of the classroom was relaxed, allowing for more creative development and freedom on the part of the students. Many new courses were added in all areas to meet individual needs and talents of the students. Such courses as cosmetology, nursing, auto mechanics, metal work, business training and practice, photography, printing, furniture upholstery, small appliance repair, commercial art, homemaking, and restaurant management, as well as all of the basics, were offered for both boys and girls.

Even the basics were restructured, allowing for more freedom of choice among the students. For example, instead of English IV for seniors, the choice was offered of a variety of semester courses such as creative writing, modern drama, senior composition, world literature, modern novel, vocational English, and communications and the media. All departments endeavored to provide more freedom of choice; and in some courses, independent studies were encouraged. All of the innovations plus good counseling and guidance made it possible for the student to have a diversified field of training available to help him develop his own inate abilities and creativity to his fullest capacity in what might be labeled a personalized education—one more likely to meet his needs and to bring him satisfaction in life. Teachers, as well as students, welcomed the innovations.

The note of caution injected into the optimistic picture was that the trend toward a creative and personalized education would fail if parents and teachers allowed the students to conclude that there was no need for the well-learned basic knowledge and skills which are so essential before one can develop his inate talents to their fullest. Neither parents, teachers, nor students should ever assume that school is just a place for entertainment or that one can be sure of a good education without desire, diligent application, and self-discipline.

What our Oklahoma schools are giving young people now is far better than the limited skills and knowledge taught and imparted in the past; and if rightly and thoroughly taught by conscientious and well-trained teachers and well received by diligent, hard-working students, well-educated young Oklahomans should be ready for the next decade of change!

Nettie Mitchell Parker, Mangum, whose career spanned over forty years, spent much of her time in the Oklahoma City system. She comments on recent progress in the state's school system, especially regarding academic freedom, increased use of technology, and the abundance of supplies in the classroom.

In the Oklahoma City schools, teachers were free to experiment in subject matter. When hand-picked committees studied projects or methods and found need for revisions, changes were made. We experienced several changes in plans of teaching, such as the departmental or the self-contained classroom.

In the latter part of the 1950's, television teaching came into existence. The role of the television was not to do away with the classroom instructor, but to assist her and enhance or enrich the students' education. In order to keep the work going in a normal situation, classrooms were equipped with a television, radio, tape recorder, film-strip machine, and record player. Records were catalogued in the building media center. Channel 13 was especially geared to the Oklahoma City curriculum, and Channel 25 was used also. Many subjects were taught by television two days per week to assist the teacher. Lessons on music, art, science, social studies, Spanish, French, history, math, and other subjects were offered via television. Workshops were organized to show teachers how to use these audio-visual materials to the best advantage.

Libraries were set up in all buildings so that children in all grades would have the full benefit of the best reading materials. Special teachers and/or aides were hired to run them. In the last few years, the wording was changed from "library" to "media center," which handled books and nonbook materials, audio-visual aids, mimeographed material, and other materials.

The city maintained a huge supply depot. Children were assessed a $4.00 per year, and the board matched that sum. Teachers ordered this amount of supplies per child each year from a prepared catalog. Each instructor was thus well equipped with supplies for a very little effort to her. Regular route trucks delivered supplies, mail, and custodial and cafeteria materials three days per week. This system of abundant supply was a far cry from what began in 1927. Education has come a long way in forty-four years.

Rae Vail Heady, Dacoma, started her teaching career in 1918 at eighteen years of age. After service in one-room, rural schools

and larger systems in Ellis and Woods counties, she, too, comments on the changing times.

There is no comparison in the warm, comfortable, carpeted, well-equipped classroom of today—with all modern teaching equipment and materials available for every subject. Modern restrooms, hot lunches, custodians to keep the building comfortable and clean, and good salaries—all are a far cry from the early classrooms, both rural and in town, where the teachers made do with the simplest equipment, carried their own lunches, built the fires, and did other custodial work. However, it was not all bad, for much learning took place in those early classrooms. For fun and pleasure, early schools had ciphering, spelling, and geography matches in which many students became proficient. Instead of candy and "pop," children had apples, peanuts, and popcorn popped on a roaring coal stove. The playground equipment was mostly provided by the children: a few marbles, a rope to jump, a twine ball, and board bats for baseball. We were fortunate to have one basketball, while today it takes many for one season.

Before and up to World War II education remained concerned chiefly with the basic subjects, where drilling and testing were expected to make one well grounded in these subjects. Today, the curriculum has changed greatly, with so many subjects and fields offered, so many new ideas and methods of teaching—some good and some not good—that often the student finds himself too involved with studies and activities. He often finds himself bewildered and unable to cope with college when he is ready to attend. I am for changes and progress in education, but only if it also gives the student the basics he needs, such as reading, spelling, and the general knowledge necessary to cope with life.

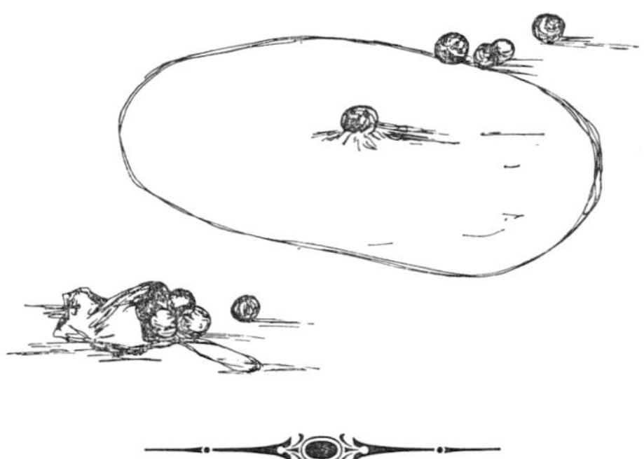

Sophia Buggs West, Coweta, had long service in the schools of Oklahoma, principally in Wagoner County. A summary of her career service perhaps typifies that of other black educators.

I attended public school and college in Mississippi and received my B.S. degree in elementary education and social science in 1938. I received my master's degree from Northeastern State College at Tahlequah in 1960. I was always deeply concerned with the educational welfare of pupils. I served thirty-eight years in the Wagoner school system, with eleven of these years spent as supervisor in the county, from 1940 to 1951. In 1940, when I began the supervision of the Wagoner County facilities, we had thirty-six Negro schools. They were one-, two-, and three-room facilities with from twenty-five to ninety-five pupils in each school. All of these schools are gone now as a result of consolidation.

I worked eight years in the Red Bird school system, where I was principal for three of those years. The last years of my teaching career were spent in the Coweta public school system. I taught fourth grade math and science. Those were some of the happiest years of my life.

Ruth T. Wynn, Wilburton, saw many changes in her forty-year career.

When I compare my last school year, 1973–74, with that of 1933–34, I see remarkable changes. My salary increased greatly. A warrant arrived on the twenty-fifth of each month; and even after deductions for teacher retirement, social security, hospital insurance, taxes, and annuity savings, I still had a take home pay which was more for one month than I made all year in 1933–34. My schoolroom was crowded with teaching materials—tests, reading readiness books, six or more different sets of readers, and volumes of math and science books. Shelves were lined with good library books. I had audio-visual equipment at my side, a record player, and, of all things, a new piano in my own room. There was no excuse for my twenty-six students not learning.

At the 11:30 lunch, I had to beg the children to eat the lovely, well-balanced meal served in an air-conditioned lunchroom. How many times I compared them with what those first graders had in 1933–34. Everyone had lunch whether he paid or not. In 1973–74, buses were provided for field trips. Mothers served refreshments at parties. The school provided ten-day sick leave yearly for the teachers. We had coffee breaks, and, would you believe it, we ordered program materials and had the money to pay for them.

Guy M. Pritchard of Stillwater continued the tradition—begun by J. C. Fitzgerald—of exposing Hillside students to the broadest education possible.

My thirty-five years of teaching experience have ranged from teacher of a one-room rural school in Lincoln County to director of the Audio-Visual Center at Oklahoma State University. But it was during my teaching at Hillside Consolidated Elementary School near Cushing that my most unusual teaching experience occurred. It involved the projects of a travel club.

Before World War II, J. C. Fitzgerald, principal of Hillside, had organized the travel club and had taken the sixth through twelfth grades on several trips in the 1930's which included tours of the United States Capitol at Washington, D.C., Mexico, and Carlsbad Caverns. In 1940 a state ruling prohibited the use of a school bus for educational tours; and the travel club, through Fitzgerald's efforts, purchased a used bus and made tours until the beginning of World War II. In 1942 I became principal of Hillside, following Fitzgerald's election as Payne County superintendent of schools. The travel club had sold the bus and had become inactive at the close of Fitzgerald's teaching there. In 1944 I had a leave of absence from Hillside to serve in the military during World War II. After I returned from service in 1946 and resumed my duties at Hillside, the travel club became active once again, but with a more limited travel program. The state department granted permission, beginning with the summer of 1947, for schools to make educational tours within the state following the end of an academic term.

During their free and leisure time after school started in the fall of 1947, the class members were constantly getting maps of Oklahoma and tracing the routes traveled previously. Such statements as "I wish we could make a map of Oklahoma large enough to mark out the routes taken last year and also plan our tour for 1948" resulted in making such a map. The map was planned to carry out our study of Oklahoma history. Our aim in making the chart was to become familiar with our state by depicting its counties, its highways, its agricultural and manufactured products, its historical and scenic places, and the names of prominent people who were born, reared, and educated in the state, and who resided in each particular county.

In September, 1947, fifteen students selected three counties each, and eight pupils chose four as their individual projects in social studies. The students selected prominent people in individual counties, such as the mayor, the secretary of the chamber of commerce, and the county or city superintendent and wrote for information about the particular county. A week was spent in deciding what information to ask for in writing to people suggested previously. No form letters were used. Although each child asked for practically the same information, his communication technique was different from any other.

The information was to be placed on a map to be prepared by students. Each child measured the height and width of the north wall of the classroom. The writer suggested that if the panhandle of Oklahoma was placed over the north door of the classroom, the map then would cover most of the north wall. After spending the arithmetic period for five days calculating the size of the chart, members of the class agreed that the map could be drawn to scale and that the panhandle could go over the north door. A map published for the *Oklahoma Stockman* was used as a guide in placing the counties, county seats, and other towns on the map. From the first of October until the first of November all classwork was taken from the information collected by the students of Hillside. No lessons were assigned from their textbook, but all subjects were correlated with the information received. Each student gave either an oral or written report (or both) over the pamphlets and printed materials received. Before accomplishing this, of course, each writer had to read the material in order to have a knowledge of the information and in order to answer questions on the subject. A discussion period was always held after a report.

The students who had selected counties on the east side of Oklahoma next to Missouri and Arkansas state lines began determining county lines. Since the township lines had been placed on the map by the students, it was now easier for them to locate the county boundaries. All work progressed from east to west until all counties had been painted. Each child did all the work on his counties. The children decided to letter each county in black and made letters one inch high. The county boundaries were also painted black. Other information was painted in various colors. When the map was finished, it had thirty-five different items of information on it.

Plans for the Hillside educational tour were made for ten nights' lodging. Each child not only wanted to visit one of the counties he had selected as a project study, but also wanted to spend the night there. Before starting on the trip, the members calculated the number of miles the group would travel each day. Also, they calculated the probable number of gallons of gasoline needed for the trip. After the route had been decided upon, each child wrote some responsible person in the city where we wanted to spend the night. The letters stated that the Hillside travel club planned to make a ten-day educational tour, beginning May 31, through Oklahoma, covering approximately thirty counties. The group would be traveling in a bus; the students would have their own bedding and cooking and eating utensils. The letter listed the day and approximate time of arrival in each city and the number of students and teachers. It was emphasized that the group would be properly chaperoned at all times. The students asked if the city had an American Legion hut, community building, school building, or gymnasium where the members might spend the night and asked if there were cooking facilities and running water. Prospective hosts and hostesses were promised that teachers would be responsible for students' conduct, the building, and the property. The group made their own rules, and the club officers enforced them.

The club traveled 1,561 miles and used 174 gallons of gas. The total cost of the travel trip was $174.73. This sum included food, insurance, admission fees, gas, and other expenses. It cost about thirty-three cents per day to feed each club member in 1948. During the summer vacation of 1947, 1948, and 1949, the Hillside travel club members visited every county in Oklahoma. The map was exhibited at the Payne County Fair, at the Oklahoma State Fair, and at a rural conference in Lincoln, Nebraska, during these years. At the exhibits, students from Hillside were on hand to explain details to interested fair viewers. Not only the students but the map itself traveled far.

Mildred C. Webb, Midwest City, tells the exciting story of the founding of a new pioneer town and school in the 1940's.

There was a loud knock at the door of our new home in a new little town—Midwest City, Oklahoma—late one June evening in 1943. A tall, bald man greeted me as I opened the door. "I'm Oscar V. Rose, superintendent of Midwest City schools. We don't have a school yet, but we will have," he said firmly. "I heard you were a teacher, and I would like for you to apply." And with that, he was gone—recruiting other teachers, I'm sure. I was anxious to teach near our home, so I dutifully resigned my art position in Oklahoma City and was hired to teach fifth grade in Midwest City.

Tinker Air Force Depot, or Tinker Air Force Base as it is now known, was being built. World War II had started, and Midwest City was growing. Enterprising builders bought land, and streets were being laid out. Homes and businesses were going up quickly for the anticipated thousands of civilian employees and military personnel at Tinker and for the builders of aircraft at Douglas Aircraft Plant. Of course, with these skilled young workers came their families and literally hundreds of children. We drove to Capitol Hill or to nearby country stores, gas stations, and laundromats, for we all needed services. Small country churches were doubled in size, and many new churches were established, and meetings were held in the schoolrooms as parents sought to continue their children's religious training. A Study Club, Lions' Club, Flower Club, choirs, and a Boy Scout troop were among the first civic organizations at work. A group of men were appointed to establish a town government with Royal Brust acting as first mayor. Everyone was a charter member of something as these enterprising Americans set about creating a working town.

There was one small county school called Sooner in what would be the Midwest City school district fifty-two; and in a nearby district, there was Soldier Creek School. Both became filled to capacity within a few weeks by children whose parents were indeed new pioneers.

Mr. Rose borrowed a school bus from Bearden Consolidated Schools and even convinced the bus driver, Oscar Bean, to move to Midwest City to help him. They were an unforgettable pair—both working for the children of the new town—often angry at each other but friends. In later years when Mr. Rose had become a national figure in educational needs of schools affected by federal installations, he and this humble man of the soil were as close friends as ever. The small school staff was still hunting teachers and buildings and buses. Little square buildings with pointed tops called hutments, precut and laid flat on big trucks, were ordered from somewhere in Texas. The date for school to open came and went, but the buildings were late in arriving. A polio epidemic postponed the beginning of school for two weeks, and the late trucks finally arrived. Mr. Rose sent out a call for teachers, their husbands, and every able-bodied interested patron to help raise the buildings; and here the pioneering spirit of these newcomers to a new town became even more evident. They labored long into every night with no pay, setting up the precut facilities in a large square. Outdoor restrooms were placed at the back of the buildings. Board walks were built, and school opened not too far behind schedule with the usual bright, eager students and the few reluctant ones one will always find.

The warmth of fall turned into the cold of winter, and we had no heat. A call went out asking parents to donate old gas stoves. They brought them in, all sizes and makes, and often stayed to hook them up. None ever exploded, we were never gassed, and we were more or less warm that first winter.

The raw pioneering proved too difficult for a few teachers, parents, and children; and they left for more settled situations. But the majority of teachers and students alike treated their experience as one great adventure, and we rose to whatever heights or endured whatever depths that came.

Speaking of depths—I have never before or since seen so much mud. Now new towns seem to build concrete streets before the houses are built; but thirty years ago, the streets remained unpaved long after the houses were built—and Midwest City was often called "Mudwest City." We waded in mud to school; we waded in mud to the restrooms; and we waded in mud to the classrooms along with 110 to 130 little or big feet. Mr. Bean and his helper often came to clean the rooms with shovels instead of brooms. A few loads of gravel for the streets eventually helped the situation, and fall and winter turned to spring.

The new town was taking shape, all laid out by special plan—an architect's dream they called it—until I'm sure it expanded far beyond the most enthusiastic builder's or architect's dream. Everywhere we looked, houses, churches, and permanent school buildings were going up. By the next year, we had overflowed our school rooms, and many of us were back in hutments or barracks. We grew a new city, new churches, stores, and even a new theater (The Skytrain) which brought us many hours of entertainment. New schools, new students, new teachers—all worked and built together.

I think now of the togetherness—the borrowed bus, the borrowed books and stoves, the cold, the crowding, the mud, the leaders who gave unsparingly of their time and were often so worried about financial affairs of the school, the teachers who taught for the joy of teaching under difficult circumstances for so little money, and lastly the students who gave their best and many of whom are now illustrious alumni and some leaders in a town they helped to build. As I look back, I would not have missed it for anything!

Mrs. Kate J. Lewis, Purcell, faced many obstacles when teaching migrant children in the western part of the state.

The most rewarding time of all my thirty-nine years of teaching were those spent with the migrant children in western Oklahoma. One year, enrollment brought nineteen Mexican-Americans and five Anglos. I felt that I faced a formidable task, since so many of the children could not speak English. I sought help from teachers who had been in the area longer than I and who had faced the same situation many times. The answers were nearly always the same—play it by ear. At the time, this was very discouraging. Added to the language barrier problem were questions of health. Though most of the migrant children remained basically a healthy lot, most of them had dental cavities and head lice. Both conditions overwhelmed me at first.

My school superintendent sought and procured federal funds for care of migrant children. He then hired a teacher's aide whose duty was to work on health and cleanliness for the Mexican-

Americans. The county health department sent us a nurse who instructed and supervised the aide. We bought boronate (louse killer) by the gallon jar; then we filled "take home" bottles of the medicine. Instructions for its use were given to older children in each family whenever possible. Sometimes, the county nurse made a home visit to instruct the mother. Many times, a bilingual pupil had to go along to act as interpreter. The greatest problem was that of reinfestation. Because of crowded living conditions, the treatment had to be repeated over and over. Toothbrushes, shoeshine kits, and lots of soap were kept stored in the shower room. Each child was taught to use these articles. Clean clothing was secured from community people who wanted to help. Too, federal funds were also used when needed for clothing. Each year, a dental check was made by the health nurse. Children with cavities were sent to the county health department's dentist. Eyes were checked and glasses secured for those who needed them. These were paid for by the local Lion's Club.

Most of the migrant children were from one to three grades behind their age group. Some over-age pupils had never been to school. Once, I enrolled five children from one family in the first grade. One boy was twelve years old and weighed 158 pounds. He became an eager learner. His eyes shone when he received his first book. In most instances, parents of these underprivileged children were anxious for their children to learn and were very co-operative with the school. At the end of three years, we saw gratifying progress. Most children had been given dental care; eyeglasses were provided for some; and cleanliness habits had improved greatly.

As we left this community to return to our home town, Purcell, we crossed a railroad track at the edge of the small town. Looking back over my shoulder, I saw a Mexican-American mother and all of her children come to the backyard brushing their teeth. This sight helped me to have a feeling of accomplishment. Not only had the children learned to practice good health habits but had also educated their parents as to their benefits. A fitting closing quote came from one child whom we called Little Joe. He remarked one day, "I want to learn to read and write, so I can show my father how."

John C. Haley, Bartlesville, reflects on his service as an administrator.

While I never ceased to consider myself a teacher, my last twenty-seven years in education were spent in administration. After military service in World War II, I returned to the classroom in Bartlesville for one semester. In 1946 I became the first vice-principal to serve College High School in Bartlesville. I worked in this capacity for eight years and then became principal of the school for the next nineteen years. I retired from that position in 1973.

As vice-principal, I had to develop my own method of counseling students, especially since I believed that persuasion was a more effective way than force in bringing improvement and change in students. This was a time before courses in counseling were available in the colleges I attended, so I had to be original. Enriched by my experience in teaching and by my military experience wherein I learned to appreciate a man for what he was, I worked hard to show an erring student a better way to happiness through the realization of his potential. In working with a student, I always tried to let him save face if he were found in error, and to do this I arranged a one-to-one situation for private consultation. If a reprimand were necessary, I tried to see that we did not part in anger. Many times, I encouraged students to think better of themselves than their actions indicated they did and to think for themselves. I sought to be consistent in my own behavior toward students (though I may often have failed in this), hoping that in this way I would encourage the development of trust. These methods worked much of the time.

During my first years as vice-principal, I was permitted to teach a class in history. In this period, I developed a course in contemporary history. Actually, it was more of a course in humanities, for we dealt with the cultural forces affecting the course of current history. There were many fine students in these classes, and they had an inspirational impact on the teacher. It was a two-way teaching situation, for I learned from them much that enabled me to serve them better.

As principal of the high school, my opportunities for teaching increased in scope. I retained the privilege of counseling with students on occasion, especially if they came to me of their own initiative and if I could act without dulling the influence of those assigned to counseling duties. My relationship with many new instructors and teachers-in-training enhanced my opportunities for teaching. Sometimes, teaching extended to parents and patrons. I made myself readily available to them for consultation and enjoyed the confidence of many. It remained a source of great pleasure for me to work with the second generation of many families, and I especially enjoyed being helpful to former students who came to me about the problems of their children.

My experiences have been varied and have included involvement in the supervision of many school events and activities, such as play production and the coaching of basketball (after a fashion) for both boys and girls. I have also had experience with fire, flood, storms, robbery of the school, and vandalism. To cite an example: I was called early one morning to rush to the school because the building was burning. I was shaving at the time; with a face half stubble, I became a fire-fighter. The closest fire department was some miles away in Oklahoma City, and the task of saving the building was left to me and a few hastily gathered volunteers. The fire had already burned out the boiler room where it had started and was spreading to the wooden portion of the brick structure when we arrived. With buckets and hose and desperate effort, we were able to contain the fire until a unit arrived from Oklahoma City. We saved the building—so the firemen told me when they ended their work some hours later—but we had no school that day. Instead, some of us put on other hats and spent the day in cleaning the place. That evening I finished shaving.

When the schools began to integrate, Bartlesville's high schools were among the first to accomplish this. It gives me pleasure to reflect upon the part I had in bringing this about in a manner that was beneficial to both blacks and whites. There was strong community support for integration, though there was also some opposition. Preparation for integrating the two senior high schools moved cautiously, and I was much concerned with reassuring the black students that they would be welcome at College High School. In the many meetings that I held with small groups of students and with individuals, I was assisted by the understanding principal of Douglass High School. Slowly, the students grew to accept me; and I was grateful for their trust.

Mary McCain, Oklahoma City, tells of her experience during the pioneering years of educational television.

Teaching on Educational Television, Channel 13, pioneering to learn how it could be utilized by the students and teachers, brought mixed emotions the entire twelve years. I taught Oklahoma history each year and government for several years. I did a weekly special elementary lesson based on social studies for two years. The first summer after the broadcasting center opened, I did a telecast, "Let's Tour Oklahoma." A year later, I did a series of telecasts on "Know Your County Schools."

There was constant experimentation, trying to discover the effective use of colors, printing, pictures, charts, maps, and creative visuals. We even had to experiment with make-up for each person who appeared on the network. We had everything to learn, but there was a feed-back each day to assist us in taking care of the weakness or failure of the lesson. You must remember that there was no color television at that time, and only two cameras were available for the studio. When one camera went out, we had to operate with just one and do the best we could. We had no taping machine. Consequently, each telecast was live. High school students were trained to run the cameras, and they worked in the studio a few hours each day. Today, some of the finest and most experienced directors and cameramen are those who started their career with Channel 13 while in high school. Sometimes teachers called to report that reception was not clear, that the print was too small, or that the teacher moved too fast for the class to keep up. There was always regret that we had to work daily to discover just what to do in every situation, but we were grateful for the information and felt that by working closely together, we could improve more rapidly. It remained trial and error for the studio teachers, the cameramen, the studio directors, and the engineers.

Once a month, representatives from all of the schools met with the first director of the broadcasting center, Mrs. Elaine Tucker; and we evaluated telecasts and received helpful ideas and suggestions from the teachers. To assure adequate preparation time, the television teacher wrote the guides to the telecast lessons a semester in advance for the students and for the classroom instructors. Each Friday, when possible, the television teachers visited one or more receiving classes. It was very valuable to talk to the students and the classroom teachers face to face, and often we came away with an idea we were eager to try.

Oklahoma history and government were enrichment lessons. I brought resource persons and elected officials from all over the state to answer key questions about their duties and responsibilities. This meant that I had to be prepared to give the lesson if there was an emergency and the resource person couldn't be present. Let me tell you about one of the amusing incidents that happened my first year teaching Oklahoma history. I had asked Elmer Fraker, executive secretary of the Oklahoma Historical Society, to be my guest and talk about cattle trails and cowboys. I visited with him in his office, and we planned the lesson. That afternoon, I began to feel uneasy about fifteen minutes before time to go on the air. I called his office and was told that he was at the broadcasting center. Of course, I had to go on the air and tell the class that our guest would be late and that I would begin the lesson. I found it extremely difficult to teach when I kept expecting his arrival momentarily; but two minutes before I was to go off the air, I looked up and Mr. Fraker was walking to my desk, saying, "Well, I'm here, Mrs. McCain." Imagine how I felt and how the students reacted when I said, "Oh, Mr. Fraker, our lesson is over; and I'll have to ask you another time." He revealed that he had been sitting in his car for thirty minutes, reading a newspaper, waiting for time to report to the studio. He had misunderstood the time—and was I sorry! Later, the teachers reported how humorous it was to the students.

Rare and unexpected situations arose as I continued using a large number of resource people. I recall that one time I was using an elected state official and had visited with him twice before the telecast. He had a complete script to follow. He was interesting and talkative, so I anticipated his telecast with much enthusiasm. He came earlier than I had requested, and he was beautifully dressed for the occasion. After we were on the air, I realized he was saying, "yes" and "no" to me and that we were not communicating. I soon discovered he was looking into the engineering area at the cameramen and had simply frozen. He seemed to be unable to talk for five or six minutes. I carried the lesson until he recovered and was able to join me in the discussion.

One regrettable telecast was one that had been carefully planned so we could use our mobile remote control truck that we purchased secondhand. The engineering crew had worked long and hard to overhaul the equipment and get it ready for the telecast at the state capitol. We were studying the executive branch of state government, and Governor J. Howard Edmondson was happy to let us telecast from the historical Blue Room. It took two days to set up equipment and even place antennas on the roof of the capitol. Everything was ready, and the governor was with us waiting to go on the air five minutes before show time. About that time, a clap of thunder sounded loudly, and there were flashes of lightning. Immediately, we knew that the lightning had struck our antennas on the roof; and we were out of luck. I shall never forget how patient Governor Edmondson was, and he told us he would come to the studio for the lesson. I well remember that he was five minutes late, unavoidably delayed, but the students really enjoyed his lesson on the responsibilities of the governor of Oklahoma.

Even now as I reminisce, I have mixed emotions about the joys, anxieties, disappointments, and thrills of being involved in the early years in what is now called instructional television. It has unlimited possibilities.

Hattie D. Tally, Altus, notes some of the changes which have occurred since World War II.

After the war was over, education began to change quite rapidly. The ideas used to train soldiers were put into the school. My schools had visual aid equipment with no films suitable to use in the classroom. It took some ten years to get the films correlated to the curriculum. Only in the last ten to twelve years have publishing houses put out their own films to supplement their textbooks. This is as it should be. It seems that films can now be utilized to the fullest.

"Time changes things" is an old adage but a true one. The children today have so much more knowledge than the children of yesteryear. Everyone, adults as well as children, are exposed to all kinds of technical knowledge; and it stays with some. Because of this, the teacher's role has been somewhat altered. The children question the teacher's statements more than they once did. I learned long before I retired always to be honest with my students. If I didn't know the answer, I told them so and went on with them to try to find the answer.

Gordon L. Paine, Lawton, discusses the transition from segregation to integration at Cameron College in the 1950's.

It was in mid-August, 1953, that Mr. Shegog, the principal of Douglass High School, and Mr. Lemuel Harkey, the principal of Dunbar Elementary School (our two all-black schools in Lawton) came to President Vernon Howell at Cameron College to request that Mr. Harkey's son, who had graduated from Douglass the previous May, be admitted to Cameron for the fall semester. Mr. Howell called me in on the conference since I was dean and registrar. We both agreed that we would like to have the young man. He had been a star football player at Douglass and was sought after by recruiters outside of Oklahoma. But we knew how Oklahoma law was written. So Mr. Howell told the men, "Gentlemen, we would like to have Lemuel, Jr., attend Cameron; but you know Oklahoma school law as well as we do. If he entered Cameron, we would be subject to a fine each day he was in attendance. I believe you can see that our answer to your request has to be 'no.'" They agreed and graciously terminated the conference. That fall, Lemuel, Jr., entered a college in Kansas on football scholarship.

Then, in the spring of 1954 came the Supreme Court decision on the matter of school segregation. That fall, twenty-six black students enrolled at Cameron. Of course, Lemuel Harkey, Jr., was not among them since he was already committed in Kansas. Members of the new group were accepted just as any other students were. I am sure that because of nearby Fort Sill and the previous integration policy adopted there our road was made easier. There was one flurry the second week of school. It came on Monday night, just as night classes were gathering. It involved no blacks. Someone said rather loudly, "Come, look what's happening." And looking out the east window, we saw a large burning cross planted on the southeast corner of the campus. Immediately there was excitement, comments, and questions: "What about that?" "That's a warning!" "What are you going to do?" To the crowd I answered: "Pay no attention to it. It is just someone playing a prank." I then turned on my heel and went about the business at hand, that of helping direct late enrollees to their proper classrooms. Whether it was a prank or not, I will never know. But the comment did serve to quiet the waters at the time. And there was never any hint or incident later which indicated that perhaps some people might be unhappy because Cameron was complying with the law.

On Saturday night of the third week of school, we had our first home football game. The center section of the east side of the stadium was fenced off and reserved for student seating. It had been thus for several years. In addition, one of the unwritten laws of our city required the black spectators to sit at the extreme south end of that east section for all games in the stadium. But near the end of the first quarter of the game, I noticed that our black students were not with the student body, nor were they with other Negroes down at the south end of the east side. They remained huddled together in a little group at the extreme north end of the east section. This disturbed me. After the game, I talked the situation over with the student body president. We both agreed that this kind of segregation was wrong. Blacks were a part of the student body and should sit with the remainder of the students. So, on Monday morning, an announcement went around to all nine o'clock classes. There was to be a meeting of all black students at 12:30 that day in room three. It was a large classroom on the first floor and the customary place for group meetings, whether student or faculty. When the group had assembled—attendance was almost 100 per cent—we told them our feelings. We were not trying to enforce an inflexible rule that must be obeyed, but were asking them, if they so chose, to sit with the rest of the student body. They were an integral part of the student body, and we would like to have all students sit together. Then we opened the meeting up for questions. There was only one. The group was aware that it was customary to hold an after-the-game "sock-hop" in the school cafeteria, and they wanted to know if they could attend. We told them that of course they were as welcome as anyone else. They were asked just to observe the rule that prohibited non-students from attending. They were asked not to bring friends along and run into embarrassment. On Saturday night of that fourth week, we had another home game. The little group did sit with the student body, and many of them did attend the "sock-hop." But they liked a little different kind of music, and their style of dance was a little different, so as time went on, fewer and fewer attended the after-game affairs, and by the season's end, all had ceased to come. But the fact that the problem was brought out into the open immediately upon its discovery and that lines of communication remained open helped to make for a good school year.

At the end of that first year, there was a higher percentage of scholastic failures among blacks than among the remainder of the student body; but we felt that more had enrolled in college than were really scholastically prepared for college competition or who really wanted to go to school in the first place. They had attended because their classmates were coming, and it was the popular thing to do. In later years, the situation corrected itself.

Neither that first year nor later was there any racial unrest or "bad feeling" on campus. As I look back, I sometimes marvel at the smoothness of the transition. Especially is this true in light of my own personal experience, which I here relate. In my first forty years of life, I had had practically no contact with blacks. I have come to realize that prejudice remains a complex problem and is deep seated. It is learned, and only through time can it be unlearned. All my life I had worked with Indians but not with other minority groups. Then, in the early 1960's on a Saturday morning, I went into a hardware store in downtown Lawton where, unknown to me, a bright, personable young man from Douglass High School had been employed part-time. As I entered, he courteously approached me and asked if he might help in some way. And quick as a flash, rebellion welled up within me, and I thought, "Why do you have to be the one that waits upon me?" I tried not to let my feelings show. I hope I was successful. But it disturbed me that I felt prejudiced. I thought that I was long past that stage. But not so! Consciously, I had complete control; but unconsciously, I still had a way to go. That feeling has not recurred since that day and was, I hope, just a part of the relearning process.

Exzetta Jones Gorman, Wewoka, relates some of her experiences in "separate" schools, her struggle to achieve "high-level" certification, and her continuing service to education.

School teaching has been a series of pleasant experiences for me. I felt it was my calling; and even though I was a small person and few board of education members felt I could control a group from a discipline standpoint, I insisted they give me a try. The board of education in the Pleasant Grove community in Seminole County, with the consent of the county superintendent, gave me my first contract. Was I a happy person? Yes!

My educational background included teacher training. I had just completed a teacher's course at Langston University in May, 1919, and was considered one of the top members of the class. After a few months, the board of education and the community at large came out in praise for the young teacher. Everything worked well. At this time, we had inspectors, and our one-room school was rated superior. I taught two years at this school and moved to a three-teacher school, Parker's Chapel. After one year in this new school, I was employed by the Wewoka board of education to teach third and fourth grades at the Douglass School.

Each summer I returned to Langston University to continue my study toward my A.B. degree, which I received in 1934 with a major in English and elementary education. As time passed and changes in the curriculum became evident, my assignments changed often. First, I taught mathematics in grades four through eight, Douglass Grade School. During the summer, I continued my study at the University of Colorado at Boulder and added library science to my study, since it was so much needed at our school. During the next change, I was assigned to teach English in grades five through eight. My work must have been satisfactory because the high school principal assigned me to teach English to grades seven, eight, and nine, in addition to my work in the high school library. I had quite a work load, but with the help of the Lord, I completed all my assignments.

As our enrollment increased, I was relieved of seventh and eighth grade English classes but taught ninth grade English and continued to work in the library. My advance study was done during the summer. After completing a special course in library science at Hampton Virginia Institute, I entered the University of Oklahoma, and on August 6, 1951, I was granted a master's degree with a major in secondary education. I continued my teaching schedule at Douglass High School until 1960 when the schools in Wewoka were integrated. I was chosen to work as librarian for the Wewoka High School and Junior High School. My work remained very interesting, and the change into the integrated system was very effective.

In 1963, at the age of sixty-two years, I retired for health reasons; however, my superintendent wanted me to do a one-semester course in remedial reading; consequently, I returned to the classroom after a rest period. Then, in 1967, the librarian had a terminal illness which prevented her from working; and the superintendent again asked that I complete a semester, which I did. This completed my work as a regular teacher, but I did substitute work until 1972, when my health prevented me working any longer. I love people, and it has been a joy working with them.

I have been involved in many civic and educational projects—local, state, and national:

1950—Vice-President of the Oklahoma Negro Teachers Association.
1960—Seminole County Teacher of the Year.
1963–67—President of the Oklahoma Federation of Colored Womens' Clubs, Inc.
1964—Who's Who in Oklahoma.
1968—Oklahoma Delegate to the National Democratic Convention in Chicago.
1963–74—Job Corps co-ordination.

William Martin, Oklahoma City, offers his account of the integration of the capitol's school system in the mid–1960's.

The Negro people of the Oklahoma City public schools attendance area were mostly attending schools dominantly black during the school year 1965–66. It was common knowledge that the Congress had passed a law designed to force integration of the blacks and whites in the public schools. This law had been interpreted by the United States Supreme Court as being no violation of the United States Constitution. The local federal district court judge had ordered the local public schools to change their attendance areas to provide for mixing of Negroes and whites in the schools, so the ratio would be much more nearly like the ratio of the general black-white population of the total attendance area. Faculty integration was also ordered. The school administration was given one year to make plans for the faculty changes.

From 1961 to 1966, the writer had been principal of Sunset Elementary School, an Oklahoma City Public School. He was assigned as principal of the summer school at Shidler Elementary, which was located in the river bottom a short distance south of the North Fork of the Canadian River. It was also an Oklahoma City public school. It was a facility used by white children during the regular term. Walnut Grove Elementary, just across the North Fork of the Canadian River to the north, was a river bottom school which black children used during the regular term. Federal funds had been provided to support partially a summer school at Shidler for both Negroes and whites. The blacks were to cross the bridge to reach Shidler by walking or by bus if needed for the one-half mile.

The principal and faculty members had met to make plans for the school. It was an integrated faculty with some teachers coming in from Shidler, some from Walnut Grove, and some from other areas. Classrooms were set up; the building and play areas were made ready for the children. There had been no mixing of the races across the river, and it was not known what would happen on the first day of school. The principal arranged for a police patrol car to be parked in the area of the Shidler School in view of those who came across the bridge on the first day of class. Faculty members were told by the principal, "Early on the morning of the first day of school, let us all be on the playground in view of the children, talking with each other. Let us pretend that we like each other, even if we do not, for the benefit of the children and as an example for them." Faculty members were on the play areas on the morning of the first day. The police car was in place. The white children came to school gradually. We saw the blacks coming across the bridge walking. We continued talking and playing our parts to make the first meeting as low key for the children as possible. The Negroes came into the play areas. The whites and blacks looked at each other, and soon all started playing and using the equipment that we had provided. A big help was that the black principal of Walnut Grove School was the assistant principal of the Shidler Summer School and was in all meetings helping make preparations and was on the playground on the first day and thereafter. That assistant principal had a great sense of humor, believed in what we were doing, and seemed to enjoy the whole program. The school secretary of Walnut Grove School was our school secretary for the summer term.

So far as was known, there were no fights that summer at Shidler. No parents came to the school to make complaints. It should be said here that the Walnut Grove area was probably one of the lowest poverty districts among blacks in all of the Oklahoma City metropolitan area. Shidler remained somewhat above the lowest poverty level, but it was still a poor neighborhood. The writer was called out of his rose garden after the summer school was completed to become acting director of elementary education of the Oklahoma City public schools. Several weeks later, he became director.

Some leaders in the school system, including some elected by the voters of the district, were fighting a delaying action in the use of the public schools to integrate the races. It became our policy in the elementary grades to do whatever we were able to do to aid in the integration process. It appeared to be the policy in the secondary schools to wait one year before taking affirmative action. Our affirmative action in the elementary schools seemed to make a big difference in later years. Our early start appeared to show our intent—our effort to see that blacks and whites had the same opportunities in the same schools as early as possible. It became the policy of the elementary schools to make each change a voluntary action in so far as was possible. We consulted all interested parties—pupils, parents, and faculty. Teachers and other school employees were interviewed to determine their attitude toward integration and their willingness to make changes to forward the program. The whites and the blacks seemed to sense our honest intent to obey and to follow the law. They seemed to feel that it was our intent in the elementary schools to follow the law because it was a good law. It was also our intent to correct an injustice.

Previously, it was the policy of the school administrative staff to hold meetings with white employees in one location and then at a different place and hour have a separate meeting with the Negro employees. There was discussion of having some joint meetings which were soon implemented. When the first joint meeting was held, the writer was an elementary school principal. He noticed that a large part of the conference was devoted to glances and stares between blacks and whites sitting in separate parts of the auditorium. We had not met and worked together, and it was only natural that we would withdraw while attempting to learn what we could of the new situation. As time passed and more joint meetings were held, we looked less and less at each other and began to establish lines of communication. Some of us began to smile and to establish friendships. When we looked at our situations in 1966, we knew that we had made much progress, and we knew that we could make much more progress. We had justice on our side, and we felt good about things that were being done and things that could be done.

As a goal, we wished to have each school faculty integrated by the same percentage as the black-white school population ratio in our system. Our first effort was to have at least one black and at least one white teacher in each school within one year. The whole situation was reviewed in a general meeting of all elementary school principals and central office leaders. This conference was followed by small group meetings of elementary school principals in building centers throughout the city. We had cookies, cake, coffee, tea, and good give-and-take in these discussions. Our general theme in the small group meetings was: "Our integration of blacks and whites in all community activities, including the public schools is one hundred years overdue; so let us get on with this business." The director of elementary education and the principals made an effort to interview teachers in the system who were interested in helping and who were willing to transfer to another school to help reach the desired ratio of black-white mix of faculties. We found good teachers willing to move. White teachers were less interested in making these moves, but it must be said that many fine white teachers and many fine Negro teachers transferred, effective the following school year. A transfer was made by having the consent of the teacher to be transferred, of each principal involved, and of the central office personnel department. Final approval rested with the superintendent and the board of education.

A test interview was conducted with each new teaching applicant to insure that she or he was willing to teach in any school in the system on her or his level of training. Many new instructors accepted positions in schools where a large number of pupils and teachers were of a race other than her or his own. Some of the leaders of the black community outside the schools complained that they were receiving too many new white teachers in their schools. They wanted some older, more experienced teachers from other parts of the school system. It was logical that they should make such a request. The reason for using the new teachers was that older faculty members with experience were less willing to transfer. Elementary schools moved forward in their work during the next years, in part because nearly all teachers had a choice in reference to transfers. In one school a training center was established, and it was necessary to transfer some instructors against their wishes; in some instances, these instructors were placed in schools they less desired because such a transfer was in the best interests of the children. Many things were done by principals to help teachers get acquainted with faculties in other buildings in order to work out agreeable changes. Some teachers called principals of schools where they would like to work. Happiness and enjoyment of work with other people remained a high priority in this whole process. We made no effort to resist the federal law as was done in some parts of the school system. We believed our attitude was reflected in pupils and parents and made a big difference in our schools and their effectiveness in teaching children.

The superintendent, assistant superintendents, and other central office employees were co-operative in working with people in the elementary schools. We were allocated some additional assistant principals; we chose some black and some white, with the approval of the personnel office, the superintendent, and the board of education. In most instances, Negroes were placed with white principals, and whites were placed with black principals, after interview and approval of all assistant principals and principals involved. All of these plans for integration were incidental to helping all pupils, teachers, and others of the community grow educationally. We concentrated on acquiring the tools for learning while creating natural situations leading to good character development.

Arlie Geymann of Muskogee, a printer and a teacher, gives an interesting account of progress in vocational education.

I first became acquainted with printing at the tender age of twelve when I started to work for *The Community Announcer*, a small-town weekly newspaper located at Oil Hill, Kansas. I graduated from Kansas State Teachers College, Pittsburg, Kansas, in 1937, with a B.S. degree in education, majoring in printing. I had never considered being a teacher at the beginning. I was interested only in becoming a better printer.

A job for a printer at the Muskogee High School became available in January, 1940; and because of the excellent facilities, notwithstanding that the salary was little better, I moved to Muskogee. I retired from this job on June 30, 1975, after thirty-five and one-half years of teaching printing and directing the various publications for the school. In the thirty-seven and one-half years of my teaching, many changes have been made. At Hot Springs, Arkansas, everything that we printed was done from hand-set type. We published a four-page newspaper about every three weeks, and everything in it was hand-set, one letter at a time, justified, locked up, and run on a slow, hand-fed cylinder press. I taught six one-hour industrial arts classes, each section numbering about thirty-six students. Over one-half of the students were girls. From this I progressed to Muskogee, where I had two Linotype machines. Thus, we now published a weekly four-page newspaper using the hot-metal composition method. Our newspaper press in Muskogee was also a hand-fed cylinder press, but it was much faster. Our headlines and ads were still set from hand-set type, but a few years later we added a Ludlow machine. This made our newspaper publishing, as well as our job-printing work, much easier.

Our classes were vocational and consisted of about twenty-five students each in two three-hour classes per day. No girls were allowed to take classes in printing because it was believed that they could not endure a three-hour vocational class. We also had a complete photo-engraving plant at Muskogee, in which we made all of our cuts for both the newspaper and the school annual, which we also printed in our school shop. Even then, as today, all of the printed materials needed for the entire city school system were printed in the school shop.

During this stage, which was just after World War II, the country was getting really fired up over offset printing. Great strides had been made and were being made daily in perfecting better inks, papers, films, presses, plates, and plate-making machines to be used in offset printing. The technique was not new, but in the past it had not really caught on. A sleeping giant had suddenly been aroused. This printing method consisted of being able to photograph anything and transfer it to a sensitized zinc plate, then offset printing it on paper, metal, or anything else.

Every summer, the trade and industrial teachers had a workshop in Stillwater. With this sudden interest manifested in offset printing, a group of instructors from several schools in the state (myself included) decided to investigate and research the possibilities of this printing method. Instead of meeting for a week at Stillwater, we decided to take a trip to Colorado Springs, Colorado, where the International Typographical Union maintained a large research center for testing new ideas and equipment and also for training union members working in the trade with the new processes and equipment. A couple of our teachers were members of the union, and they had secured an invitation for us to visit the center.

Needless to say, this trip turned out to be one of the highlights of my career. I saw for the first time the tremendous ideas, equipment, and processes that were developing for this new printing method. New processes and computers were setting "cold type" from huge typesetters with memory tape banks which were automatically adjusting for left, right, or center line-up and which could flush left or right as desired and in whatever style or size typeface that was wanted. Original typists could be setting type in New York, and the machines across the country would be putting it on photo paper for instant paste-up. Great advancements were not just confined to the typesetting, but similar improvements were being made in the construction of cameras, in plate making, and in press development.

Well, I could readily see that there was going to be a great need for outstanding printers, technicians, machinists, and others for this trade. Good students had to be influenced to enter the printing trade programs over the nation. The job opportunities would be unlimited. But, alas, upon my return to Muskogee, my optimism waned. Having been involved in so many instances of attempting to work with the board of education to find money with which to upgrade the print shop, I knew that the economy budgets that public schools must live with would never permit us to buy even the meager equipment necessary to implement the new program in a very minor way. However, with the passing of the Vocational Act of 1963, which gave matching funds to schools for vocational education, we were able to add some of the equipment that I spoke of earlier. Upon my retirement this last year I left a well-equipped print shop of which Muskogee should be proud—I know I am!

In conclusion, in my thirty-seven and one-half years of teaching printing, many changes were made. From my first teaching job at Hot Springs, where all the printing was done completely from hand-set type and slow, hand-fed presses, I progressed to Muskogee where "hot metal" processes, photo-engraving, faster hand-fed presses—and, later, automatic presses—all letterpress equipment was used. Today most of the work in the shop is produced on photo-composed typesetting machines, is photographed on film, is transferred to presensitized aluminum plates, and is printed on automatic offset presses at speeds of 7,200 to 9,000 sheets per hour. Girls are now back in the print shop—and, I might add, are a very vital part of this program. They are participating in all phases of the work—design, layout, paste-up, photo-composing, plate-making, and press work.

Many teachers and administrators facilitated progress in the state's educational system with their service outside, as well as inside, the classroom. Most participated in professional organizations which helped develop quality programs. A mere listing of the professional activities of the contributors to this project would fill the volume, but a partial listing of the contributions of one leader might be representative. Gerald Stubbs, Stillwater, played an important part in securing the "better school" amendments of the 1940's. The account below is a summary prepared by J. C. Fitzgerald, another of Oklahoma's leaders in education.

Gerald Stubbs was one of the leaders in the organization and development of the Oklahoma Education Association. He was president of the association in 1944–45 and provided leadership in developing an improved method of financing public education in the state through four amendments to the Oklahoma Constitution. Those of us who were active at this time remember well that the teachers carried petitions and secured sufficient signatures to call a special election on the four "Better School Amendments." The state Chamber of Commerce challenged the signatures and fought the amendments all the way to the Supreme Court, but the court held the petition signatures valid. Then the teachers campaigned for approval of the amendments by the people at the special election and were successful in securing passage of all four. This was perhaps one of the most significant events in our state history as far as education is concerned.

During the 1945 session of the legislature these amendments had to be vitalized and made active by the legislature. Again, President Stubbs, along with other educators, was successful in securing state appropriations four times as large as any previous appropriations for education, although today the sum would seem quite insignificant. This step, nevertheless, established a means for state support of public education rather than forcing districts to depend almost entirely on local ad valorem taxes.

Mr. Stubbs's leadership and hard work are reflected in numerous organizations for educational improvement, and these efforts have continued throughout his life to the present time. He was one of the leaders in the establishment of the Oklahoma Retired Teachers Association and the Oklahoma Teachers Retirement System which provides the benefits to retired instructors. Again, petitions were carried by teachers; and the state constitution was changed to permit state retirement systems. Again, the teachers responded, and success was gained. One significant benefit from this amendment was that it not only made possible a retirement system for teachers, but also made it possible for other groups to establish systems of retirement. It is doubtful that many retired policemen, firemen, or other public employees realize or appreciate the fact that but for the teachers' efforts in amending the constitution, these groups would today be without any retirement benefits. Mr. Stubbs also was a founder of the Oklahoma State School Boards Association, which has had a steady growth and influence in involving lay persons in the solutions of problems affecting their children and the public schools.

Another teacher who made contributions outside the classroom was Kate Frank, Muskogee, who on one occasion had to "fight" (successfully) for her professional life.

I became active in professional associations in 1932. From 1932 to 1943, I served the teaching profession as president, Northeast District Classroom Teachers Association; president, Department of Classroom Teachers Association of the Oklahoma Education Association; and president, Oklahoma Education Association. I also had been National Education Association director from Oklahoma, member of the NEA budget committee, member of the executive board of the Commission for the Defense of Democracy Through Education of the NEA (was a member when I was "fired"), and delegate to the NEA Business Assembly for twelve years. I had been very active in carrying out the policies of the associations of which I was a member and held official positions. This required that I become very knowledgeable about school finance, policy making of school administration, budgets, and taxation for schools.

School administrators let the classroom teachers know that their place was in the classroom and that they were to ask no questions about salary schedules, budgets, sick leaves with pay, textbooks, and reasons for dismissal of instructors. A few even got "fired" for the activities outside the classroom. I was one of them. At a special called meeting on Wednesday, May 19, 1943, the board of education of my school system voted three to one not to reappoint me for the school year of 1943–44. No reason was given for my dismissal, except that I was a troublemaker. The board did not criticize my classroom performance. I had no previous warning that my activities in lobbying for better teaching conditions for instructors and improved educational opportunities for all children did not meet the approval of the board. The first that I knew about being "fired" was reading of the event in the evening newspaper. I was shocked. The community was surprised. My professional friends all over the nation couldn't believe it had happened. I received an official notification from the board two days later.

I notified Donald DuShane, executive secretary of the Commission for the Defense of Democracy Through Education, of the action of the board. I also notified H. B. Allman, chairman of the Tenure Committee of the NEA. They came at once to make an investigation of my dismissal and to try to get the board to rescind its action. The board would not reverse its decision. After thorough investigation, the Commission and the Tenure Committee, announced that in their opinion I was an efficient teacher. Dr. DuShane conceived the plan that I should stay at home until the citizens had an opportunity to speak at the next school board election. His plan was to tell the teachers all over the United States the true story of my dismissal and to form a "Kate Frank Defense Fund" by asking for volunteer contributions to the fund to pay me each month the same amount of money that I would have received if I had been teaching. I didn't approve of the plan at first. I told Dr. DuShane that I could get a job somewhere else, but I followed his plan because I believed it would benefit the profession. Teachers and professional associations contributed $4,800 to the fund. The plan worked. The same board of education that voted to not re-employ me in 1943 voted to rehire me in January, 1945, for the remainder of the year. The board continued to employ me until I retired in 1954. There is not a board of education anywhere that could have treated me any better than I was treated after re-employment.

I owe my professional life to Dr. DuShane for his advice and encouragement. His plan for me was effective. I am glad that I followed it for the profession and myself. Dr. DuShane died very suddenly in the spring of 1945. As a memorial to him, the teachers created a "Donald DuShane Defense Fund" to help teachers who had been dismissed as I had. There was a balance of $900 in the Kate Frank Defense Fund in January, 1945, when I was re-employed. The $900 was the first contribution to the "Donald DuShane Defense Fund." This story is written to let the young teachers know what the "Donald DuShane Defense Fund" is and how it originated. A booklet "You're Fired! It Might Have Been You" was published by the Tenure Committee of the NEA which gives the background and details of the "Kate Frank Case."

VII

A FUNNY THING HAPPENED ON THE WAY TO SCHOOL

The following short passages reflect the humorous incidents that only children, it seems, can manufacture. While teachers often carried a full class load, which meant "burning the midnight oil" to get all papers graded and all lesson plans made, and remained responsible for extracurricular activities as well, incidents like those recounted below often made the labors more enjoyable by making the days more interesting. No doubt, teachers sometimes

wondered what would happen next, what the "little ones" would say or do next.

Vivian Smith, Elk City, who taught in several one- and two-room schools, remembers the pranks that children played on her.

One boy gave me a live snake. I was teaching a spelling class, and two boys kept making noise. I asked them what was the trouble. One boy said, "He has a snake." Thinking that it was a rubber snake, I put my hand behind me and said, "Give me that snake." He did—you can guess the rest.

One Monday when I went to school, there sat in my chair the biggest jackrabbit I ever saw, paws on the desk, wire glasses over his eyes. I left him there all day.

A. Willard Brokaw, Shawnee, came from Wyoming to Oklahoma in 1925 to work in the Shawnee schools and spent forty-two years in the same system. He recounts several amusing stories.

During my tenure as a high school teacher, I assisted in extracurricular activities, principally in dramatics. I well remember when we were presenting a musical play with an Indian theme. One of my students played the part of a young brave whose costume was a single feather and a breechclout. He was embarrassed, but as fast as other Indians were killed in battle, he retrieved their items of clothing; and by the end of the play, he wore the full regalia of a chief.

During the agonies of the great depression of the 1930's, children came to their classes inadequately dressed for the winter.

Our PTA chairman visited the schools to help distribute suitable clothing which had been gathered in community social service projects. She found a sixth grade boy who came walking to school barefooted in an inch or two of new-fallen snow. She was horrified. She asked me to explain why I had not properly cared for his need. I responded by taking him to a clothing store where the manager had expressed a desire to help in such a problem. He fitted the boy with a fine pair of stout shoes. The next morning the social service chairman again came to my office to report that the boy was still barefooted and walked to school in the snow! She asked me why had I not done my duty? I sent for the boy. Sure enough, he was barefooted. I asked him why he was not wearing his new shoes to school. "Oh," he said, "I had other shoes. I didn't need shoes. I just like to feel the snow on my bare feet!"

In my latter part of my assignment as high school principal, my duties included the supervision of a class of secondary-level in-patients in the Shawnee Indian Tubercular Hospital. The class was accredited to the high school. When students began to meet requirements for graduation and participated in the commencements, a strong bond of friendship evolved between the young students and me. Our class atmosphere was flavored by a relaxed camaraderie among us. I remained curious about the Indian sense of humor. During my youthful years, Indians in current cartoons confined their remarks to "ugh!" I asked the class if Indians always said "ugh." One of the boys answered, "No, sometimes, they say "ugh, ugh!"

Sophia Buggs West, Coweta, served for years as a supervisor to the rural black schools in Wagoner County.

I really enjoyed my eleven years as a supervisor in Wagoner

County. Once, I visited a one-room school and was talking to the students, complimenting them on their good discipline. One small boy raised his hand and asked to speak. I said, "Yes?" He said, "Miss, you ought to be here when you ain't."

Mary Romine Meyer, Fairview, excelled in her instruction but had trouble carrying a tune.

I always knew that I was no singer. But one day, I undertook to lead the children in the singing of "America." When I finished the song, a girl in the back of the room raised her hand and said, "Miss Romine, I knew the words to that song; but I knew it by a different tune."

A. D. Hefley, McAlester, taught his first school in Nale (Pittsburg County). Imagine his horror when, on his first day:

I was outside busily engaged in cutting the day's supply of wood when I heard a terrific scream coming from the direction of the outhouse.

Wilburn, age six, had been excused a few minutes before to make his morning call. Another student was running toward me and screaming, at the top of his voice: "Come quick, Wilburn is dying." I threw down my axe and ran toward the little building.

The farmer-carpenter who had been employed to erect the little house had adults in mind when he cut the holes in the seat of the structure. Little Wilburn had lost his balance, had fallen through the aperture, and was standing knee-deep in the streaming soil beneath.

I saw that the gravity of the situation called for a quick decision and immediate action. I grabbed a pole which was lying on the ground nearby, backed off, gave a hefty heave-ho, and knocked the building down. I thrust the pole beneath the soggy ground and yelled for Wilburn to get "a-straddle" of the pole where I could pull him to safety.

I then faced another decision. What must I do with Wilburn. Obviously, I couldn't take him inside the school building, and it was freezing cold outside. Would he freeze to death on the two-and-one-half-mile walk home? I decided to send one of the older pupils home with him. Luckily, they had a cold but safe journey; nothing fatal happened.

Kate J. Lewis, Purcell, tells of one young man who followed common sense when enrolling for courses.

It was enrollment day, and I was enlisting library aides. Afterward, we held a short meeting to chart a work schedule. Homer, a high school junior, was present. I hadn't remembered enrolling a boy. "Homer," I asked, "did you sign up for library?" "Yes, Ma'am," he replied. "Here it is on my card." Sure enough, there on his enrollment card was "Bookkeeping."

Mrs. Lewis also recounts the following anecdotes:

Little Leroy once rushed panting from the playground to ask, "Mrs. Lewis, is this yesterday?"

Once I made Larry stay in at recess to finish his penmanship. After finishing, he handed the paper to me with these words, "Mrs. Lewis, you're still welcome at our house."

Roger had evidently failed to listen to my instructions on how to write his paper. "What do I do?" he asked. "Listen when I'm explaining," I answered, none too patiently. "What does that mean?" he further inquired. "It means to listen when I'm talking," I abruptly replied. Roger's comeback was, "Heck! You talk all the time."

Beulah Morris, Nowata, had her hands full one day in a Nowata County school while trying to deliver a lesson on Aesop.

The following incident stands out in my memory. It shows my neglect as a teacher in my beginning years. I sometimes failed to make things clear to my pupils. In this case, a map, with explanations to the children, would have been so helpful. This I did not use, and what followed is what happened in a third grade class: We had studied for several days something of the life of Aesop and a number of his fables. At the conclusion of the study we were having a review. One of the first questions I asked was "Where was Aesop born?" After an instant, a little boy's hand shot up. I called on him. His answer was, "In oil." Well, I almost laughed aloud—it struck me as so funny. But the answer seemed to mean nothing unusual to the other children. I then said, "No, it wasn't in oil but in Greece." He then said, "What's the difference between oil and grease (Greece)?"

On the question of "adultry," Faye M. Duke of Alva relates the following story.

The most startling bit of information I ever received was from a test on American literature. In introducing this study to my students, I explained that American literature is the only major literature of the world that started on an adult, mature level. All others had their beginning in folk literature and had evolved. On a test over the first part of our study, a lovely and delightful young lady (to reveal her name would betray a confidence) wrote these words: "American literature is unique in that it is the only major literature of the world that had its beginning in adultry."

The imagination, if not the "book learnin'," of grade school children is demonstrated in this series of stories submitted by Christine Millsap of Weleetka.

Once, I had the second and third grade art classes drawing pictures of Pilgrims for a display. One child asked, "who are these people, Mr. and Mrs. Pilgrim?"

For Lincoln's birthday, I read my classes stories of his greatness and then asked for stories of their own. One child wrote, "Abraham Lincoln was born in a log cabin which he helped his father build."

Once, while the kids were working on a written test, I asked Johnny if he found the questions difficult. He snapped back, "Oh, no, it's the answers that get me."

Another time, I spent a whole period talking to the class about Eskimos. The next day I asked, "Who lives up north where it is cold?" Waving his hand frantically, one child said, "Old Santa Claus."

Once when we were studying about proteins, I asked, "What do we find in meat and beans?" One girl answered, "In beans it's rocks and dirt. Mother always has to wash them before cooking."

PROJECT CONTRIBUTORS

The list below identifies those teachers who contributed reminiscences for the ORTA collection which will be housed in the archives of the Oklahoma Historical Society. If known, the home town of the participant is given.

Adaline Abbott
Shattuck

Whitt K. Abbott
Muskogee

Theresa W. Abram
Oklahoma City

Blanche Alexander
Pauls Valley

Hazel Allen
Pawnee

Gertrude Allenbaugh
Meeker

Paul J. Alyea
Tulsa

Julia M. Avritt
Oklahoma City

Jewell Bailey
Valliant

Helen B. Baldwin
Longdale

Beth Ball
Enid

Dorothy M. Ballew
Walters

Ruby R. Barber
Midwest City

Gladys Eaton Bartholomew
Norman

Viola Barton
Enid

Florence B. Bass
Beaver

Clara Bateman
Pawnee

Lloyd Leroy Bateson
Prague

Neoma Martin Bateson
Prague

Cynthia L. Beach
Muskogee

Richard H. Belcher
Beaver

Theta Hunt Benton

Freda Bergman
Okeene

Daisy L. Bernet
Ralston

Cassia C. Berry
Emporia, Kansas

Dora Berry
Sayre

Zelma Bickers
McAlester

Ella Mae Blackburn
Walters

Mattie Blackwell
Prague

Edith May Blaylock
Arnett

Frances Margret Bobo
Pauls Valley

Lee Boccher
Kingfisher

Lula Page Bonebrake
Norman

Ruby Helen Bonnell
Sayre

Birdie Bowman
Lawton

Emma C. Box
Ada

Joyce Bradfield
Ponca City

Inus Brecheen
Hollis

Arthur C. Brodell
Cleveland

A. Willard Brokaw
Shawnee

Katherine D. Brokaw
Shawnee

Carrie Lou Brothers
Atoka

Doris Brown

Opal Hartsell Brown
Lawton

Thelma H. Browning
Owasso

Nina O. Brumfield
Midwest City

Mary A. Buffington
Stillwater

Ruby B. Burke
Beaver

Chelsea O. Burkett
Noble

Edna Bybee
Pawnee

Opal Callahan
Norman

Geordia Coffey Camp
Oklahoma City

Bess Campbell
Krebs

Letha M. Campbell
Oklahoma City

Roberta M. Carpenter
Red Rock

Earl Franklin Carter
Collinsville

Mary Etta Carter
Tecumseh

Zelma Carter
Sapulpa

Agnes E. Cassity
Beaver

Margaret Castelaz
Tulsa

Mae D. Chapman
Yukon

Johnnie Bishop Chisholm
Tishomingo

Lucile D. Claiborne
Lawton

Ray Claiborne
Lawton

Elsie Claunch
Enid

Goldie Lemon Coffey
Muskogee

Eunice S. Coffield
Drumright

Elizabeth Fay Cole
Tulsa

Myrtie Collins
(deceased)

Jontie Combs

Maybelle Conger
Oklahoma City

Isabel D. Cook
Muskogee

Pearl Copelin
Mangum

Kate Baldridge Corey
Bristow

Vera Smith Cornelius
Oklahoma City

Hugh D. Corwin
Lawton

Clifford E. Costley
Oklahoma City

Mabel Baldwin Couch
Chelsea

Isabelle J. Cox
Oklahoma City

Lillie Mae Cozart
Porter

Bonnie L. Crabb
Shawnee

Ida G. Creekmore
Tulsa

Zula D. Crocker
Wagoner

Lillian Clark Cronkhite
Watonga

Grace S. Crow
Temple

Mary Gretchen Crowder
McAlester

Willa L. Crumble
Chandler

Zoe Calvert Crutchfield
Elk City

Genevieve Brasel Cunningham
Fairview

Vera M. Cunningham
Hollis

Ruby Lee Curry
Broken Bow

Algie P. Curtis
Oklahoma City

Christine M. Davis
Kingfisher

Gretel Fulton Davis
Tonkawa

Jane Elizabeth Davis
Norman

Roy H. Davis
Muskogee

Lydia Dawson
McAlester

Agnes M. Deck
Idabel

Frances Davis Dickens
Watonga

John W. Divine
Perry

Ora Dollins
Wilburton

Edna Donley
Oklahoma City

Alma B. Doughty
Oklahoma City

Nettie Doughty
Fairview

Billy M. Douthill
Miami

Maude A. Drake
Alva

Ella Draper
Tishomingo

Faye M. Duke
Alva

Euna Durham
Gordonville

Lelia Dyson

A. L. Ebersole
Perry

Anne D. Ellis
Idabel

Mary C. Ellis
Cheyenne

O. H. Ellis
Cheyenne

Ella H. Engelken
Alva

Mary Lena Evans
(deceased)

Zinia M. Evatt
McAlester

Hazel S. Exline
Laverne

Zelma Lee Farris
Stroud

Bertha Sills Fast
Del City

Pearl H. Faulk
Tulsa

Mildred Feikes
Canton

Villa E. Fender
Bartlesville

W. L. Findly
Kingfisher

Anna B. Fisher
Alva

Ina Dale Fisher
Woodward

J. C. Fitzgerald
Stillwater

Willa Frances Flue
Durham

Eva Lee Fobes
Sapulpa

Walene G. Folks
Moore

May Parry Forneris
Coalgate

Ima Foster
Mangum

Ura Foster
Mangum

Agness Francis
Eric

Cassandra Blasdel Frank
Oklahoma City

Kate Frank
Muskogee

W. A. Franklin
Ponca City

Ethel Fread
McAlester

Pauline Rives Freeny
Tulsa

Laura M. French
Alva

Doris E. Fry
Stilwell

Savannah Buggs Fuller
Coweta

Ruth Gallaher
Wellston

Eunice M. Gamble
Texola

J. M. Gamble
Texola

Jim Gammill
Ada

Delbert Garner
Wilburton

Johnnie Garner
Wilburton

Ayliffe Garrett
Erick

N. L. George
Oklahoma City

Arlie J. Geymann
Muskogee

A. Gibson
Purcell

Mabel Gillian
Chandler

Geen Gilmour
Kingfisher

Mary Gilmour, R.N.
Kingfisher

Chloe H. Glessner
Oklahoma City

Exzetta Gorman
Wewoka

H. D. Gound
Stilwell

Mary Grant
Idabel

Wilma E. Gray

Thelma Green
Shawnee

Pauline Greenshields
Seattle

Susie Griffin
Atoka

Nina May Grimes
Walters

I. C. Gunning
Wilburton

Irene M. Hagar
Ada

Alma Halcomb
Atoka

John C. Haley
Bartlesville

Alberta Hamilton
Miami

Grace M. Hannah
Prague

Ruth Harper
Madill

Claude C. Harris
Muskogee

Edgar E. Harris
Owasso

Rubeal Foster Harris
Chandler

Vallie W. Harris

Violet Horn Harris

Dollie Harrison
Coweta

Matitia B. Harrison
Watonga

Azalee Hart
Bristow

Gwen Hart
Tulsa

Addie M. Haston
Sapulpa

Yna Vey Hatchett
Meeker

Beulah E. Hathaway
Aldridge

Elizabeth M. Hays
Oklahoma City

Rae Wilma Heady
Dacoma

A. D. Hefley
McAlester

Marie Hoskins Heiskell
Washington

Eunice E. Heizer
Blackwell

Jennie M. Higgins
Coweta

Fleta M. Hill
Mangum

Jessie May Hines
Lawton

Evelyn C. Hoch
Alva

B. D. Holbert
Oklahoma City

Effie C. Holbert
Oklahoma City

Flecia G. Holcomb
Oklahoma City

Gladys Holcomb
Bristow

Louise Holler
Cleveland

Pauline P. Holloway
Tulsa

Ruth A. Hoodenpyle
Walters

Othello Hooker
Walters

George J. Hooper
Tulsa

Kate Eads Hopkins
Stilwell

Mrs. Adam Hornbeck
Shawnee

Faye Sandlin House
Tulsa

Opal T. House
Elk City

Ruth B. Houston
Lawton

Edith Cross Howard
(deceased)

Elizabeth Howard
Sapulpa

Nettie Belle Howe
Midwest City

Edna Mae Hrdy
Prague

Irene Hromas
Enid

Lois F. Hubbard
Crawford

Jess S. Hudson
Tulsa

Bessie M. Huff
Muskogee

Oscar E. Huffines
Sulphur

Bethie A. Hulsey
Kinta

Nell Ives
Alva

Grace Jameson
Walters

Della J. Jenkins
Moore

James P. Jenkins
Moore

Lucille Jenkins
Meeker

Marguerite Jimerson
Miami

Louise Joachims
Alva

Trixie June Johnson
Prague

Beatrice J. Jones
Tulsa

Livonia Jones
Stillwater

Olia Jones
Prague

Ruby Mae Jones
Tulsa

Vera C. Jones
Port

Nell W. Jordan
Meeker

Violet Jordan
Aline

Standifer Keas
Midwest City

Elizabeth H. Keef
Krebs

Irene H. Keen
Norman

Paul V. Keen
Norman

Bessie T. Kelley
Grimes

Chella L. Kent
Sayre

Thomas A. Kent
Sayre

Ilene Badger Ketch
Kingfisher

Herbert C. King
Kingfisher

William C. King
(deceased)

Elsie Grace Kirkpatrick
Shawnee

Clara Knight
Meeker

Edythe M. Knosp
Perry

Beauton Kooken
Temple

Mabel N. Kotchavar
Blackwell

Ethel Ann Kunke
Oklahoma City

Genevieve L. Kysar
Sayre

James Earl LaFon
Norman

Edna Lawler
Idabel

Pearl Ince Laxson
Temple

Gussie Tucker Lay
Tulsa

Edith Layton
Pawhuska

Susie K. Leierer
Fairview

Alto Lewallen
McAlester

Fannie E. Lewis
Stilwell

Ila Lewis
Willow

Kate J. Lewis
Purcell

Gertrude Lollar
Purcell

Nobel O. Long
Enid

Margy Maloney Lorenz
Okeene

Gladys Lovell
Tulsa

Elsie W. Lowry
Atoka

George W. Lowry
Atoka

Glessie Luker
Moore

Nellie Elizabeth Lunday
Pawhuska

Nell Main
Billings

Gertrude E. Major
Enid

Louise Major
Enid

Lucy Jane Makoske
Stilwell

Adah Mantooth
Noble

Maceo L. Marshall
Muskogee

Archie O. Martin
Stillwater

Bernice Cox Martin
Alva

James T. Martin
(deceased)

William Earl Martin
Oklahoma City

Edna Wharry Mason
Bethany

Pearl Matlock
Enid

Mary McCain
Decatur

Violet B. McClain
Tulsa

Edith A. McClure
Delaware

Vernon H. McClure
Delaware

Fern F. McCormick
Perry

Mildred P. McCoy
Chandler

Clara V. McFall
Oklahoma City

Arcie Alice McFalls
Idabel

Ferdinand D. McFalls
Idabel

Bessie McGee
Wilburton

Lois Waugh McGuckin
Blackwell

Clover McIntosh
Lehigh

Margaret H. McLaurine
Muskogee

Lee T. McMahan
Mangum

Florence McMullen
Alva

Ethel E. McPhaul
Muskogee

Dorothea Meagher
Edmond

William J. Mellor
Oklahoma City

W. C. Merritt
Maysville

Margaret M. Metcalf

Mary Romine Meyer
Fairview

Dr. Mabel Miles
Tulsa

Gwendolyn Miller
Norman

Christine C. Millsap
Weleetka

Okla Gunter Mitchell

Clara E. Moon
Oklahoma City

James B. Moore
Vista, California

Katharine L. Moore
Sapulpa

Myrtle Moore
Duncan

Freda Morgan
Commerce

Beulah Morris
Nowata

Hallie C. Morris
Coweta

Gladys Morrow
Walters

Claire B. Moulin
Chandler

Effie Fae Nagel
Adams

Rebacca Nalley
Muskogee

Lennie J. Nelson
Lawton

Bonnie Nesser
Elk City

Lucille B. Newby
Alva

Reba Miles Newell
Stroud

Ruby Nicholson
Stroud

Gladys Nunn
Muskogee

J. Myron Oates
Tulsa

Veta P. Oates
Tulsa

Neal E. O'Brien
Elk City

Martha Thelma Olive
Mangum

Ann Otis
Walters

Edna S. Owen
Reydon

Bonnie A. Paine
Lawton

Gordon L. Paine
Lawton

Benn G. Palmer
Owasso

Elizabeth Palmer
Owasso

Nettie Mitchell Parker
Mangum

Jewell Parsons
Okmulgee

Bessie M. Patterson
Ponca City

Zella J. Patterson
Langston

Gertrude May Patton
Duncan

Carl E. Paul (deceased)
Muskogee

Mable Percy Paul
Fairview

Carrie Lee Peeler
Elk City

Cassie Annie Pershall
Maramec

Thelma Peters
Muskogee

Cecile M. Peterson
Watonga

Addie Mae Pettit
Hartshorne

Macy Pever
Cheyenne

Emma M. Pierce
Bethany

Dicie Pinkerton
Pryor

Theodore L. Pittenger
Muskogee

Thelma F. Poff
Elk City

Lillian Pope
Enid

Grace Potter
Kremlin

Guy M. Pritchard

Bea A. Proffitt
Fairview

Anna Rylant Quisenberry
Elk City

Bennie Evans Raine

William A. Ranck
Oklahoma City

Edna Martin Ray
Fairview

Maynee E. Reavis
Shawnee

Arley Remeth Reeder
Bristow

Theo Edge Reeder
Bristow

Addie Reid
Bristow

Eleanor Knopp Reser
Blackwell

Anna Laura Reynolds
Elk City

Ruth Rice
Pauls Valley

Virgie D. Richardson
Muskogee

Grace H. Richmond
Ada

Mildred D. Rickard
Oklahoma City

Helen M. Riedt
Hartshorne

Grace B. Riggs
Anaheim, California

Pauline Lovell Riley
Moore

Dorris M. Ring
Red Rock

Marie Roberson
Owasso

Imogene Self Roberts
Stringtown

Lillian Roberts
Miami

Murray A. Roberts
Muskogee

Pearl Moree Robertson
Nowata

Sarah J. Robinson

Ambrose L. Rochel
Muskogee

Lavon D. Rochel
Muskogee

Charles E. Rogers
Moore

Ethel Rogers
Sayre

Kathryn Rogers
Moore

Allie Belle Root
Tulsa

Harriett Ross
Stillwater

Lottie Ross
McAlester

Archie Royse
El Reno

Boston Archie Russell
Muskogee

Ruby Sands
Shawnee

Opal A. Scales
Muskogee

Frances L. Schirmer
Pawhuska

Beryl Lucille Schumann
Lawton

Barbara Y. Schwabe
Tulsa

George Sanders Scott
Muskogee

A. O. H. Setzepfandt
Tulsa

Pauline A. Sharpe
Edmond

Anna Shepherd

Byron L. Shepherd
Tulsa

Gertrude J. Shero
Wilburton

Ruby W. Sherrick
Ramona

Jane W. Shewey
Orienta

Opal Shipman
Stilwell

Arthur L. Shuck
Weatherford

Ollie T. Sides
Sayre

Mamie Simmons
Elk City

Vera Mae Simmons
Ada

Edna A. Simpkins
Elk City

Minnie Slaton
Putnam City

Arta Lee Smalley
Haywood

Ann P. Smith
Duncan

Annetta Smith
Muskogee

Glenn R. Smith
Clinton

Julia B. Smith
Norman

Kate Snow Smith
Okmulgee

Marguerite Isbell Smith
Oklahoma City

Mayrie K. Smith
Elk City

Otis G. Smith
Shawnee

Roe L. Smith
Elk City

Vivian Smith
Elk City

Ethel L. Snodgrass
Nowata

Helen Weston Snow
Claremore

Susie B. Spears

George E. Spraberry
Prague

Ada Warfield Spurlock
Coweta

Vesta D. Stacey
McAlester

Grace Lucille Stambaugh
Chester

Harry Stambaugh
Chester

Virginia M. Stapley
Stillwater

Juanita Starr
Stilwell

Lucille Starr
Stilwell

Berthé A. Stebler
Muskogee

Nellie Stebler
Muskogee

Maxine Stevens
Moore

Lucy T. Stewart
Erick

Maud E. Stimpson
Walters

Martha Stockton
Blackwell

Esther C. Strickland
Erick

Clifford Andrew Strozier
Tulsa

Gerald Taylor Stubbs
Stillwater

Susie H. Sunderland
Tulsa

Lydia Swain (deceased)
Muskogee

Lillian L. Swale
Oklahoma City

Hattie D. Tally
Altus

Mrs. Cecil Tautfest
Tonkawa

Emma H. Teel
LeFlore

Flossie B. Templeton
Tulsa

Viva L. Thacker
Stringtown

Edith K. Thiessen

Mrs. Ben Thomas, Sr.
(deceased)

Mabel L. Timberlake
El Reno

Edna Tipler
Lawton

Myrle Trammell

Lois P. Tucker
Nowata

Loy Pollan Tullis
Miami

Lonnie T. Vanderveer
Inglewood, California

Mildred M. Varner
Walters

Dolores Viers
Fairview

Elsie Voth
Fairview

Florence Knight Wallace
Altus

Lucile W. Walta
Kingfisher

Walter Glen Ward
Shidler

Josie Washichek
Shawnee

Bessie M. Watson
Ada

Cathelene Watson
Okmulgee

Jeryl A. Watson
Okmulgee

Lila G. Watson
Miami

Loyd R. Watson
Ada

Tom Watson
Ada

Lola D. Wauchope

Cora Rowell Waugh
(deceased)

Golda W. Webb

Mildred C. Webb
Midwest City

Emma Weinmeister
Okeene

Esther Weinmeister
Okeene

Nell B. Welch
Tulsa

Edith H. Wells
Elk City

Beulah S. Wertz
Muskogee

Leo Bradley Wertz
Muskogee

Sophia Buggs West
Coweta

Clarrissa E. Wheat
Chickasha

Tinye Wheeless
Olustee

Vera Wheeless
Olustee

Buena Vista White
Muskogee

Lois White

Mary A. White
Muskogee

Louise M. Whitham
Tulsa

Henry C. Whitlow
Tulsa

Pearl Wickham
McAlester

Lois Wiley
Muskogee

Bertha Williams
Muskogee

Pearl L. Williams
Purcell

Ollie M. Willowby
Elk City

E. B. Wilmer
Sallisaw

Bernice Wilson
Cache

Marion Ralph Wilson
Ralston

Thelma Doughty Wilson
Fairview

Wilma G. Wilson
Miami

Dion Wood
Duncan

Ellen Wood
Watonga

Ione Martha Wood
Muskogee

Robert H. Wood
Watonga

Daisy Woodring
Fairview

Minnie A. Worel
McAlester

Ruth T. Wynn

Leona E. York
Hitchcock

Eva Mae Young
Crawford

Edith Zondler
Perry

INDEX

Abbott, Adaline: narrative by, 80–83
Academic freedom: 192, 227–30
Ada, Okla.: 8, 108
Adair County, Okla.: 88
Adamson, Okla.: 164
Administrators: duties and problems of, 205–207; conflicts with faculty, 227–30
Ahloso, Okla.: 108
Alcott school (Stillwater, Okla.): 91
Alex, Okla.: 32
Allen, Hazel: narrative by, 89–90
Allen, Okla.: 45–46
Allman, H. B.: 229
Altus, Okla.: 211
Alva, Okla.: 7, 18, 125–26, 128, 130, 236
Anadarko, Okla.: 73
Antlers, Okla.: 56
Apache, Okla.: 76
Atoka, Okla.: 86
Atoka County, Okla.: 85–87

Baker, Rebecca: 83–84
Ball, Beth: narrative by, 105–108
Banks, John: 16–17, 102
Barber, Ruby R.: narrative by, 188–92
Bartlesville, Okla.: 205
Barton, Viola Martin: narrative by, 100–102
Bateson, Lloyd: narrative by, 17
Bean, Oscar: 201
Bearden Consolidated Schools: 201
Beaver County, Okla.: 101
Beckham County, Okla.: 52–53, 170
Becker, Rozella: 143
Bennett, Archie: 81
Berry, Cassia: narrative by, 58–59
"Better School" Amendments: 11, 226–27
Bethany, Okla.: 167
Bickers, Zelma: narrative by, 19
"Black Blizzards": 163
Black shoals: 46–48, 75, 121, 195, 211–22
Blackwell, Okla.: 20, 31, 59, 67
Blair, Okla.: 170–71
Blue Back Spelling Book: 40
Bradfield, Joyce: narrative by, 31
Bristow, Okla.: 121
Brokaw, A. Willard: narrative by, 232–33
Brodell, Arthur C.: narrative by, 19–20, 55
Buffalo, Okla.: 100
Buffalo Mountain, Okla.: 164–66
Buffington, Mary: narrative by, 63–64, 115–17
Bureau of Indian Affairs: 173–74

Burkett, Chelsea O.: narrative by, 24–26
Buzzard Roost School: 75–76
Bynum, Jim (wealthy merchant who individually raises teacher's salary): 104–105
Byrds Mill, Okla.: 39

Caddo County, Okla.: 73–76, 97, 99
Calvin, Okla.: 46
Cameron University (Lawton, Okla.): 30, 170, 181, 211–15
Camp, Geordia Coffey: narrative by, 48–49
Canadian County, Okla.: 145–47
Canadian River: 156, 218
Cayuga, Okla.: 134
Cedar Vale School: 97–100
Cement, Okla.: 73–76
Central State University (Edmond, Okla.): 7, 27, 32, 61, 168, 181
Centralia, Okla.: 30
Certification, of teachers: 5–6, 8, 12–13, 15, 18, 19, 21–38, 41, 46, 61, 64, 73–74, 86–88, 92–93, 103–104, 112, 115, 117, 122, 128, 145, 156, 181, 215–16
Chandler, Okla.: 117
Chelsea, Okla.: 29, 109
Cherokee Indian Nation: 4, 55, 88–90, 93, 111–12
Cherokee Indian Schools: 4, 88–89, 111–12
Cheyenne, Okla.: 51, 184
Cheyenne-Arapaho County, Okla.: Schools in, 48
Cheyenne-Arapaho Reservation School, Okla.: 128–30
Chickasha, Okla.: 30, 141
Chickasaw Indian Nation: 119
Chickasaw Indian Schools: 4
Chigley, Martin: 40–41
Chilocco High School: 173
Choctaw Indian Nation: 46, 85
Choctaw Indian Schools: 4, 40–45
Church of Christ: 57–58
Civilian Conservation Corps: 150–51
Claiborne, Lucile Danner: narrative by, 181–83
Claiborne, Ray: narrative by, 170–71
Claremore, Okla.: 83
Cleveland, Okla.: 55
Cleveland County, Okla.: 19, 24
Coal County, Okla.: 39
Coalgate, Okla.: 21, 46
Coffey, Goldie Lemon: narrative by, 161–62
Coffey, George: 48–49
College High School (Bartlesville, Okla.): 205–207
Colleges and Universities: founded, 7–8
Colony, Okla.: 142
Comanche County, Okla.: 142–45, 172–73
Comanche County Retired Teachers Association: 46
Combs, Jontie: narrative by, 31–32
Community centers: schools as, 167, 169, 182, 187
Compulsory attendance laws: 9
Concho, Okla.: 129
Consolidation of schools: 7–8, 12–13, 89–90, 112, 185, 195
Contracts, of teachers: 15, 30–33, 147–51, 159
Cornelius, Vera Smith: narrative by, 145–47
Cotton County, Okla.: 60, 170, 181–82
"Cotton" schools: 70, 77–80
Couch, Mabel B.: narrative by, 29–30, 34–35, 108–11, 136–37, 155–56
Counselors: duties and problems of, 205–207
Coweta, Okla.: 78, 195, 233
Cox, J. M.: 54
Cox, Mary: 54
Creek County Fair: 167
Creek Indian Schools: 4, 56–58
Crews, Ethel: 85
Criswell, Elroy: 55–56
Cronwell, Okla.: 88
Crooked Oak School (Okla. County, Okla): 184

Crutchfield, Zoe Calvert: narrative by, 94–97
Curriculum, of Indian schools: 4; set by territorial legislature, 5; changes for, 188, 191–92, 194, 216
Cushing, Okla.: 175–79

Dacona, Okla.: 193
Davis, Jane E.: narrative by, 32–33
Dawson, T.: 34
Delaware County, Okla.: 134–36
Dempsey School: 187
Depression Era: education during, 9–10, 138–79; New Deal and, 150–51
Dewar, Okla.: 171
Dewey County, Okla.: 128–30
Discipline, in schools: 59, 187–88
Donley, Edna: narrative by, 21–24
Doughty, Nettie: narrative of, 183–84
Douglass High School (Bartlesville, Okla.): and integration, 207
Douglass High School (Oklahoma City, Okla.): 88
Douglass Elementary School (Wewoka, Okla.): 215
Douglass High School (Lawton, Okla.): 212
Doxey (Okla. Terr.): 54
Drake, John: 104
Draper, Ella: narrative by, 52
Dugouts, homes of early settlers: 53, 55
Dugout schools: 48, 51–52, 101
Duke, Faye M.: narrative by, 18, 236–37
Dunbar Elementary School (Lawton, Okla.): 212
Dunbar High School (Hobart, Okla.): 88
Duncan, Okla.: 31
Durant, Okla.: 8, 86
Du Shane, Donald: and academic freedom, 229–30
Dust Bowl: 161–62
Dust storms: 161–63, 175; effects on schools, 146–47, 149

Eagle Chief Creek, Okla.: 126
East Central State University (Ada, Okla.): 8, 35
Edmond, Okla.: 7, 159, 168
Edmondson, J. Howard: 210–11
Education, in Oklahoma: 3–14; in the territories, 3–7, 38–71; in one-room schools, 3, 8, 12, 16, 26–27, 46, 48–52, 55, 56–60, 62–66, 73–82, 85–88, 101, 105–13, 116–20, 122–36, 145–47, 159, 164–66, 168–70, 183–85, 196, 215, 234; higher, 7–8, 13; in the early statehood era, 72–137; in the depression era, 138–79; in the modern era, 180–230; current trends in, 182–96; impact of technology upon, 193, 196, 208–11; of migrant children, 203–205; vocational, 223–26
Educational television: impact on education, 208–11
Elk City, Okla.: 18, 52, 94, 156, 232
Ellis County, Okla.: 81–82, 194
Elm Grove School (Major County, Okla.): 122–25
Emahaka Indian School: 83
Emerson School (Roger Mills County, Okla.): 184
Enid, Okla.: 100, 105
Erick, Okla.: 51, 54
Evans, Mary Phipps: narratives by, 56–58

Fair Oaks School: 84
Fairview, Okla.: 122, 130, 183, 234
Fairview High School (Fairview, Okla.): 122
Federal aid to education: 10, 12–13, 138, 186, 204, 218
Field trips for students: innovative out-of-state towns, 175–79
Fitzgerald, Elizabeth: 175
Fitzgerald, J. Connor, narrative by, 175–79; organizer of tours for students, 175–79, 196–97; summarizes the contributions to education of Gerald Stubbs, 226–27

Five Civilized Tribes: education of, 4–6; *see also* individual tribes
Fobes, Eva Lee: narrative by, 166–67
Forneris, May Parry: narrative by, 21
Fort Sill, Okla.: 88
Four-H clubs: importance of, 63, 117, 167, 169, 173, 182
Fox, Walter: 111
Fraker, Elmer: 209–10
Francis, Agness: narrative by, 51–52
Francis, Okla.: 46, 119
Frank, Kate: narrative by, 227–30
Franklin, W. A. (author of "Reflections of the Ghost of a One-Room Rural Schoolhouse."): 64–66
Friends Academy (Gate, Okla.): 101
Friendship School (Washita County, Okla.): 54, 94–97
Fund raising: for school supplies, 101–102
Future Farmers of America: 172

Gage, Okla.: 80; school of, 82
Gate, Okla.: 101
Gertz: 45
Geymann, Arlie: narrative by, 223–26
Glessner, Chloe H.: narrative by, 97–100
"God Bless America": 179
Gold, G. M.: 104–105
Gorman, Exzetta Jones: narrative by, 215–17
Grady County, Okla.: 32
Grand Center School, Okla.: 64
Grant County, Okla.: 59
Greer County, Okla.: 185
Grimes, Nina May: narrative by, 60–61

Haley, John C.: narrative by, 205–207
Harkey, Lemuel: 212
Harmony school (Leflore, Okla.): 70
Harper County, Okla.: 100
Harris, Okla.: 88
Harris, Claude C.: narrative by, 119–20
Hart, Azalee: narrative by, 121
Hartshorne, Okla.: 20, 164
Haskell County, Okla.: 39
Haskell High School: 173
Hatchett, Yna Vey: narrative of, 154–55
Hay's Chapel, Okla.: 77
Hay's Chapel Demonstration Club: 77
Headrick, Okla.: 28
Head Start program: 110
Heady, Rae Vail: narrative by, 193–94
Hefley, A. D.: 15; narrative by, 16–17, 102–105, 234–35
Heizer, Eunice: narrative by, 20, 59–60; poem by, 67–68
Hembrce, Hugh: 56
Henryetta, Okla.: 49
Higgins, Jennie Hays: narrative by, 77–80
High Bridge North School (Latimer County, Okla.): 70–71
Highview school (Highview, Okla.): 75–76
Hill Fleta M.: narrative by, 184–88
Hillside Elementary School (Perkins, Okla.): 197–200
Hillside High School (Perkins, Okla.): 175–79
Hillside Travel Club: 175–79, 197–200
Hines, Jessie May: narrative by, 30–31, 141
Hinton, Okla.: 97–98, 142
Hobart, Okla.: 88
Hog Creek, Okla.: 73; school of, 74
Holbert, B. D.: narrative by, 87–88
Holdenville, Okla.: 46
Holman, Fannie: 45
Homestead Club: 173
Hominy, Okla.: 31
Hot lunch programs: 139–40, 144–46, 155–56, 160, 186, 196
Howard, Elizabeth: narrative by, 140–41
Howe, Nettie Belle: narrative by, 73–77
Howell, Vernon: 212
Hudson, Jess: narrative by, 27–29
Huffman, Emma: 81
Hughes County, Okla.: 45–46, 56

Idabel, Okla.: 17
Independence School (Lincoln County, Okla.): 63
Indiahoma High School (Comanche County, Okla.): vocational agriculture in, 172–74
Indian Camp School (Osage County, Okla.): 117
Indianola, Okla.: 103
Indian schools: 3–6, 38, 40–46, 49, 56–58, 83, 88–89, 111–12, 117, 128–30, 161; vocational agriculture in, 172–74
Indian Territory: 52, 85; education in, 3–6, 38, 40–46, 49, 56–58, 83, 88–89, 111–12, 117, 161; vocational agriculture in, 172–74
Integration, of schools: 58–59, 207, 211–22
Iowa Indians: 161
Ireton District, Okla.: 32
Isabella, Okla.: 122

Jefferson Grade School (Lawton, Okla.): 142–45
Jefferson School (Stillwater, Okla.): 91
Jenkins, Lucille: narrative of, 153–54
Johnson, Charley N.: 53
Johnson, Isaac N.: 53
Jones Academy (Indian school): 173–74
Jones, Livonia: narrative by, 139–40
Jones, Ira Lee: 181
Justice, Okla.: 120

Kate Frank Case, The: 227–30
Kay County, Okla.: 55–56, 167–70
Kelso, Charles A.: 63
Kelso, Ulysses Grant: 63
Keokuk Falls, Okla.: rum-runners at, 84
Kersey, A. D.: 56
King, Herbert C.: narrative summarizing William C. King's contribution to education in Oklahoma, 46–48
King, William C.: 46–48
Kingfisher College (Kingfisher, Okla.): 105
Kingfisher County, Okla.: 46–47, 105–108
Ku Klux Klan: schoolrooms as meeting places of 106–107, 108
Kysar, Genevieve L.: narrative by, 141–42

Lahoma, Okla.: 58
Langston University (Langston, Okla.): 7, 87, 215, 216
Latimer County, Okla.: 68, 70
Lawton, Okla.: 142–45, 170, 181, 211
Laxson, Pearl: narrative by, 156–59
Leader, Okla.: 45
Leader, Otis: 45
Leedey High School: 156
Leflore, Okla.: 70
Leslie district (near Fairview, Okla.): 133
Lewis, Fannie Ross: narrative by, 88–89
Lewis, Kate J.: narrative by, 151–52, 203–205, 235–36
Lewis, T. T.: 103–104
Lexington High School: 26
Lincoln County, Okla.: 63, 115–17, 159, 196
Lincoln School (Stillwater, Okla.: 91
Literary Clubs: importance of, 63, 107–108
Little, Okla.: 119
Little Wolf School: 80; destroyed by tornado, 82–83
Log Schoolhouses: 3, 55, 73, 83

McAlester, Okla.: 15, 16, 19, 21, 39, 46, 68, 102–103, 117, 234
McBee, Nellie: 164
McBee, Pete: 164
McCain, Mary: narrative by, 208–11
McCormick, Fern Folger: narrative by, 26–27
McFalls, Arcie Alice: narrative by, 17
McGucker, Lois: narrative by, 55–56
McIntosh County, Okla.: 49

McMillan, Okla.: 40
Major County, Okla.: 122–25, 130–33
Mangum, Okla.: 26, 184, 192
Maramec, Okla.: 55
Marshall County, Okla.: 52
Martin, Bernice Cox: narrative by, 125–28
Martin, Ed: 122
Martin, Flora: 122
Martin, William: narrative by, 217–22
Mason, Edna: narrative by, 167–70
Meeker, Okla.: 153–54
Mekasukey Indian School: 83
Mendenhall, Blake: 165
Meno, Okla.: 58
Mexican-Americans: the teaching of, 142–45, 203–205
Meyer, Mary Romine: narrative by, 234
Miami, Okla.: 134
Midwest City, Okla.: 73, 188; founding of, 200–203; establishing schools in, 200–203; as "Midwest City," 202
Migrant children: education of, 142–45, 203–205
Mill Creek, Okla.: 54
Millsap, Christine: narrative by, 237–38
Missionaries: educational efforts of, 4
Missionary work: teaching compared to, 161
Mitchell, Okla Gunter: narrative by, 111–12
Mobeta Trail, Okla.: 53
Model School program: 8, 120, 135
Modern Era: education during, 180–230
Moore, Katharine Clark: narrative by, 35–36
Moral and spiritual values: teacher's responsibility for imparting, 183
Morris, Beulah: narrative by, 236
Morrison High School: 26
Morrison, Okla.: 26
Mound Valley, Okla.: 145–47
Muskogee High School: 223–26
Muskogee, Okla.: 45–46, 119, 152, 161, 223, 227–30

Nagel, Effie: narrative by, 163
Nale, Okla.: 103, 234
Narcotics, and the schools: 190
National Council for Accreditation of Teacher Education: 23
National Education Association: 228–30
Neill, H. E.: 95
New Deal (effects of, on education): 10, 150–152
North Eagle School (Woods County, Okla.): 126–28
Northeast District Classroom Teachers Association: 227
Northeastern State University (Tahlequah, Okla.): 8, 195
Northwestern State University (Alva, Okla.): 7, 82, 122, 128
Nowata, Okla.: 30, 93, 152, 236
Nowata County, Okla.: 90, 108–110, 183, 236

Okeene, Okla.: 58
Okfuskee County, Okla.: 35
Oklahoma (history of education in): 3–14
Oklahoma Board of Education: 120; licensing of teachers, 8, 22–23, 24, 25, 26
Oklahoma Chamber of Commerce: opposition to "Better School" amendment, 226
Oklahoma City: 21, 48, 87–88, 97, 141, 145, 162, 182, 184, 192–93, 217–22; public schools of, 217–22
Oklahoma College for Women at Chickasha, Okla.: 26
Oklahoma Education Association: 11–12, 23–24, 159, 226, 228
Oklahoma Historical Society: 14, 92, 209; acquires reminiscences by Oklahoma retired teachers, 14
Oklahoma Retired Teachers Association: 175, 227; donates collection of

reminiscences to the Oklahoma Historical Society, 14
Oklahoma State School Boards Association: 227
Oklahoma State University (references to Oklahoma Agricultural and Mechanical College included): 7, 19, 70, 90–94, 117, 142, 172, 196, 224; Congregational Church first classroom for, 91; Technical Institute of, 92; scene of first graduation in Oklahoma, 92
Oklahoma Stockman, 198
Oklahoma Supreme Court: upholds "Better School" Amendments, 226
Oklahoma Teacher: 64
Oklahoma Teachers Retirement System: 227
Oklahoma Territory (education in): 5–7, 46–48, 52–53, 55, 58–60, 90
Oklahoma, University of: 7, 25, 26, 28, 88
Okmulgee, Okla.: 49
Okmulgee County, Okla.: 171
Old Central (at Oklahoma State University): oldest college building in Oklahoma, 90; scene of first graduation in Oklahoma, 92; museum for Oklahoma Historical Society, 92
One-room schools: 3, 8, 12, 16, 26–27, 46, 48–52, 55, 56–60, 62–66, 73–82, 85–88, 101, 105–13, 116–20, 122–36, 145–47, 159, 164–66, 168–170, 183–85, 196, 215, 234; compared to modern primary schools, 110; sod smokehouse used for school, 56
Open classroom (experiment with): 188
Osage County, Okla.: 31, 115, 117
Outlaws: 39, 48

Paine, Gordon L.: narrative by, 211–15
Parent-Teacher Association: 11–12, 169, 233
Parker, Mettie Mitchell: narrative by, 26, 192–93
Parker's Chapel School: 215
Patton, Gertrude Gates: narrative by, 31
Pauls Valley, Okla.: 37
Payne County, Okla.: 89, 161, 175–79, 200; County Fair of, 200
Pawnee, Okla.: 89
Pawnee County, Okla.: 55
Perkins, Okla.: 161
Perry, Okla.: 27, 55
Peterson, Cecile: narrative by, 128–30
Pettit, Addie: narrative by, 20–21, 164–66
Phillips, Josephine: 109
Phillips University: 26
Pittsburg County, Okla.: 117, 164–66, 234
Pleasant Grove, Okla.: 215
Pleasant Valley, Okla.: 47
Ponca City, Okla.: 31, 64
Pond Creek, Okla.: Teachers Institute held in, 60
Pontotoc County, Okla.: 45, 108
Practice teaching: expensive in lieu of, 93
Prague, Okla.: 17
Prairie View College: 87–88
Printing (as a vocational field): 223–26
Pritchard, Guy M.: narrative by, 196–200
Professional Standards Board (for teachers): 24
Purcell, Okla.: 151, 203, 205, 235

Ramona, Okla.: 114–15; school of, 114
Ray, Edna Martin: narrative by, 122–25
Ray's Arithmetic: 40
Reavis, Maynee E.: narrative by, 112–13
Red Bird School: 195
Redden, Okla.: 86
Red Oak, Okla.: 68–71
"Reflections of the Ghost of a One-Room Rural Schoolhouse": 64–66
Rice, Ruth: narrative by, 37

Riverside School: 75, 119–20
Roger Mills County, Okla.: 51, 156, 161–62, 184
Rogers, Addie May: 48
Rogers County, Okla.: 34
Roosevelt, Franklin D.: and the New Deal, 152
Rose, Oscar V.: 200–203
Ross, Lottie: narrative by, 39–45
Rothhammer School: 78
Rowell, Cora: 55–56
Ruby School (Nowata County, Okla.): 183
Rural Schools: 5–7, 8–9, 12–13, 35, 46, *passim*
Russia: impact on education in the United States, 188–92

Salaries: in education, 12–13, 32, 46, 82, 88, 92–94, 98, 101, 104–105, 110, 113, 116–18, 122, 126, 129–31, 140–41, 145–48, 151–53, 157, 159, 161, 163–64, 166–68, 185, 189, 191, 196; discounted during the depression, 140–41, 145, 147–48, 151–52, 163, 166, 168
Salem, Okla.: 49
Salt Creek School (Nowata County, Okla.): 108–109
Salvation Army: assists schools during the depression, 144
Sand Creek Subscription School: 83
Sands, Ruby: narrative by, 61–63
Sapulpa, Okla.: 35, 140–41, 166
Sayre, Okla.: 53, 141
Scales, Opal A.: narrative by, 45–46
"School at Old Bluff Center" (poem by Eunice Heizer): 67–68
School Code of 1913: 8
School Code of 1949: 11
School Code of 1971: 11
Schools: *passim*; consolidation of, 7–8, 12–13, 89–90, 112, 185, 195; segregated, 46–48, 75, 121, 195, 211–22; current instructional trends of, 182–83, 187–88
Schwarte, Jennie: 143
Segar (Indian Territory): 53
Seminole County, Okla.: 83–84, 112, 119–20, 215
Seminoles: educ. by, 4
Sentinel, Okla.: 49
Sequoyah County, Okla.: 111–12
Sequoyah High School: 173
Sharpe, Pauline T.: narrative by, 159–61
Shattuck, Okla.: 80
Shattuck public schools: 83
Shawnee, Okla.: 61, 112, 232; Indian Tubercular Hospital at, 233
Sherrick, Ruby Wallace: narrative by, 114–15
Shidler Elementary School: 218–19
Simpkins, Edna Alice: narrative by, 52–54
"Six-thru-three plan": 9
Smith, Julia B.: narrative by, 147–51
Smith, Marguerite Isbell: narrative by, 162
Smith, Vivian: narrative by, 18–19, 232
Snodgrass, Ethel L.: narrative by, 152–53
Snow, Helen Weston: narrative by, 83–85
Social life, schools and: 136–37, ff.
Sod house: 80
Sod schoolhouses: 73
Sod smoke house (used for school): 56
Soldier Creek School (Midwest City, Okla.): 201
Sooner School (Midwest City, Okla.): 201
South Gale School: 25
Southeastern State Normal: 8, 26
Southeastern State University (Durant Okla.): 8, 26, 86
Southwestern State University (Weatherford, Okla.): 70
Spaulding, Okla.: 56–58
Spring Hill, Okla.: 115
Sputnik, and education: 188–92
Starr, Belle: 39, 44
State aid to schools: 9–11, 112–13

Stillwater, Okla.: 7, 63, 70, 88, 90–94, 139–40, 168, 175, 196, 224, 226
Stilwell, Okla.: 88
Stimpson, Maud: narrative by, 90–94
Stringtown, Okla.: 85
Stringtown High School: 86
Strozier, Clifford, Sr.: narrative by, 68–71
Stubbs, Gerald: summary of accomplishments of, 226–27
Subscription Schools: 45, 49–52, 83, 111, 119
Sunset Elementary School (Oklahoma City, Okla.): 218
Supplies: availability of, the 1930's compared to the 1970's, 186–87
Supreme Court of Oklahoma: upholds "Better School" Amendments, 226
Supreme Court of the United States: and integration of schools, 212, 217
Surplus commodities: use of during the depression, 154, 155–56
Sweetwater, Oklahoma Territory: 54
Swinton's Readers: 40
Sylvan Seminary: 52

Tahlequah, Okla.: 8
Talala School: 34
Tally, Hattie D.: narrative by, 211
Teachers: certification of, 5–6, 8, 12–13, 15, 18, 19, 21–38, 41, 46, 61, 64, 73–74, 86–88, 92–93, 103–104, 112, 115, 117, 122, 128, 145, 156, 181, 215–16; shortage of, 7, 8, 10; salaries of, 12–13, 32, 46, 82, 88, 92–94, 98, 101, 104–05, 110, 113, 116–18, 122, 126, 129–31, 140–41, 145–48, 151–53, 157, 159, 161, 163–64, 166–68, 185, 189, 191, 196; contracts of, 15, 30–33, 147–51, 159; motivation of, 15–22, 83, 102–103; status of, 191, 211
Teacher Education and Professional Standards Commission: 23–24
Teachers Institute: 60
Teacher retirement law: 11
Teaching: in one-room schools, 3, 8, 12, 16, 26–27, 46, 48–52, 55, 56–60, 62–66, 73–82, 85–88, 101, 105–13, 116–20, 122–136, 145–147, 159, 164–66, 168–70, 183–85, 196, 215, 234; effects of World War II on, 23; effects of the depression on, 147–51; military and, 190–91
Technology: impact on classroom instruction, 193, 196, 208–11
Television (used in schools): 193, 208–11
Temple, Okla.: 156
Territorial Era: education during, 3–7, 38–71
Texas County, Okla.: 163
Textbooks: free textbook laws, 9, 11
Thacker, Vera: narrative by, 85–87
Thiessen, Edith Koons: narrative by, 130–33
Tinker Air Force Base (Okla.): 200
Tin Top School (Cheyenne–Arapaho reservation): 128–30
Tonkawa, Okla.: 7, 169
Transient families: education of, 142–45
Tucker, Elaine: 209
Tullis, Loy Pollan: narrative by, 134–36
Tulsa, Okla.: 27, 29, 33, 68

Union District (Okla.): 168
United States Congress, and laws providing for integration of schools: 217
Universities and colleges: founded, 7–8
University of Oklahoma: 7, 25, 26, 28, 88, 216
University Preparatory School (Tonkawa, Okla.): 7
Urban schools: 6, 9, 12–13ff.

Valley View District (Okla.): 32
Vietnam War (impact on education): 189
Vocational agriculture: 171–74
Vocational education: development of, 223–26

Wagoner County, Okla.: 77, 121, 195, 233
Walnut Grove Elementary School (Okla. City, Okla.): 218–19
Walters, Okla.: 60–61, 90
Washington County, Okla.: 114–15
Washita County, Okla.: 48, 94–97, 142
Watonga, Okla.: 128, 130, 142, 171
Watson, Bessie McBroom: narrative by, 108
Watson, Jeryl A.: narrative by, 49–51
Waugh, William H.: 55
Weatherford, Okla.: 7
Weatherford Normal School: 74
Webb, Mildred C.: narrative by, 200–203
Welch, Nell Terrell: narrative by, 33–34
Weleetka, Okla.: 237
West Junior High School (Muskogee, Okla.): 46
West, Sophia Buggs: narrative by, 195, 233–34
Western District Baptist Association: 48
Wetumka Indian School: 49
Wewoka, Okla.: 83, 120, 215
Whiskey stills: 130, 152
Whitefield, Okla.: 39
Wickham, Pearl: narrative by, 117–19
Wilburton, Okla.: 70–71, 196
Wilburton High School (Wilburton, Okla.): 70
William Woods College: 46
Wing Spring: 26–27
Wingo, Okla.: 54
Wister, Okla.: 70
Wood, Ellen Watson: narrative by, 142–45
Wood, Robert H.: narrative by, 171–74
Woods County, Okla.: 100, 125–28, 194
Woodward County, Okla.: 100, 162
Works Progress Administration: 143
Wynn, Ruth T.: narrative by, 196

Yale, Okla.: 89
Young, Eva Mae: narrative by, 161–62
"You're Fired! It Migh Have Been You" (reports on the Kate Frank Case): 230